THE POLITICAL AND STATISTICAL HISTORY OF GUJARAT

THE POLITICAL AND STATISTICAL HISTORY OF GUJARAT

TRANSLATED FROM THE PERSIAN OF

ALI MOHAMMED KHAN

THE REVENUE MINISTER OF THE PROVINCE

TO WHICH ARE ADDED

COPIOUS ANNOTATIONS

AND AN

HISTORICAL INTRODUCTION

JAMES BIRD

GYAN

Published by

Gyan Publishing House
5, Ansari Road
Daryaganj, New Delhi-110002
Phone: 011-47034999, 9811692060
E-mail: books@gyanbooks.com

Distribution Network
gyanbooks.com
India, USA, Canada, UK, Australia, France

ISBN : 978-81-212-3899-1 (PB)
First Published, London, 1835

2nd Impression 2020

Printed at: Gyan Press, Delhi.

The
Political and Statistical History of Gujarat
Author: James Bird

THE POLITICAL AND STATISTICAL HISTORY OF GUJARÁT,

TRANSLATED FROM THE PERSIAN OF

ALÍ MOHAMMED KHÁN.

THE REVENUE MINISTER OF THE PROVINCE;

TO WHICH ARE ADDED,

COPIOUS ANNOTATIONS,

AND AN

HISTORICAL INTRODUCTION

BY JAMES BIRD, ESQ.

PUBLISHED UNDER THE SUPERINTENDENCE OF THE ORIENTAL TRANSLATION FUND OF GREAT BRITAIN AND IRELAND.

LONDON:
RICHARD BENTLEY, NEW BURLINGTON STREET,
Publisher in Ordinary to His Majesty,
TO THE ORIENTAL TRANSLATION FUND, &c.
M.DCCC.XXXV.

Oriental Translation Fund

LONDON.

INSTITUTED 1828.

UNDER THE PATRONAGE OF HIS MOST GRACIOUS MAJESTY

WILLIAM THE FOURTH.

THIS COPY

WAS PRINTED FOR

THE RIGHT HONORABLE

LORD GLENELG, F.R.S. M.R.S.L.

A MEMBER OF THE ROYAL ASIATIC SOCIETY,

AND

A SUBSCRIBER TO

The Oriental Translation Fund.

TO

THE HONOURABLE

MOUNTSTUART ELPHINSTONE.

DEAR SIR,

While translating the following history, I frequently reflected that whatever leisure and opportunity I possessed, for accomplishing this task, had chiefly arisen from the liberality of public measures, and the impartiality of private patronage, during your government at Bombay. To no one so appropriately as you, therefore, could I dedicate these pages; and, while I feel gratified in giving testimony to the utility of encouraging individuals, disposed to study the languages of the East, I am sensible that few can better judge the imperfections of my present undertaking than yourself. I fear to offend your delicacy of sentiment, by speaking of public principle in the language of eulogium ; but I should ill consult the interests of the public service, or appreciate my own feelings, could I be silent, after having obtained the situation I lately held, for no other reason than having complied with the terms of your government orders, promulgated to promote the study of oriental languages among the Europeans.

Though the acquirement of these, and the cultivation of oriental literature, may be of use, in enlarging our views of general history and geography, they serve a yet more important purpose, in this country, by removing the prejudices of early education, by interesting the feelings of Europeans for the welfare of Asiatics, and disposing the former to treat as equals those whom they had been taught to consider as inferiors. These advantages were duly estimated by your administration : during which to have possessed such acquirement was to obtain reward. Every good government will keep sight of such enlightened policy, if it regards the efficiency of its servants, or the happiness of its subjects ; though I regret to observe an ill-judged economy, in this matter, has been of late ordered by authority from home. The love of distinction is, with some, a more powerful incitement to exertion than even the hope of emolument; and for such the establishment of the Royal Asiatic Society and Oriental Translation Fund holds out powerful inducements; but, with the majority, the last will be found to be the more influential passion, and should be turned to good account by rulers, who wish to conciliate a conquered people.

In ascribing this much to you, I must not forget what I owe to your successors, for having afforded me every facility in completing the present translation. The late Sir John Malcolm, who had himself so successfully cultivated oriental literature, and was ready to encourage others, placed at my command the services of the native whom I mention in the preface; and I am under similar obligations to the Right Honourable the Earl of Clare.

It is incumbent on us, as rulers of India, to possess an accurate knowledge of its customs, manners, religious opinions, history, and commerce; and regarding the early state of such there is yet a wide field of interesting research. The influence of the Greek kingdom of Bactria on Sanskrit literature; the knowledge which the Romans possessed of India, and the state of their commerce with the country; the intercourse of the primitive Arabs and eastern Christians with the Hindús; the incorporation of foreign tribes with the aborigines; the institutions of their civil society; and rules of their military policy, are subjects of intense interest, that may be successfully elucidated by closely studying the Greek and Roman authors, in connexion with Sanskrit literature, and the historical and geographical books in Arabic and Persian. In the introduction, prefixed to the following translation, I have endeavoured to clear up the obscurity that exists in one portion of Indian history; and, if such obtain your approbation, it will gratify,

Dear Sir,

Your obedient servant,

JAMES BIRD.

London, 1st September, 1834.

CONTENTS.

PAGE

Preface 1

Historical Introduction, illustrating the Constitution of Hindú Society, and the state of India, from the end of the Tenth to the beginning of the Thirteenth Century . 5

Preface to the Mirát Ahmadí, or Mirror of Ahmad; a History of Gujarát 91

SECTION I.

Preliminary Observations on the State of Gujarát . . 102

The beginning of the Kingdom of Gujarát, under its Rájás; and the foundation of the city of Patan, sometimes named Anhilwárah, or Nahrwálah 137

The Capture of Somnáth by Sultán Mahmúd Ghaznaví . 146

The Sovereignty of the Baghílah race at Nahrwálah; and the Edifices erected by Siddha Rájá Solankí Jey Singh . 154

The Triumph of the Faith, and the establishment of the Mohammedan Religion in the country . . . 160

The Reign of Sultán Kutbu-d-dín Mubárak Sháh, son of Alá-ud-dín Khiljí 165

The Reign of Sultán Mohammed Toghluk Sháh . . 168

PAGE

The Reign of Fíroz Sháh Toghluk III. of Dehlí, cousin of Mohammed Toghluk 170

The Reign of Ghiásu-d-dín Toghluk II., grandson of Fíroz, also called Fíroz Sháh IV. . . . 172

The Reign of Sultán Abúbekr Sháh, grandson of Fíroz III., and that of his uncle, Mohammed Toghluk II. . . 173

SECTION II.

The Government of Zafir Khán, son of Wajíhu-l-Mulk, with the Foundation of the Gujarát Metropolis, and the reign of the Gujarát Kings 174

The Reign of Ahmad Khán, grandson of Muzaffir, and entitled Ahmad Sháh 186

The Reign of Sultán Mohammed Sháh I. . . 195

The Reign of Jalál Khán, entitled Kutbu-d-dín . . 197

The Reign of Sultán Dáod, uncle of Kutbu-d-dín . . 201

The Reign of Sultán Fat'h Khán, entitled Mahmúd Bígarrah 202

The Reign of Khalíl Khán, entitled Muzaffir Sháh II., or, The Clement 219

The Reign of Sultán Sikandar . . . 229

The Reign of Sultán Bahádur 232

The Reign of Sultán Mahmúd II., son of Latíf Khán . 253

The Reign of Ahmad Khán II., son of Latíf Khán, grandson of Shukár Khán, son of Sultán Ahmad I. . . . 273

The Reign of Sultán Muzaffir III., commonly called Nathú, the last of the race of Gujarát Kings . . . 287

SECTION III.

A General Account of the celebrated Descendants of Sáhibi Kirán Amír Taimúr Kúrkán, who have reigned in Hindústán 290

PAGE

The commencement of Insurrection in Gujarát, the arrival of the Mírzás in the country, the termination of the power of its Kings, and its incorporation with the Kingdom of Hindústán, under Jalálu-d-dín Mohammed Akbar . 301

The Capture of Súrat 318

The return of the Imperial Banners to the Capital of Agra, and the appointment of Khán Azíz Koká to the Government of Gujarát, with Wajíhu-l-Mulk Gujarátí as his Díwán 324

The arrival of the Emperor, in nine days, from the seat of Government, then at Fat'hpúr . . . 328

The return of the Emperor to his Capital, after conferring the Government of Gujarát on Khán Azíz Koká a second time 339

The Government of Shahábu-d-dín Ahmad Khán, and the Díwánship of Prágdás, with the flight and return of Muzaffir Sultán to Gujarát 348

The Government of Itimád Khán Gujarátí, with the Díwánship of Abú-l-Kásim, and the capture of Ahmadábád by Sultán Muzaffir 354

The Government of Mírzá Khán, with the defeat of Muzaffir, and capture of Ahmadábád. The exaltation of Mírzá Khán to the rank of Five Thousand, and the title of Khán Khánán, with the foundation of the Fat'h Bágh, at the town where the battle was fought. The Díwánship of Khoájáh Abú-l-Kásim, and the order for adopting the Iláhí Era in the country of Hindústán . . 370

Copy of the Imperial Firmán for the establishment of the Iláhí Era 382

Copy of the Order regarding Veneration for God and attention to the Government Regulations . . 389

PAGE

The Government of Mírzá Azíz Koká for a second time in Gujarát, and copy of the Order which was issued abolishing the Transit Duty on articles of commerce . . 405

Sultán Muzaffir, surnamed Nathú, excites the Jám, or landholder of Nawanagar, to raise a tumult; the latter is defeated, and Júnagarh taken . . . 412

The seizure and suicide of Sultán Muzaffir; the Pilgrimage of Mírzá Azíz Koká to Mekka; the Government of Prince Sultán Morád, with Súrj Singh as his deputy, succeeded by that of Mírzá Azíz Koká, on his return from the Pilgrimage, and the death of Akbar . . . 420

PREFACE.

MOHAMMEDAN historians generally tire the patience of the reader by too minute a detail of sieges and battles, of murder and intrigue, without relieving the fatiguing sameness of their narratives, by the more pleasing and instructive accounts of individual character, or the policy and domestic manners of a people. The author of the "Mirát Ahmadí," who gives us a political and statistical history of the Gujarát province, must be exempted from this general censure. He commences with the early history of the country, under the Hindú Rájás, in the tenth, eleventh, and twelfth, centuries of our era ; and has briefly sketched the Mohammedan invasions, which, at this time, happened under the kings of Ghazní and Ghór. After narrating its subsequent conquest, in the thirteenth century, by the Patan kings of Dehlí, and the rise of native Mohammedan princes in the province, he details its political management by the Moghul emperors, from Akbar to Aurangzíb. He then minutely describes the contests and disturbances, which, from the death of Aurangzíb, A.D. 1707, to the defeat of the Mahrattas by Ahmad Sháh Abdalí, A.D. 1761, tended gradually to destroy the prosperity of the province; and concludes his history by an Appendix, containing an account of the various sects of Hindús and Mohammedans, the different parganahs, and the most remarkable places of religious resort. This last portion gives a connected history of the Mahratta transactions in that quarter; and ends with the settlement, at Baroda, of Dámají Gaikwár, and the death of Bálájí Bájí Ráo, after the unfortunate battle of Pánipat.

The materials of this work were collected by Mohammed Alí Khán, the Imperial Díwán, or revenue minister of Gujarát; who, in his preface, gives us a short biographical account of himself. He has there stated, that this history was brought to a conclusion in A.D. 1756; but it was not, in fact, completed until A.D. 1762, or Hij. 1175. As the author commenced collecting materials in A.D. 1748, he must have dedicated fourteen years of attention to its composition. His style is more laboured and verbose than that of most Mohammedan historians; but what it wants in elegance is compensated by general accuracy of facts, and research. In his account of the Rájás, he has added little or nothing to the information which had been previously communicated by the historian Abu-l-Fazl; though this is a period regarding which we could wish to have received more detailed accounts.

I shall therefore endeavour to supply this deficiency, by giving a sketch of the state of Hindú Society, at this time; and, though such be not so complete as I could wish, it can be filled up by the discoveries of future inquirers. Previous to doing so, it is necessary to say something regarding the manuscript of the work. I am not aware that a copy of the Mirát Ahmadí is to be found among any of the existing collections of Persian books now in Europe. The one from which the translation is made was transcribed at Ahmadábád, A.D. 1822, by Narsain Dás, of the Kait tribe. In rendering it into English, I have had the advice and assistance of the very learned Persian Secretary of the Satárah Residency, Mír Khairát Alí, commonly called Mushták; who, had he lived in other times than ours, and under a different system, would, in consideration of his knowledge of the Persian language and of Mohammedan history, have risen to offices of great rank and emolument.

HISTORICAL INTRODUCTION;

ILLUSTRATING

THE CONSTITUTION OF HINDÚ SOCIETY,

AND

THE STATE OF INDIA,

FROM THE

END OF THE TENTH TO THE BEGINNING OF THE THIRTEENTH CENTURY.

Origin of the Southern Hindús.

THE Hindús, south of the Narbadá river, are now amalgamated in religion; and possess a general system of faith and literature, which may be termed Brhámanical Hindúism. There was a time, however, in the history of the peninsula, when they consisted of distinct tribes, who were not Hindús; and this is recognised in their traditionary histories, or indicated by their copper-plate grants of land. Even so late as the Mohammedan invasion, under Mahmúd of Ghazní, the prevailing system of faith, in the provinces of Gujarát, Khándesh, Aurangábád, Bíjapúr, and the Konkans, appears to have been the heterodox one of Hindúism, or the Jaina religion. This will sufficiently account to us why so many remains of this faith, as may be seen in their cave temples, are yet found on the western side of India. But to trace the progressive steps by which this religion was extended from the south-east to the north-west[a] would be foreign to this sketch of Hindú history in more recent times.

The obscurity of their history, from the end of the tenth to the end of the twelfth century.

The interval from the first great battle between the Mohammedans and Hindús, to the establishment of the Patan empire of Dehlí, or from A.D. 977 to 1193, is a time of great obscurity in the history of India. Excepting the names of individual Rájás, who at this period opposed the kings of Ghazní and Ghór, Mohammedan authors give but little information regarding the state of the country. That little, however, when compared

(a) The close affinity between the Hálí Kanara letters and those of Cave inscriptions justifies the conclusion. The Cave temples on the Island of Salsette are yet called the Caves of Kanara; and I possess a Sanskrit grant of land, found at Bhándúp, on that island, in which the Rájá, then reigning at Tanna, specifies his court was composed of five Ministers; one of which, Srí Karna, was particularly consulted on making peace or war in the Karnatic. The Rájá's name is Chín Rájá Deva, who claims descent from the Rájás of Tagara, and from the same family as that of the Sanskrit grant translated by Sir W. Jones (*A.R.* I. p. 357). This dates anterior to the grant now in my possession, which is dated Sáliváhana, 948, A.D. 1026. A branch of this family, or the Silhára tribe of Rájpúts, was at the same time reigning above the Gháts. The capital was Panalla, near Kolápúr.

with the traditionary history of the Hindús, and the list of dynasties supplied by the copper-plate grants of lands, written in Sanskrit, and found throughout India, will enable us to form an opinion of the civil constitution and state of Hindú society in those times.

No work deserving the name of History known among them.

No work deserving the name of History can be said to exist among the Hindús[b]. The lists of their kings, the legends of their holy places, with the traditional histories of provinces and of religious leaders or sects[c], when extensively compared, will give us some insight into the migration and distribution of tribes, or the nature of their civil society. But such can be of little use in history, without some means of fixing the chronology of events to which they relate.

Utility of Sanskrit grants and Mohammedan annals in illustrating their traditions.

It is here that Sanskrit grants and Mohammedan annals come to our aid, in discovering truth. The accounts of even the most recent transactions are so clouded by mythology, that without such we

(b) The Rájá Taringiní is a Sanskrit history of Kashmír, the substance of which has been given to the world (see *A. R.* XV.) by the learned Professor Wilson; but, as it bears much internal evidence of being traditionary and inaccurate, I cannot make it an exception.

(c) These are called, in Sanskrit, Rájá Vansávalís, Máhátmyas, and Charitras.

cannot discriminate between history and fable. The exaggerated notions of chronology among the people, and the pretended antiquity of their gods, have led to the blind endeavour of adapting their domestic history to the fabulous ages of the world, and tended to involve both in almost impenetrable darkness. Other sources of exaggeration will be found in their traditions; of which the most constant is confounding individual revolutions with the general history of India. Such may be discovered most frequently in traditionary accounts of provinces, where the history of the native princes is ignorantly blended with that of their foreign conquerors.

Sanskrit geography of the western coast.

The western coast of India, from the Indus to Dariyá Bahádurgarh, appears to have been known to Sanskrit writers of early times by the name of Sauráshtra, Gurjara, Abhíra, Konkana, and Govaráshtra. The first division extended from Hingula, or Hingláj, in the great western Run, to Jambúka, or Jambúsír, on the Narbadá. From hence to the Tápí, or Taptí river, was Gurjara; and from this, southwards to Devagarh, the country was called Abhíra, or the region of Shepherds[d]. Konkana extended southwards from Devagarh to Sadáse-

(d) See Ward's *Hindoos*, III. p. 450; and Wilford's *Geography of the Puránas*, *A.R.* VIII. p. 336.

ogarh; and from hence to Bahádurgarh was Govaráshtra[e]. The southern divisions, now enumerated, also bore the general name of Ahikshetra, or country of Snakes; which is called, by Ptolomy, Adisatra, from the mountains of which the Chaberas, or Cávery river, has its origin. It was also known to the Sanskrit writers by the name of Maru[f], or the wilderness; from which the Greek and Roman traders, by adopting the Arabic article *Al*, and inflecting the word, obtained the appellation of Limyrica, or Almúrika. Abhíra was distributed into several minor divisions; as Berbera[g] or Marahta, from the Taptí river to Bassein; Virata, from hence to Bankút; and Kiráta, from Bankút to Devagarh. The latter name implies the region of Foresters; and was also

(e) Govaráshtra was the country about Goa, and is the same as the district otherwise named Hayaga. Some geographers would extend its northern limits on the Bombay side of Sadáseogarh, and thus contract those of the Konkana.—See Wilson's *Kashmír, A. R.* XV. p. 47; and Grant Duff's *History of the Mahrattas,* I. p. 4.

(f) It is so named in a grant of land by Crishna Ráya of Vijayanagar, or Bijnaggar, dated Sáliváhana, 1448; A.D. 1526.

(g) Berbera is the Barbarike of Arian's Periplus. The name of Berbera was originally applied to a more northern region, as were most of the Sanskrit geographical divisions known in the south; plainly indicating that the Bráhmans introduced the language and the customs from the north.

applied to the western part of Gondwána, which was distinguished, however, by the appellation of Kiráta Chanda.

A.D. 977, war with the Hindus, who are defeated.

When the Mohammedans, under the first king of Ghazní, Násir-ud-dín-Sabuktagín, carried their arms against the Hindús, they were opposed by an allied army of Rájpúts, commanded by the Rájás of the Panjáb, Dehlí, Kanauj, and Kálanjar. The confederate army of the latter, amounting to a hundred thousand horse, accompanied by many elephants, was led to battle by Jaipál I., chief of the Panjáb, and son of Chait or Chaitra Pál. His country extended from Sirhind, south-east, to the river of Alishang in Kábúl, north-west, or the district of Lamghán. The kingdoms of his allies were situated near the Jumna and Ganges, and could not have exceeded in extent the modern provinces of Dehlí, Agra, and Allá-hábád. The opposing armies, having met near Lamghán, fought a battle, which was gained by Sabuktagín. If we may believe the accounts, the Rájpúts, though numerous as the locusts of the wilderness, proved themselves very inferior soldiers, when tried against their opponents. The latter, though few in number, were confident in themselves; and Sabuktagín, by successively bringing up fresh squadrons of cavalry against the enemy's centre, succeeded in breaking their line. After this had been effected, the whole of the Hindús gave way, and left the Mohammedans an easy victory.

Causes which rendered them inferior in war to the Mohammedans.

The latter appear to have been so unequal in number to their enemies, that, knowing, as we do, the bravery of the Rájpúts, and their utter recklessness of life, we might well doubt whether the armies were so disproportioned as represented by Mohammedan authority. Causes, however, were at this time existing, in the constitution of Hindú society, which rendered the Rájpúts inferior in war. The Mohammedans, stimulated by religious zeal and elated by the success of conquest, had triumphantly carried their arms and their faith from the shores of the Mediterranean to the banks of the Jaxartes. Every successive conquest had enriched their leaders; and the secret springs of avarice and ambition equally impelled the soldier and his chief to support fatigue or encounter danger. The whole were, consequently, a devoted band of warriors, consecrated to the support of a common cause, and had been long accustomed to exertion. The Hindús, on the contrary, though bound together by religious faith, viewed it more with superstitious awe than worldly enthusiasm; and, though ready to sacrifice their lives on the funeral pile, when fortune forsook them, were more disposed to propitiate her favour by vain ceremonies than secure success by daring efforts. Other causes were not wanting to destroy unanimity, and paralyse their spirit; of which deliberative councils of war, to which the priesthood were admitted, and the inferior equipment of their cavalry, were the principal.

Councils of war.

Multiplicity of opinion is no where more inimical to success than in war. One brave and active commander, who has mastered the affections of his soldiers, and can control their wishes, leads them against an enemy with a confident daring that can do all but ensure victory; whilst a confederated body, without any singleness of effort, wastes the time in frivolous discussions, or finds the bravery of its numbers rendered nugatory through the jealousy or caprice of its leaders. It was the custom, as would appear, among the Hindú chiefs of those days to assemble their feudal retainers on occasions of great public emergency, or when the national safety and religion were threatened from without. The confederate leaders submitted in part to the guidance of a common chief, who had, as we learn, the title of Pál, or Protector; though we are left to surmise whether he was entitled to the office by birth or raised to it by election. The last was probably the right on which he held his command; and, if so, it gave those he commanded undue influence over his authority. To add to the difficulty of his situation, he was, moreover, thwarted in his measures by the Bráhmans, or priesthood; who had a voice in the national councils, which took cognisance of his proceedings. We are told by Ferishta, that Sabuktagín, on first advancing towards India, had fought a previous skirmish, in which he was successful; and, after consenting to return to Ghazní, was to receive a tribute for his forbearance. No sooner, however, had the Mohammedans retired, than the Bráhmans advised that the treaty should not be ratified. Jaipál, on reaching Lahore, imprisoned the persons whom Sabuktagín had sent to receive the money; though the noblest Kshatrís, or Rájpúts, who also formed part of the council, remonstrated against so impolitic a proceeding. At this time, it was the custom for the Bráhmans to be seated on the right, and the Rájpúts on the left, of the throne. The former, who kept in subjection the minds of a superstitious people, could enforce their advice by appealing to popular prejudices; but the latter, with more wisdom, and with the natural manliness of their character, said, "The troops have not forgotten the terror of the enemy's arms; and Jaipál may rest assured that Sabuktagín will not brook such an insult, without a dreadful revenge[h]." The issue soon proved the truth of the prediction; and Jaipál, by not listening to their advice, brought on fresh disasters, with the return of the Mohammedans.

Inferior equipment of the Hindú cavalry.

The latter, we are told, were better mounted than the Hindús, who were unable to withstand their charge. The motley cavalry of feudal chieftains, brought together on emergency, could not well sustain the superior weight of northern horses and their riders, when these had been long trained to the exercises of war, and taught to act in concert. The Rájpút vassals were an ill-equipped and worse-commanded body of national militia, who performed military service as the price of a feudal fief[i]; and, though sometimes called out in cases of internal warfare, were little prepared or inclined to face the standing army of a foreign invader.

State of India at this time.

Hindústán was, at this time, apportioned among various tribes of Rájpúts; whose grants still remaining, as memorials of

(h) Briggs's *Ferishta*, I. p. 17.

(i) See Colonel Tod's *Military Service of Rájastan*, I. p. 147.

their sway, enable us to form some opinion of their general distribution. Many of the tribes, now known, do not appear to have had an existence till some time subsequent to the first invasion by Sabuktagín, as proved by the tenor of their gifts of land. We may enumerate the Chohan and Rahtore tribes among those who had not then risen into notice; though their own vanity, and the pretensions of their poetical legends, would claim for them a higher antiquity[k]. The earliest seat of the former appears to have been Sámbar, or Sákambharí, north-west of Ajmír; as Vella Deva, or Bil Deo, was probably the first of the family. The first of the Rahtore tribe was Yasovigraha, or Srí Pál, who calls himself a prince of the Solar race; plainly intimating that the appellation of Rahtore had not yet been adopted; though the third in descent from him, Srí Chandra Deva, who conquered the realm of Kanauj, might have assumed it soon after. Previous to this time, the prince of Kanauj, who was leagued in the confederacy against the Mohammedans, had the appellation of Korah; but regarding the tribes to which the other confederates belonged

([k]) See Colebrooke's translation of an Inscription from the Fíroz Lát, *A.R.* VII. p. 180. in reference to the former; and *Asiatic Researches*, IX. p. 441. XV. p. 461. regarding the latter.

nothing certain can be fixed, before we obtain multiplied translations of Sanskrit grants in the north of India. Bengal was ruled, at this period, by the Voidya monarchs, who had their capital at Nuddea, on the Ganges. In the south of India, the kingdom of Pandya, or Madura, now on the decline, sank under the rising fortunes of the Chóla kings of Tanjore, who also reduced the ancient kingdom of Chéra[l]. The south-western part of Upper Kanara, or Karnáta, near the Krishna, was possessed by the Yádavas, who appear to have been a pastoral people. They were confined on the west by the Siyálara[m] or Silhára tribe of Rájpúts, who had for their capital Panalla, near Kolápúr, and were in possession of the greater part of the country, on the sea-coast. On the north, and in the province of Khándesh, the Silháras were bounded by a branch, if not the original stock of the Chálukya family, who claimed descent from the Yádavas. Their capital was Mánkhet, apparently the same as that now called Mángarh, or Mánikgarh. They assumed

(l) See Professor Wilson's able Introduction to the M'Kenzie Collection.

(m) Two grants from this family are in my possession, and two have been already published.—See *Asiatic Researches*, I. p. 357; and Bombay *Literary Transactions*, III. p. 393.

the high-sounding titles of Rájá of Rájás, in a grant of land[n]; and styled themselves Parama Bhattárak, Parama Ishwar, or Supreme Lords. Their religious faith was the Jaina; but the person who received the gift was a Bráhman of the Bharadwája tribe of Rig Veda. Whether this family of the Chálukya had any connexion with the former Rájá of Tryambak, called, in Khándesh, the Gaurí, or Gaulí Rájá[o], must be mere matter of opinion: but this much is certain, that another branch of it was established, about this time, in Nahrwálah; and that their previous settlement in Khándesh, as ascertained by this grant, is fatal to the authenticity of the Mirát Ahmadí's account of their origin in Gujarát. The Gohila tribe had previously established themselves in Málwá, and may claim the celebrated Rájá Bhoja[p], as a member of their family. Not long after, the Parmara had succeeded them in this quarter, and were probably their descendants[q].

([n]) Grants of land by Kákka Rájá, dated Sáliváhana, 894, or A.D. 972.

([o]) Wilson's M'Kenzie Coll. Intr. c. vi.

([p]) See Translation of Inscriptions from Abú, *A. R.* XVI. p. 322.

([q]) Grants of this tribe, dating A.D. 1134, translated by Mr. Colebrooke.—*Trans. R.A.S.* vol. I. p. 231.

Government of the Rájás.

The different principalities, into which India was divided, were of greater or less extent; and were called Mandalas, or districts. The sovereign of a large tract was styled Mahá Mandala Ishwar, or a Chakravartí Rájá, signifying lord of an extensive country, and indicating that he ruled over several minor tributaries. The latter were named Mandaladesas[r], and are sometimes mentioned in the Mohammedan histories by the appellation of Mandalik Rájás. No historical records of their form of government having been preserved to our time, we can only judge of it by the analogy of institutions yet existing among the Jhárejás of Kach, and the tribes of Rájpútána, which are very similar to the feudal system of Europe. The several members of a chief's family would, at his death, be entitled to a certain appanage of his demesnes; and every district, so acquired, would constitute a distinct principality; subject to a similar division, at the decease of the principal, as had taken place in the original possession. Every minor tributary would thus, in time, possess a body of kinsmen, standing in the same relation to him as he and his brothers bore to a common ancestor; and would be called the

(r) Cavelly Boria's *Account of the Jainas, A. R.* IX. p. 246.

Bháiad, or brotherhood of the chiefs and of their kinsmen. Such is the present state of government in Kach; and a similar constitution existed, in former times, among the members of the different tribes, as clearly indicated by grants of land. The individuals of the original family had the unlimited authority of their own lands; were guardians of the public peace, and charged with the chastisement of general enemies; whilst the kinsmen were bound to attend them, in time of war, as the price of the possessions they enjoyed.

Such were the discordant materials of the Hindú army that opposed the Mohammedans; and, when we consider the state of India at this time, there is no cause for wonder why the latter experienced so little opposition in conquering it.

A. D. 1001. Mahmúd of Ghazní's first expedition to India.

Mahmúd of Ghazní, who had succeeded his father Sabuktagín, was a bigoted adherent to the Sunní[s] faith; and a stickler regarding points of doctrine[t]. The idolaters of India were, therefore, the object of his aversion; and he had not long succeeded to

(s) The Sunnís are those who believe the Mohammedan traditions, and follow the three first Khalifs; and the Shías are the followers of Alí and the twelve Imáms. The Turks adhere to the former, the Persians to the latter.

(t) Life of Firdausí, in the Tazkerat-us-Shoará, or Lives of the Poets, by Daulat Sháh.

the throne before he led his first crusade against the Hindús. Accompanied by ten thousand horse, he left Ghazní in the month of August; and, marching against his father's former opponent, Jaipál I., met him at Pesháwar. The Hindú army, which consisted of twelve thousand horse and thirty thousand foot, supported by three hundred elephants, was defeated with the loss of five thousand men. Jaipál and his kinsmen were made prisoners; but, as the former had been twice defeated, and was deemed unworthy of reigning, he resigned the throne to his son Ananda, or Ananga Pál, and expiated his misfortunes by giving up his life on a funeral pile. Mahmúd obtained much plunder on this occasion; and the personal jewels taken from Jaipál were estimated at eighty thousand pounds. After this victory, the Mohammedans invested and reduced the fort of Bahtinda, situated among the Bháttís or Shepherds, in the most easterly and inaccessible part of the Panjáb kingdom. Jaipál generally resided at this fort; and probably did so as a measure of security, though Lahore appears to have been his capital.

After the first expedition, the king of Ghazní
A. D. 1005. Hij. 396. established Mohammedan governors in the country of the Panjáb; and made a treaty

with Ananga Pál; who, as we may infer from the Mohammedan accounts, was to pay an annual tribute. The minor Rájás, who had borne allegiance to the chief of Lahore, now refused to give their proportion of this contribution to Ananga Pál; but were encouraged by the latter, who might urge this as an excuse for not forwarding the stipulated sum due to the conqueror. One of the refractory tributaries was Rájá Vijaya Ráya, or Bíjí Ráy, who resided at Bhátnah[u], now called Bhatnír; situated on the northern extremity of the Bikánír desert. The display of so much resistance among his tributaries made Mahmúd undertake his second expedition against the Hindús.

The army accordingly marched, by Multán,
Second Expedition. against Bhátnah[x]; and, on reaching the territory of the Bháttís, was met by a force,

(u) The Habíbu-s-Sair calls it Batnah, but Colonel Briggs's Translation of Ferishta has Bhateea. It is the same place as that called Bhulneer in Arrowsmith's Map.

(x) See Ferishta, the Habíbu-s-Sair, and Price's Mohammedan History, on the authority of the Kholásata-l-Akhbár. Ferishta makes Mahmúd march to Bhátnah, Hij. 395; and the following year against Multán, to punish its refractory Mohammedan governor. The latter did not take place until after the war with his father-in-law, Elík Khán, if we may trust the other authorities. The Habíbu-s-Sair, and Kholásata-l-Akhbár, were written more than an hundred years prior to Ferishta, and are, in this matter, more trustworthy.

commanded by Vijaya Ráya; who, having strongly posted himself, bravely checked the progress of the Mohammedans for three days. The latter, at length prevailing, invested the fortress; from which the Rájá fled, perceiving it was no longer tenable, and left only a small garrison of his troops to continue the defence. It was soon after taken by assault; and the chief, Vijaya Ráya, when pursued and sur rounded, preferred running his breast against a sword to being made a prisoner.

A. D. 1007. Hij. 398. Third Expedition.

The crusades against the Indians were, for a time, suspended; as Mahmúd's father-in-law, Elík Khán, had invaded Khorásán, and demanded his attention. After this matter had been settled, the interest of religion called him back to Hindústán. The Mohammedan rulers of Multán, established there by the kings of Ghazní, were permitted to continue the government in their families, on the payment of a tribute to their liege lords. The grandson of the original chief at length succeeded to the office, and, swerving from his allegiance, abandoned the tenets of the faithful. This induced Mahmúd to undertake his third expedition[y].

(y) This, according to Ferishta, would be his fourth expedition: but that author, who has closely followed the Tabkát Akbarí, having misplaced the expedition to Multán, as noticed in a former

But the rebel, who sought and obtained the aid of Ananga Pál, on this occasion, seeing the army of the latter defeated and dispersed, thought of purchasing his master's pardon; and obtained it, by a profession of implicit obedience for the future, and the promise of an annual tribute of twenty thousand golden dirhems[z].

A. D. 1008. Fourth Expedition.

But, though transgression of the faithful might be forgotten, the backsliding of an idolater could not be overlooked. Ananga Pál had assisted, in rebellion, Mahmúd's governor and tributary; and the latter was now resolved to revenge the insult. The former had timely warning of his intention; and sent ambassadors to invite the assistance of the Hindú princes of the country. The latter now considered the expulsion of the Mohamme-

former note, here repeats the story of a renegado Hindú, named Sewakpál, having swerved from his allegiance. There was no such person, as appears; and the mistake has arisen from having placed the expedition to Multán before the war with Elík Khán, instead of after it. We are not informed how this Sewakpál obtained power; and in some manuscripts he is called Záb-Sah, being an evident error of the copyist's for Nawá-Sah; signifying "grandchild," a name which was applied to the revolted governor of Multán, Abul Fattah Daod, the grandson of Shaikh Hamíd Lodí. Price, in his Mohammedan History, has also mistaken the name, and calls him Nowásah Sháh.

(z) Briggs's *Ferishta*, vol. I. p. 41.

dans from India as a sacred duty; and hastened, with their contingents, to the neighbourhood of the Panjáb. A greater army than had yet assembled took the field, and, as Ferishta tells us, numbered, among its leaders, the Rájás of Dehlí[a], Kanauj, Kálinjar, Goaliár, Ajmír, and Ujain. The Mohammedans had marched from Ghazní in the beginning of spring, and met the Hindús, in the neighbourhood of Pesháwar, west of the Indus. After the armies had rested for forty days in sight of each other, and the Mohammedans had entrenched their camp, as some security against the hosts of the enemy, Mahmúd resolved on giving battle. To commence the attack, he detached a body of archers to skirmish on his front; but these were soon driven back by the Kahkres, or Gakkars, a warlike tribe, then inhabiting the salt range, or Johd mountains, between the Behut (Hydaspes) and Indus, and who are the ancestors of the modern Jauts. Such was the fury with which these barbarians made their onset, that, rushing pell-mell into the lines of the Mohammedans, they committed dreadful carnage among the latter; of whom four or five thousand fell victims, according to various accounts. The Gak-

([a]) The seat of government in the Dehlí province appears to have been Mírát.

kars, described to have had their heads and feet bare, were armed with various weapons; but such was the impression of their desperate effort, that Mahmúd began to think of retiring from his entrenchments, when, fortunately for the cause of Islám, the elephant, which carried Ananga Pál, frightened by the naphtha balls, turned and fled. The death or flight of a leader, among eastern armies, is the signal for a general retreat; and the panic of the Hindús, who saw their chief retire, becoming general, they gave way in every quarter. Five thousand Arabian horse, with ten thousand of the Turkish and Afghán cavalry, uninterruptedly pursued the fugitives for two days and nights; during which, it is said, twenty thousand Hindús were slain[b]. Thirty elephants were taken, and the king obtained much other booty.

If we might trust Ferishta's authority, Mahmúd, at this time marching into the mountains between the sources of the Rávi (Hydraotes) and Beyáh[c] (Hyphasis) rivers, captured the celebrated fortress of Nágrakót, then called the Fort of Bhím. It was not, however, till the fol-

(b) *Ferishta*, vol. I. p. 47.

(c) Called, in Sanskrit, Vipása; from which the Greeks got Hyphasis.

A.D. 1009. lowing year, Hij. 400, according to the Tabakát Akbarí and Habíbu-s-Sair, that this expedition was undertaken; and, as the hostile armies, prior to the last battle, had consumed three or four months in operations west of the Indus, it is not probable that Mahmúd could have marched into India at the commencement of the rainy season[d]. The fortress of Nágrakót had been for ages the object of Hindú veneration; and not far distant from it there are temples, near one of those extraordinary spectacles of nature, a burning fountain, for which the ignorant have a superstitious and idolatrous regard. The last is known by the name of Jwálá-Mukhí[e], or "the effulgent countenance."

Fifth Expedition. When Mahmúd invested Nágrakót, which was his fifth expedition, the temples were filled with wealth and jewels; the pious offerings, by rulers of the neighbouring kingdoms, that had been thus accumulating for many years. Such was the vast booty obtained, by

([d]) The Hij. year 399, given for the march to Pesháwar, or the previous year A.D. commenced the 5th September, A.D. 1008; and, as the spring season, when he left Ghazní, would not commence till A.D. 1009, he must have spent the summer in Kábúl, and set out for Hindústán about October.

([e]) In Mandelslo's *Indian Travels*, p. 14, it is mentioned by the name of Kala Maka.

this expedition, that the conqueror, on his return to Ghazní, prepared a magnificent festival; and, having caused his pavilion to be pitched without the city, exhibited, to the assembled multitude, a golden throne and other ensigns of luxury, which the spoils of Hindústán had enabled him to prepare.

As the Afgháns, inhabiting the mountains of Ghór, employed Mahmúd's attention in the succeeding year, the war against the Hindús was for a time suspended. But another crusade against idolatry was, according to Ferishta, undertaken to Thánesar, near Dehlí, in Hij.
A.D. 1011. 402; though the Habíbu-s-Sair says, that, after the conquest of Nágrakót, the most urgent solicitations for peace were made by the paramount sovereign of the Hindús, who promised an annual supply of fifty elephants, and a remittance of tribute to the treasury at Ghazní. Mahmúd so far complied with the proposal, it is said, that the commercial intercourse between the subjects of the adverse powers was renewed. The account of this
Sixth Expedition. expedition[f] to India is, that the king

(f) Ferishta makes Mahmúd march back from Ghór, to attack Multán in the previous year; and if such had taken place, it would constitute the sixth expedition. It is mentioned in the

Tabkát

of Ghazní, hearing of Thánesar being held in equal veneration by the Hindús, as Mekka by the Mohammedans, resolved to march against it, and destroy the idol Jagsoma, which was worshipped there. As a treaty existed between Ananga Pál and Mahmúd, by which the former was bound not to molest the Mohammedans in their march through the country, the latter sent to the Rájá, according to Ferishtá's account, informing him of his intentions, and requesting that safeguards might be given to protect his towns and villages from the camp-followers. It is something new, indeed, in politics, to find one of the parties to a treaty, entered into for mutual advantage, commanding to have that portion of it fulfilled which suits their wishes; whilst an open avowal is made, that there is no intention of abiding by the remainder. Such, however, is the statement of this affair by the author just quoted; and, as Ananga Pál is said to have prepared an entertainment for the king of Ghazní, this assertion casts suspicion on the narrative of the expedition, which bears more the impress of fiction than of history.

Tabkát Akbarí, from which Ferishta borrowed; but it is not noticed by the prior authorities, which I possess. Having, therefore, doubts regarding it, I have rejected his account.

Part of the two succeeding years was spent in sending an army into Jurján; and in political discussions with the Khalif of Baghdad, regarding the surrender of the Khorásán province, and the city of Samarkand, to the government
A.D. 1014. Hij. 405. Seventh Expedition.
of Ghazní. Another crusade against idolatry was at length resolved on; and Mahmúd led this, the seventh one, against Nárdain, the then boundary of India[g], or the eastern part of the Hindú Kúsh; separating, as Ferishta says, the countries of Hindústán and Turkistán, and remarkable for its excellent fruits. The country into which the army of Ghazní marched appears to have been the same as that now called Káfiristán, where the inhabitants were, and still are, idolaters[h]; and are named the Siáh Púsh, or black-vested, by the Mohammedans of latter times. In Nárdain there was a temple, which the army of Ghazní destroyed; and brought from thence a stone covered with certain inscriptions, which were, according to the Hindús, of great antiquity[i].

(g) Habíbu-s-Saír.

(h) Consult Mr. Elphinstone's *Kabool,* Vol. II. p. 127, for an account of this people.

(i) Briggs's *Ferishta,* I. p. 65.—There is again much confusion in Ferishta's account of this expedition, which he places in Hij.

Mahmúd, in returning to Ghazní, marched along the southern face of the mountains of Hindú Kúsh: till hearing that the ruler of Pansír, now called Panjshír[k], was an infidel, and possessed some of those elephants called the elephants of Sulaimán, he advanced against this place, plundering and murdering the inhabitants.

The murder of the king of Khawárazm (the ancient Chorasmia), who was Mahmúd's brother-in-law, called the attention of the latter to that quarter: and the affairs of that state, having been thus thrown into confusion, occupied the chief part of his time for the three succeeding years. At the expiration of this period, Hindústán, with its dependencies, was doomed,
Eighth Expedition. for the eighth time, to become the theatre of the king of Ghazní's operations. After collecting a numerous army from Turkistán, Máwará-un-Nahr, (Transoxiana) and Khorásán, the followers of which, in aiding the crusade, were as much instigated by avarice as religion, Mahmúd marched for Kanauj in the spring

Hij. 412; and makes Mahmúd march to Bulnat, Hij. 404; though the narratives evidently refer to the same places and transactions.

([k]) This is the name of the river which joins that of Ghúrband, and gives name to a pass which leads through the Hindú Kúsh from Kábúl to Turkistán.

of Hij. 409[1]. The author of the Habíbu-s-Sair tells us that, besides the king's regular troops, twenty-thousand Mohammedan crusaders formed part of the force, destined to destroy the devoted country, and the yet remaining strongholds of idolatry. Kanauj is described as distant from Ghazní a journey of three months: and the Mohammedan army followed, as would appear, the route of Peshawar, to the attack. Ferishta makes the troops march from hence directly to Kanauj, and afterwards to Mírát: but here his ignorance of geography has so confused the account, that the army moves about, in all directions, without any obvious reason. After having passed the Indus, and entered Hindústán, the Mohammedans first attacked, according to the Habíbu-s-Sair, a strong fortress; of which the ruler, a person of rank and consequence, and an idolater, is said to have submitted, and adopted the faith of Islám. The name of this fortress is not given, but

(1) Ferishta, and the Habíbu-s-Sair. As the spring season is, however, mentioned, and as Hij. 409 commenced the 20th May, A.D. 1018, Mahmúd must have left Ghazní in the end of the preceding Hijira year 408; which would correspond with the spring of A.D. 1018. Mohammedan historians, not attending to the fact of the seasons, west of the Indus, being the same as those in Europe, and forgetting the particular commencement of the Hij. years, are constantly committing such blunders.

appears to have been the same as Mírát[m]. From hence the army marched, along the banks of the Jumna, to another fort not named[n]; the same, as we learn from other sources[o], with Máhwan, near Matra; and which was the capital of the Rájá of Bindrában. The then governing Rájá in this province was Kúlchand, who attacked the Mohammedans, and was defeated. This unfortunate Hindú chief, after the issue of the battle, fled, along with his wife, and was pursued; when, seeing no means of escape, and doubtless to avoid pollution, he first murdered his partner, and then slew himself. Eighty-five elephants were taken by the Mohammedans. The troops next advanced against Matra, or Mathurá, not far distant, and then the most venerated place of Hindú worship. Here the people of Ghazní were so struck by the magnificence of the buildings, that, says my authority[p], no words can express it. The palaces and other buildings, which were many,

(m) Ferishta quotes the Habíbu-s-Sair, in asserting that the Rájá of Kanauj adopted the faith of Islám; but this history makes no such assertion: and it is evident, from a comparison of the two accounts, that Ferishta has transferred the narrative of the Habíbu-s-Sair regarding this nameless fort, and made it applicable to Kanauj.

(n) Habíbu-s-Sair.

(o) Ferishta.

(p) Habíbu-s-Sair.

are described as being built of stone and white marble; and such was the feeling of wonder excited in the mind of Mahmúd, that, while writing to the nobles of Ghazní, he said, "Should any one propose to build such a town, he could not do so in two-and-twenty years, with the assistance of the most skilful architect, and after expending millions of dínárs." But bigotry stifled, in the breast of Mahmúd, every nobler feeling; and though the art of the architect could raise his admiration, it could not make him generous to stay the work of destruction. The solidity of the temples alone resisted his efforts: the idols were broken down; jewels were carried away of immense value; and every thing combustible was given to the flames. Twenty-six days were thus spent: the king marched along the bank of the Ab-Gang, or Ganges, where he captured seven fortifications, and arrived at Kanauj on the eighteenth of Shabán[q], or end of December. Six or seven months had elapsed since the army left Ghazní: the Panjáb rivers on the route had, at this season of the year, impeded its advance; and the solicitude of all was relieved by seeing before them the object of their wishes. The Rájá of Kanauj, who is called by some Koráh[r], and by others

(q) Habíbu-s-Sair. (r) Tabakát Akbarí.

Jaipál[8], warned, no doubt, by the fate of Matra, and perceiving the hopelessness of resistance, sued for peace, and paid a tribute ; though it is asserted, by other accounts, that he fled. This was followed by fresh conquests; where the blood of the idolaters was made to flow, that the intolerant spirit of Islám might be gratified.

The recital of the enormities committed during these barbarous expeditions sickens and fatigues the mind by the sameness of the narrative ; towns were captured and set on fire ; temples destroyed; idols broken, or converted into currency, when found of precious metals ; the inhabitants pillaged and carried into captivity ; while commerce and cultivation were totally ruined and neglected. Such were the numbers of the captives carried away, after the sack of Matra, that a slave was sold in the Mohammedan camp for ten dirhems, or about five shillings of English money. Yet the unsatiable mind of Mahmúd was not satisfied with the sufferings he had inflicted on idolatry, or the wealth he had acquired ; and, when affairs in other quarters left his thoughts at liberty, he

(8) The Habíbu-s-Sair calls him Jaipál ; who is the same, no doubt, as Jaipál II. the son of Ananga Pál : but otherwise called Koráh, from the appellation of his tribe.

again turned his attention to India. Two more expeditions were undertaken against the devoted country; one of which was directed against the fort of Kálinjar, and the other to the temple of Somnáth, in Gujarát. The former was undertaken to revenge the attack on the Rájá of Kanauj; who, in Mahmúd's absence, was put to death by Nanda Rájá of Kálinjar, as he had submitted to the Mohammedans, and accepted their alliance. It is difficult to reconcile the conflicting testimony of the original authorities[t] in this matter; though it appears, that, puzzled by the contradiction of dates given for this event, they have made two separate expeditions to Kálinjar, where only one took place[u]. About the time of Mahmúd's seventh expedition, the paramount sovereignty of India had been transferred, at the death of Ananga Pál, to his son Jaipál II[x], who, if not the Rájá of Kanauj, is the same as he who fled when the Mohammedans approached that city. If the

A.D. 1022. Hij. 413. Ninth Expedition.

Review of events preceding it.

(t) Ferishta and the Tabakát Akbarí.

(u) The author of the Tabakát Akbarí places Mahmúd's first march to Kálinjar, Hij. 410, or the year after he had taken Kanauj; but Ferishta gives Hij. 412 as the date. The second march is placed, by the former, Hij. 413, and by the latter, 414: but either one or both must be wrong.

(x) See Briggs's Ferishta I.

Koráh family were not the original lords of the latter, but to which opinion I incline, the Rájá, who brought on himself the hostility of the neighbouring princes, was one who had gained the good will of the king of Ghazní, and was appointed to the office. But, be the truth of this transaction what it may, we are told that, when the Mohammedan army approached the banks of the Jumna, Jaipál II. who had repeatedly fled before the standards of Islám, now assisted by Nanda Rájá of Kálinjar, took up a position on the eastern bank, with the ostensible motive of giving battle. The Hindú host of horse and foot, though far exceeding in numbers their opponents, and supported by six hundred and forty elephants, struck with panic, decamped during the night; but, the story of their being routed by eight persons[y], from the army of Ghazní, is too ridiculous to deserve notice. While the Mohammedans advanced to Kálinjar, their march was distinguished by the usual excesses; the fortress was invested and besieged; and peace was, after a time, purchased by a money contribution and a present of three hundred elephants.

The last crusade against idolatry, in which the king of Ghazní was engaged, was an expe-

(y) See Ferishta and the Tabakát Akbarí.

dition to the temple of Somnáth, situated near Diú, in the province of Gujarát. Poetry and fable have been alike employed to adorn the narrative and magnify the importance of this conquest. But, if the record of past events borrows more from fancy than memory, and substitutes amusement for instruction, the order of knowledge is inverted; and, where history ought to have commenced, fable has not yet terminated. In this matter, doubt is better than credulity; and, if we hesitate to give assent to much that has been said of Somnáth, we will not insult the spirit of philosophy. The district

The religious sectaries who worshipped at Somnáth.

of the Gujarát peninsula, now called Bábrewár, of which Billáwal Patan is the chief town, was formerly known by the name of Patan Somnáth. It derived this appellation from the title of a celebrated idol, whose temple existed in the neighbourhood; and the Bráhmans of the country assert, that here Siva was worshipped under the symbol of the Linga, or Phallus[z]. The symbol then venerated was one of the twelve famous Lingas, or Phalli, which were of old set up in different parts; and of which Mahákál, at Ujain, and Rámnáth in Southern India, are well known to Mohammedan history. The former was destroyed by

(z) Appendix to the Mirát Ahmadí.

Shams-ud-dín Altimsh, two hundred years after the time of Mahmúd of Ghazní; and was, we are told, formed on the same plan as Somnáth[a]. This is conclusive evidence that the assertion of the Bráhmans respecting the temple of Somnáth is correct; and Mahádeo, or Siva, was the deity, who, under the title of Swayambhú Náth[b], or Swayam Náth, the self-existent, was there worshipped. On the authority of the Habíbu-s-Sair, this idol was formed of cut stone, five cubits in height; of which three cubits were visible, and two were below the surface. The Hindús then venerated the idol more than any other[c]; the attendants washed it daily with water brought from the Ganges[d];

([a]) This great temple, in Málwá, was destroyed A.D. 1233. See Briggs's Ferishta I. p. 24.

([b]) Derived from three Sanskrit words, स्वयं *Swayam*, of himself, भू *Bhú*, existing, and नाथ *Náth*, Lord; but which is sometimes, for sake of brevity, pronounced Swayam Náth, without the medial radical. This would be written by the Mohammedans سویمناته *Swayam Náth;* which, by the neglect of the points and the reduplicated ي *ya*, becomes سومناته *Somnáth*. But Colonel Vans Kennedy, remarking on this note, says that the name is rather derived from सीम and नाथ, lord of the moon; a name of Siva under which he is generally worshipped.

([c]) Habíbu-s-Sair.

([d]) Rauzatu-s-saffá, quoted in the Mirát Ahmadí.

the revenue of ten thousand villages[e] was assigned for the support of its temple ; two thousand Bráhmans performed the ceremonies of its worship ; five hundred dancing women, with three hundred musicians, were ready to perform before it ; many smaller images of gold and silver, in the temple, surrounded this the greatest of the gods ; and three hundred barbers were waiting to shave the devotees who sought admittance to the holy place. Such was the popularity of this obscene worship ; such the fanaticism of its followers, that the princes of Hindústán devoted their daughters to the service of the temple[f]; and, at the occurrence of an eclipse, sometimes as many as a thousand individuals came to perform their devotions. The religion was of old common to Arabia and India ; and there is reason for believing, what the early Mohammedan authorities assert, that Lát, worshipped by the idolaters of Mekka, was a similar deity as the Swayam Náth of the Hindús[g]. Du-

(e) My copy of the Habíbu-s-Sair says ten thousand, and is supported in this account by the appendix to the Mirát Ahmadí, which quotes the authority of the Rauzatu-s-saffá : but Colonel Briggs's Ferishta says only two thousand.

(f) Ferishta.

(g) The Habíbu-s-Sair quotes the following verse from Shaikh Faríd-ud-dín Attár, as an authority for this opinion :—

"The army of Mahmúd found in Somnáth the idol whose name was

ring the seventh century of our era, the worship of Siva, if not prevalent, was at least known in the west of India[h]; and existed, for some time after, in friendly union with the heterodox faith of Jaina. But to trace the origin of the two sects, their connexion, enmity, and disunion; or to show by what means the last gained ascendency, would occupy more space and attention than can be here devoted to this interesting subject.

The fame of the temple of Swayambhú Náth at length reached the ear of Mahmúd; who, several years, had been projecting another expedition, for the destruction of the vain idolaters. Accompanied by thirty thousand horse, besides many volunteers, he left Ghazní the
A.D. 1025. October 7. Tenth Expedition. 10th of Shabán, Hij. 416[i]; and in the middle of the following month, arrived at Multán. An inhospitable desert lay on the

was Lát." Herodotus (B. III. c. 8.) notices Alilat as one of the idols worshipped by the ancient Arabs; but makes it a female deity, by identifying it with Urania. The name of this goddess is probably from the Arabic الهة Iláhat, which signifies the horned Moon, and the Sun. The assertion of the father of history is, therefore, reconcileable with the opinion of Mohammedan writers regarding the idol at Mekka, which was, they say, a male deity, and the same with Swayam Náth.

(h) See translation of an inscription from Abú, dated Samvat 727, A.D. 671.

(i) Habíbu-s-Sair.

route to Gujarát; water and provisions were to be carried where none could be procured; and twenty thousand camels were laden with supplies. The army came to several fortifications in the desert, which submitted without resistance; sacked Ajmír; passed Nahrwálah; and arrived, at Somnáth, in the month of Zulhijjah. Here
A.D. 1026. the Mohammedans beheld a large fortress, whose walls were washed by the sea. The people within, anxious to view the strangers, crowded to the battlements; the Mohammedans advanced, and dispersed them with their arrows; and an attempt was made to scale the walls. The Hindús, who now returned to the works, rendered the last abortive; and continued a brave resistance till night made the besiegers retire. On the following day, the siege was renewed; the place captured; and five thousand Hindús slain in the storm. A few, by escaping in a boat, saved themselves from the vengeance of the enemy. Mahmúd, on entering the temple, observed a covered apartment, whose roof was supported by six pillars set with jewels[k]; and here stood the idol.

([k]) (Habíbu-s-Sair.) This apartment was the recess, which is placed at the extreme end of the temples dedicated to Siva. Six pillars are as many as could be, in all probability, studded with jewels, and no more are mentioned in my copy of the

The latter was broken in pieces by the king's own hand; and orders were given to his attendants, that the pieces, carried to Ghazní, were to be cast before the great mosque in honour of the triumph obtained by Islám. By this expedition incalculable wealth was collected, and exceeded many thousand dínárs; though the story of the jewels found in the belly of the idol is the invention of some narrator, who loved fable more than truth. Mahmúd returned to Ghazní by the route of the Sind desert, where his army suffered greatly from the scarcity of forage and water; and, though information was brought him that Parama Deva[l], greatest of the Indian Rájás, lay with an army on his way, he pursued his march, not deeming it advisable to follow him. After much labour and suffering, the troops arrived at Ghazní in the following year[m].

A.D. 1030. Four years subsequent to these events, this great conqueror breathed his last. He had attained his sixty-third year, and died of stone

the Habíbu-s-Sair. Others, who have fancied that this description applied to the whole body of the temple, enumerate the pillars from thirty-six to fifty-six.

(l) This was a title signifying supreme lord, and was applied to the Rájá of Nahrwálah.

(m) Tabakát Akbarí.

in the bladder; a disease, which, at this period of life, is equally common in its attack, as it is suited to wear out the last energies of a vigorous constitution. Mahmúd, in stature, was of the middle size; in face, strongly marked with small pox [n]; in spirit determined; in disposition vindictive and unforgiving; a wrangler in the religious doctrines of Islám, yet a follower of its most superstitious sect; possessing vanity, to patronize learning as a mean of extending his fame, though avarice, a stronger passion, made him forget his purpose [o]; obstinate, bigoted, and energetic, he could at once awe the minds of the seditious, and secure the support of his subjects: who, loving him as a saint and their leader, shed tears of regret when he left his sceptre to weaker hands.

Character of Mahmúd.

Extent of the empire of Ghazní at his death.

With the declining power of the race of Sámán, the kings of Ghazní, from the humble situation of provincial governors, had raised themselves to extensive dominion. The quarrels of neighbouring states gave them a pretext for the necessity of interference; and, though not scrupulous in this matter, they justified the march of their troops into other coun-

(n) Ferishta.

(o) See the Tazkaratu-s-Shoará, by Daulat Sháh, for his treatment of Firdausí.

tries, as state expediency and self-preservation, while their only motive was a hope of adding to their territory, through the weakness of those they pretended to assist. The provinces of Ghazní[p], Kábúl, and Balkh, with part of Khorásán, had been bequeathed to his children by Sabuktagín; but such was the extent and rapidity of the conquests made by Mahmúd, that, in no less than thirty years after, the empire of Ghazní extended from the Persian Gulf to the sea of Aral, and from the mountains of Kurdistán to the Satlaj. With the exception of Khúzistán and Fárs, yet remaining possessions of the nearly extinguished race of Bawaihi[q], this mighty kingdom included the whole of Persia, Transoxiana, and the Panjáb; while it embraced every variety of climate, through twenty degrees of latitude and thirty of longitude. The decease of its founder was the signal for its decline; which was equally rapid as its rise.

Character of his successors. At the death of Mahmúd, two sons were left to dispute the succession to his throne; but, as these were twins, whose priority of right was only established by a few hours, each con-

(p) The province of Ghazní is the same as that called Zabulistán, when distinguished from Kábúl.

(q) See Gibbon's Roman Empire, vol. x., p. 83, where they are called Bowides.

sidered his claim equally legitimate, and resolved to decide it by the sword. The will of their father had been evinced in favour of the elder; and, though his dying wish indicated him for his successor, the younger was little disposed to yield obedience to a decision, which he considered, no doubt, founded on caprice. Mohammed, the name of the former, mild and winning in his manner, had secured a father's affection by filial duty and implicit obedience; and though Masúd, the younger, had more striking qualities to sway the multitude, they were little calculated to win a parent's love, though they might occasionally command his regard. The former, though gentle and tractable in disposition, possessed little besides which might command respect: the other, bold and independent in his language, might sometimes offend his father; but, distinguished for feats of strength, loved for liberality, and admired for his valour, won the hearts of the army and the nobles, and calculated with certainty on success. The Khalif of Baghdád had been privately instructed by the late king of Ghazní that, in addressing him, he was to insert the name of the Prince Mohammed before that of Masúd. The letter was read aloud in court, at Ghazní; some of the nobles, in their zeal for the cause of the latter, expressed indignation and surprise at the circumstance, but the answer of Masúd to them was characteristic of the man. "Concern not yourselves," said he; "when swords are truest, we may write what follows[r]."

Accession of Masúd.

Mahmúd contemplated, as would appear, the contest of the brothers for his throne; and arranged, as far as circumstances would permit, that his favourite might find every facility for possessing himself of Ghazní. Masúd, who had been sent to rule the most westerly dependencies of the empire, had his seat of government at Ispahán; while Mohammed, nearer to the capital, directed the affairs of Transoxiana, and resided at Jurján[s], in the ancient Hyrcania, south-east of the Caspian. When the intelligence of his father's decease was brought to the latter, he immediately set out for Ghazní, and was crowned with the approbation and aid of the late king's relations, who executed his will in this respect. The wishes of the army and the nobles, however, were all in favour of Masúd, who, leaving governors in the provinces of Persian Irák, made all possible

(r) Ferishta.

(s) Jurján, on the Caspian, must be carefully distinguished from Jurjistán, Ghirjistán, or Georgia, which also formed part of the Ghaznían empire.

expedition in advancing to Khorásán, with the intention of asserting his right to the throne. Mohammed made preparation to oppose him, and marched to Taki-ábád, not far distant from Ghazní; but the nobles, having formed a conspiracy, seized and confined him; while they
A.D. 1030. October. hastened to join his more fortunate rival. The aspirations of the younger were realized; the conspirators joined him at Herát; the army marched by way of Balkh to Ghazní; the elder brother was blinded, as the greatest mercy which can be extended to a rival in the east; and the crown of Ghazní encircled the brow of Masúd.

Notwithstanding the many eminent qualities which distinguished this prince, and which appeared to indicate him as born for dominion, his administration proved less vigorous than was anticipated, and the extent of the empire was considerably reduced during his reign. The causes which occasioned such things were perhaps beyond the possibility of control. The pastoral tribe of Turkmáns had found a brave and active leader in the person of Toghrul Beg, sprung from the race of Saljúk; and, while these warlike barbarians were professing obedience to the king of Ghazní, they continued to commit aggressions against his people and his power. Though long superior, the troops of Ghazní had now met their equals: victory did not always accompany their standards; and the northern parts of the kingdom were all but severed from the monarch's control.

The rise of such formidable rivals proved an auspicious event for the feeble states of India, by directing the attention of the Ghazní government to other parts of its possessions. But, though Masúd was no longer able to afflict Hindústán with the desolating warfare which had been carried on by his father, the country was not altogether exempted from foreign invasion. An expedition was undertaken against the fort of Hansi, sixty miles west of the river Jumna, and then the capital of Sewalik, or that mountainous country which separates the province of Dehlí from the sources of the Ganges. The place was taken; the troops advanced to Sonpat, of which the ruler Depál, or Deva Pál Harnát[t], fled; and a Mohammedan governor was established in the

A.D 1036. Expedition to Hansi.

([t]) This is the title given him by the Tabakát Akbarí; but Lieut.-Col. Briggs's Ferishta calls him Depal Hurry. We may conclude that this person was a follower of Buddha, as his title of Harinath is a designation of that deity, who, in the Sanskrit inscription from Buddha Gayá, or Bahár, is called Hari, and Harísa. (See *A.R.* I. p. 284.)

place. After ordering the idols to be broken, Masúd went in pursuit of the fugitive Rájá; who, being surprised by the king, lost most of his army, and escaped with much difficulty. The troops soon after returned to Ghazní; and Majdúd[u], the younger son of Masúd, was appointed to the government of Multán, and the Indian dependencies of the empire.

While the aggressions of the Saljúk Turkmáns were daily becoming more daring, Masúd, with singular infatuation, neglected to pursue those vigorous measures, suited to check encroachments on his territory. Though the nobles endeavoured to dissuade him from undertaking the expedition to India, representing that the troops might be more properly employed in expelling the Turkmáns from Khorásán[x], he would not attend to this good advice, and suffered in the end for his obstinacy. In his absence, the power of his formidable enemies had increased; the property and lives of his subjects were made their sport; and, as one of his nobles said, "though once but ants, they had become adders[y]." The several members of the subjugated race of Bawaihi, who, as lieute-

(u) In Colonel Briggs's Ferishta he is sometimes called Madood.

(x) Habíbu-s-Sair. (y) Ferishta.

nants of the king of Ghazní, continued to conduct the government of Persian Irák, took this opportunity of regaining their independence, and excited a rebellion. Masúd, too late perceiving that all these causes threatened to dismember his empire, marched against the Turkmáns. Several engagements were fought with various success, till the army of Ghazní, marching to Sirakhsh, in Khorásán, was opposed by the latter, and met with defeat. The king soon after withdrew to his Indian possessions, with a view of recruiting his army, and repairing his losses ; but the troops, becoming discontented on the road, mutinied, and dethroned their leader. His blind brother Mohammed was now elevated to the vacant throne, and Masúd sent to prison, where he was soon after assassinated.

A.D. 1042. Sultan Modúd. The blind Mohammed did not long retain his newly-acquired dignity. Modúd, the son of Masúd, was not without suspicion that his uncle had been privy to his father's murder. The former received the news of this event by a letter from his uncle, who affected to lament a brother's death ; and the answer to the fratricide was as biting and sarcastic, as condolence was ill-dissembled and uncalled for, in his nephew's opinion : " May God lengthen the days," said he, "of so merciful a king, and grant that his mad son Ahmad gain glory in the practice of regicide, till he obtains his reward at our hands!" At this time, Modúd was at Balkh, whither he had been sent, after his father's defeat and retreat to India. Indignant at his uncle's supposed hypocrisy, this prince, on first receiving intelligence of the event, was anxious to march directly on the Panjáb, that he might revenge his father's murder. From this he was dissuaded by his friends ; who induced him first to go to Ghazní, and take possession of the ancient capital of his ancestors. His approach was hailed with acclamation by the citizens, who thronged to meet him. From this he hastened to the banks of the Indus, to oppose his uncle's army, which had marched from Lahore. The struggle of the parties was soon decided ; a battle was fought between them, in which Modúd was victorious ; and his father's murderers were put to death. There was now no rival to oppose his pretensions to the throne of Ghazní, except his brother Majdúd[z] ; who had been left, as before noticed, in the government of the south-eastern states. Hansi was, at this time, the capital of the younger brother, who

(z) Habíbu-s-Sair.

refused to bear allegiance to the elder. The latter had failed by persuasion to bring the other to obedience, and had no choice left him but to trust to the sword for the issue of the contest. A force was sent to the Panjáb; when Majdúd, hearing of its approach, left Hansi, and hastened to oppose it. Soon after, however, he was found dead in his bed, without any previous complaint; and left his brother undisputed possession of the kingdom.

The Hindús regain possession of several subjugated places.

Revolt among its principal governors, increasing encroachments by the Saljúk Turkmáns, and the domestic quarrels of its princes, had much embarrassed the affairs of the Ghazní government. The Hindús were not slow in perceiving this change in the power of their conquerors; and, having experienced nothing from their government in the height of its prosperity but insult and dishonour, were glad to perceive the day of retribution approaching, and hastened to assist in its downfall and disgrace. Priestcraft was at work with the credulity of the people, and zealots of all parties perceived it was their interest to unite against their oppressors. A numerous host was collected, under the command of the Rájá of Dehlí and his confederates; and Hansi, Nágrakót, and Thánesar, were retaken; the dilapidated temples were rebuilt; idolatrous rites re-established, and the Mohammedans of Lahore narrowly escaped the horrors of a storm. While the relative power and knowledge of parties, since those days, has turned much in favour of us as conquerors, the principles of human nature, and the incitement to action, are indelible and unchangeable; and the lesson ought not be forgotten by those who have succeeded in possession.

A.D. 1043. Review of the state of India at this period, and the distribution of the country among its Hindú rulers.

In order to fill up the periods of fable, and bring down its history to the time when Mohammedan annals of India commence, the Voidya monarchs of Bengal, cotemporary with the Rájpút princes bearing the title of Pál, are made to succeed them in the general system of Hindú chronology. This, as will presently be explained, is founded on misconception and ignorance. The last but one of the Voidya Rájás, Lakshmana Sinha, is well known to Mohammedan history as Lakamir, and gives name to an era in Bengal. Their original seat of government was Naddia[a]; but Gaur, or Laknauti, on the left bank of the Ganges, near Malda, afterwards became their capital. Cotemporary with this state was that

(a) They resided, as would appear, at Naddia, situated near the junction of the Jellinghi and Kásimbázár rivers.

of Benares and Gaur; which was governed, in the reign of Mahmúd of Ghazní, by Rájás of the Buddhist persuasion; of whose former existence and belief the urns found at Sarnáth, four miles north of Benares, and the inscription on the statue of Buddha, afford us unequivocal proof[b]. The contiguous Hindú principality, north-westward, was Kálinjar, tributary to the Buddhist princes of Benares; and further eastward than that the kings of Ghazní do not appear to have advanced. The first of the Benares family, Bhúpála, otherwise named Mahípála, was succeeded by his sons Sthirapála and Vasantapála, who erected the temple of Sarnáth[c]. If the Srí Deva Pála, of the Mongír grant and inscription from Buddal[d], be not the same person

(b) See *A. R.* Vol. V. p. 132. The date of the inscription, commemorating the construction of edifices dedicated to Buddha, is Samvat 1083, A.D. 1027. Of the princes named, the first was Mahípál, whose sons were Sthirapála, and Kámapála.

(c) On the genealogical list of this family, see *A.R.* V. p. 133, and Vol. XV. p. 465.

(d) *A. R.* Vol. I. p. 123 and 133. The date of the first is the 33rd year of the Rájá's reign, and not of the general era called Samvat, which commences fifty-six years before Christ. It was the custom for the Balhara emperors, or Lord Protectors of India, to date their reign from the last of their predecessor: and of this we are informed by the two Mohammedan travellers of Renaudot, who wrote in Hij. 596, A.D. 1173. It has been usual to place the date of these travels as far back as the end of the ninth century of

as the last, though differently entitled, he certainly succeeded this family, not long after A.D. 1027. Ten years subsequent to this time, the name of Yaso Pála occurs. He issues his commands in the fort of Karrah [e], but ruled the realm of Kausamba, or Rangamatty, situated on the Brahmaputra river. This can be no other than Srí Deva Pála, who was mighty lord of the great Sugats or Buddhists, and had for his subjects the Gaur, Khoso, Laasata, and Bhoto, or the people of Bahar, Kassay, Lhassa, and Bhútan. He travelled on his pilgrimages from the sources of the Ganges, at Kedar Náth, to Gúkerna on the ocean [f], and overran the kingdoms on his route. These conquests were not permanent; but the occurrence of such indicates the unsettled habits of the military class of Hindús in those times. As the prince who made them is said to have acted according

of our era, or Hij. 264; simply because the commentator, Abú-Zaid al-Hasan, of Siraf, has mentioned a revolution which happened in China at this time. But, as the original manuscript contained observations on the extent and circumference of Damascus, and of other cities subject to Núra-d-dín, uncle of the celebrated Saladin, with the date when it was written, Hij. 569, the evidence goes to prove that the travels could not have taken place earlier than the end of the eleventh or twelfth century of our era.

(e) See *A. R.* IV. p. 433.

(f) The Gúkerna mentioned in the grant is Gúkerna on the Malabar coast, and not Gokernak on the frontiers of Kashmír.

to the Shástra, or the law, and emulated a God in his actions, he may have thus received the title of Srí Deva Pála ; while his other title of Yaso Pála would express his celebrity. On the west of India, Dhúrlabha Chalukya had abdicated, at Nahrwálah Patan, in favour of his son, or brother, Bhíma Rájá I ; and made his pilgrimage to Gayá. One of the Gohila family occupied Ajmír, and, in the south of India, the Belál princes, who afterwards took possession of Dwárá Samudra, had swerved from their allegiance to the Chóla Rájás, and founded a new state north of the Krishna [g].

Appellations of the Rájpúts at this time.

There is nothing more perplexing to the reader of oriental history than the variety of names by which individuals are in different places designated ; and this practice has been a fruitful source of error, from the period when Greek historians first made known to us the history of Persia, even to the present day. An acute discrimination of the analogy and differences of historical facts, and an extensive knowledge of the several revolutions and rise of kingdoms which took place, can alone guard us against the commission of mistakes in this matter. In no part of oriental research will such be found more necessary than in our

(g) See M'Kenzie Collection, Vol. II. p. 13.

inquiries after the early history of the Hindús; when individuals are sometimes designated by the appellation of their tribe, at others by their religious or military titles; and, as synonymous terms are indiscriminately used for the last, the causes for confusion are numerous, and their effect not easily prevented. Rájáputras had at this time the appellation of Verma, or Varman, which was the customary designation for the military tribe, as that of Sarman[h] pointed out the Bráhmans, or sacerdotal class. The former, at the present day, is used to distinguish the Arracanese Buddhists of Kshatrya or Rájpút origin, as Dr. Leyden informs us[i]: and this similarity of appellation, among tribes west and east of the Brahmaputra river, is one of many facts, which go to establish their common origin. These Rájpúts, called "Verma Kshatrya," in a Sanskrit grant[k] by Jaya Chandra, the last Hindú ruler of Kanauj, were sometimes entitled Bhúmihara Bráhmans[l], or lords of the soil. Among the Rihans, or Burmese priests, they are

(h) These are the barbarian philosophers of the Greeks, who were called Sarmanæ. See *Opera Clementis Alexandrini*, edit. Sylburg. fol., p. 305.

(i) *A. R.* Vol. X. p. 231.

(k) The date of this grant is Samvat era 1234, A.D. 1177. See *A. R.* XV. p. 450.

(l) In the Buddal inscription, *A. R.* I. p. 134.

called Biammas, and are thought to be the first inhabitants of the earth.

A member of the Silhára tribe of Rájpúts, having the appellation of Gonka Rájá, had conquered Kirhata Kúndí Desh, Múta Konkun Desh, and the country about Merij[m]. His son Mara Sinha Rájá, who appears to be the same as Marichand of Dekhan tradition[n], reigned at Panala, and is styled Maha Mandala Ishwar, or master of an extensive region, and lord of the city of Tagara. About fifty years subsequent to this, the Rájás who ruled over the Gantúr and Palnad districts, near the mouth of the Krishna, were also styled Gonka[o]; and, though these had the additional appellation of Chóla, the probability is in favour of their relationship with the earlier Rájás, who ruled further west on the banks of that river.

A.D. 1058. Conquests in the Dekhun.

The Chalukya, or Solanki tribe of Rájpúts, had been established in Gujarát and Khándesh some time prior to the destruction of Somnáth. A branch of this family had come from the westward at that time; and,

A.D. 1078. Chalukyas of Kalyani.

(m) Sanskrit grant in my possession, dated Sálivâhana 980, A.D. 1058.

(n) See Scott's *Ferishta,* Vol. I. Introduc. p. XI.

(o) See Introduc. to the M'Kenzie Collection, p. XCI. and CXV.

not long after, one of them conquered the territory of Kuntala[p] desa, or the country about Kalyani and Banawasi. The person who made these conquests was Víra Raya, who had also the appellation of Bhuvana Malla Víra ; and was, as the inscription tells us, the foe of the kings of Chóla[q]. The reign of one of this family is remarkable for a revolution in the Jaina religion of the Dekhan ; by which the well known sectaries and followers of Siva, who are called Lingayats, were first established in the country. Vijala Raya, the individual then reigning, endeavouring to repress the extension of this belief, was put to death by the enraged followers of its founder, Chenna Básava[r].

Rahtore family established at Kanauj.

Mohammedan conquests had so disorganized the petty principalities on the banks of the Jumna and Ganges, and so upset the constitution of Hindú society, that a favourable opportunity was left for a military adventurer to establish a new dynasty in the Doab. The last of the Koráh family, who ruled Kanauj, had drawn on himself the hatred of the neighbouring Rájás by accepting a Mohammedan alliance, and was put to death as unworthy of the Hindú name. This

(p) See Introduc. to the M'Kenzie Collection, p. CXV.

(q) See *A. R.* IX. p. 428.

(r) Básava Purána extracted in the M'Kenzie Collection, Vol. II. p. 10.

was the cause of Mahmúd of Ghazní's ninth expedition to India. From that time the vacant throne of Kanauj was to become the prize of any one who had the inclination and power to contend for it. A candidate at length appeared in the person of Srí Chandra Deva; who, only six years prior to the revolution which extinguished the Jaina religion in the Dekhan, "conquered by his own arm the unequalled kingdom of Kanyákubja or Kanauj[s]." His grandfather, Srí Pál, otherwise named Yasovigraha, claimed descent from the solar race[t]: from which we learn that the appellation of Rahtore, by which this family became celebrated in the annals of India, could not have been assumed prior to the conquest of Kanauj by Srí Chandra Deva. This prince visited the holy places of Kási, Kúsika, and northern Kosala, which are now known to us by the names of Benares, the Kúsi river in Bahar, and the modern Fyzabad in Oude. Conquest could not have been the object of these visits, as the power of the recently acquired sovereignty was curbed, on the south-east, by the Pál princes of Benares; and the evidence of grants seems to establish

(s) See incriptions and grants relative to this family, *A. R.* p. 447, and Vol. IX. p. 441.

(t) See *A. R.* Vol. IX. p. 441.

that, while the conquests of the latter were extended to the south, along the sea coast, those of the former were carried westward into Málwá.

A.D. 1088. Rise of the Hindú kingdom of Warangal.

The state of Warangal, in the Dekhan, which became celebrated in the Mohammedan annals, was established by a feudatory, or relative, of the Chalukya family of Kalyani. The person who accomplished this was Kakateya Pralaya; whom some genealogies make the son of Bhuvanika Malla, the same as Víra Raya.

Review of Ghazní affairs from the reign of Modúd.

After the death of Modúd, in A.D. 1049, the prosperity of the Saljúk Turkmáns continued to increase, while the fortune of the house of Ghazní was on the wane. During this period no extensive conquests were made in India, though there were occasional aggressions committed on its borders. Nágrakót was retaken in the time of Sultan Abdúl Rashíd; and, during the reign of Sultan Ibrahim, possession of some places in the Panjáb was obtained. The kings of Ghazní, however, had lost a great part of their paternal possessions on the west; which had been wrested from them by Toghrul Beg and Alp Arslan, the victorious leaders of the Turkmáns. The former, for a time, escaped total expulsion from their ancestral property, as Masúd III. of Ghazní had married the daughter of Malik Shah Saljúk, otherwise named Jalál-ud-dín, or the glory of religion. But the limits of the empire were now so contracted that the royal family resolved to reside in India, and made Lahore[u] their capital. An officer was soon after sent to carry on a crusade against the Hindús; during which, it is said, he passed the Ganges: but there is cause for doubting whether the Mohammedan successes, in the then weakened power of the Ghazní monarchs, could have been very great, against the vigorous Hindú leaders who ruled the kingdoms of Kanauj and Benares.

Hindú rulers of Kanauj and Benares.

Srí Deva Pála was succeeded in the government of Benares and Gaur, by Rájá Pála, who had been appointed Yava Rájá[x], or successor, previous to his father's death; and the throne of Kanauj was occupied by Madana Pála, son and successor of Srí Chandra Deva. We cannot but regret that the time of Srí Deva Pála's death may not be accurately ascertained; but, knowing that he reigned thirty-three years, and having identified him with Yaso Pála, whose ascertained date is A. D. 1037, we shall not be far wide of the truth by fixing the accession of his successor in A.D. 1070. The states of Kanauj and Benares were distinct at this time; the

(u) Ferishta.

(x) See Mongír grant, *A. R.* I. p. 128.

general title of the ruling family in the former being Chandra, while all the princes of the other bore the appellation of Pála ; and Mohammedan authorities recognise the two separate governments of Kanauj and Mongír. The last, which comprised Benares and Gaur, extended its authority not long after into Orissa and Dravira. In as far as the wealth and power of those who governed influenced the literature or religion of the Hindús, we may reasonably regret the want of their history : though we have lost little by the absence of other details, which would present the same unvarying narrative of robbery and oppression, that are characteristic of quarrels among a semi-barbarous people.

A.D. 1105. Conquests by the Rájás of Gaor.

The sovereignty of Benares and Gaur had been transferred, as would appear, to Srí Súra Pála ; who succeeded Rájá Pála. During the reign of this prince, the countries of Útkal, the Húns, Dravira, and Kunjara, were subdued, and annexed to the kingdom of Gaur [y].

In the transcript of the inscription, which informs us of these conquests, Gurjara is read for Kunjara; but, as neither western Gujarát nor the small district of this name in the Panjáb can be the countries intended, an error has probably crept into the copy, by which Kunjara, or

(y) See Buddal Inscription, p. 13. *A. R.* I. p. 136.

a country abounding with elephants, has been converted into Gurjara. The country of Kunjara is that now known by the name of Tipperah, east of the Ganges; where the people, being of Scythian origin, were appropriately enough termed Húns [z]. Útkal is the province now called Orissa, east of the Godaveri river; and Dravira [a], though limited in its most confined sense to the eastern shore of the Peninsula, between the Palar and Koartilair rivers, has been here extended to include the maritime part of Telingana.

By the traditionary history and native annals of Orissa, the fact of its invasion, from the north, about this time, is sufficiently well authenticated [b]. The Vansávalí, or genealogical list of

(z) The sea coast, at the summit of the bay of Bengal, from point Godaveri to Cape Negrais is known in the Puránas by the name of Kalinga, or a country abounding with creeks. In the end of the first century of our era, it was so known to the Roman traders: for Pliny tells us, that the people called Calingæ coast hard upon the sea (Book 17, chap. XVII). In chap. XIX, he gives a most accurate description of them: "When you are over the Ganges, the first region upon the coast that you set foot into is that of the Gandaridæ and the Calingæ, called Parthiales: (Quest. Thus named from the people having the manners of Parthians?) The king of this country hath in ordinary for his wars eighty thousand foot, one thousand horse, and seven hundred elephants."

(a) It originally included Arcot and Madras.

(b) See Mr. Sterling's account of Orissa, *A. R.* XV. p. 267.

its princes, has erroneously brought the invader from the banks of the Godaveri, or lesser Ganges, and styles the new race Gangá-Vansa. The person who subdued the province was named Serang Deo, or Chor Ganga; and was probably the same as Súra Pála of Gaur. It is impossible to determine whether the invasion of Orissa was conducted by the Supreme Rájás of Gaur in person, or by their military ministers; but no doubt can exist that the change of dynasty in the former was effected through the influence of one or other from the latter. The cognate origin of the letters of the Mahávalipuram inscription[c], and those of the Bhali alphabet, or sacred character of the Burmese, and the tradition that the temples there were executed by the Dharma Rájá, or a northern prince, are other proofs confirming the authority of the Buddal inscription, with regard to the conquests which were effected in the south.

A.D. 1152. Death of Sultán Bairam of Ghazní. The Mohammedan possessions in India during this reign.

Masúd III. of Ghazní was eventually succeeded by his son Bairam, who is more distinguished for the patronage

(c) Mahávalipuram, now known by the name of the Seven Pagodas, is situated to the south of Madras. An account of the inscriptions, by Dr. Babington, will be found in Vol. II. *Trans. R. A. S.* p. 258; and further information may be collected from the papers of Messrs. Chambers and Goldingham; *A. R.* Vol. I. p. 145, and V. p. 69.

he extended to literature than for the conquests he made. His death happened after a reign of thirty-five years; during which time he alternately occupied Ghazní and Lahore as his capital. In this reign the Arabic version of Bidpay's fables, called the Kalíla wa Dimna, which had been translated from Pehleví by Abdallah ben Mokaffa, was rendered into Persian. Many learned men at this time found a liberal patron in Sultán Bairam, who united to an uncommon desire for knowledge a noble and generous disposition[d]. The poet Shaikh Nizámi was one among the many who experienced the benefit of such enlightened liberality.

Soon after his accession to power, Sultán Bairam was engaged in an expedition to Lahore, for the purpose of chastising Mohammed Bahlin, the refractory Viceroy of India; who had been appointed to the government by his rival brother, Sultán Arslán. The Viceroy was defeated and made captive: but, being subsequently pardoned and reinstated in the government, effected several conquests in the country of Sewalik. Having soon after excited a rebellion, Mohammed Bahlin was again defeated near Multán, and perished in his flight.

(d) Ferishta.

Succession of Jaya Chandra, the last Rájá of Kanauj. Partition of the kingdom of Gaur some time previous to this event.

Jaya Chandra, the last Hindú sovereign of Kanauj, and one of the most celebrated characters of Rájpút history, was at this time appointed Yava Rájá, or designated successor and associate in the empire of his father, Vijaya Chandra[e]. He is well known in the legendary history of the Rájpúts as the rival and enemy of Prithvi Ráyá, prince of Ajmír, between whom a contest for pre-eminence, as supreme potentate of India, was continually kept up, till the Mohammedans, under Mohammed Ghorí, interfered and ruined both.

Some time previous to the accession of Jaya Chandra, the supreme power of the Pál princes of Gaur had terminated with Náráyan Pála, the last of his race: and to this cause we may ascribe the contests which followed between

(e) See translation of a grant of land by Mr. Colebrooke in *A. R.* IX. p. 441. The person who made the grant was the last Rájá of Kanauj, who, by some error, is there called by the name of his father Vijaya Chandra Deva. It is plainly stated in the grant that it was given on the occasion of his inauguration as Yava Rájá; and here Vijaya Chandra Deva could not possibly be meant; since the Mohammedan annals inform us that Jaya Chandra, when slain in battle by the troops of Mohammed Ghorí, had attained extreme old age. It is evident from another grant by this family, (*A. R.* XV. p. 449,) that Vijaya Chandra and Jaya Chandra were father and son; but Mr. Wilson, in his comments, appears to be wrong when he assigns the first grant to Vijaya Chandra.

Jaya Chandra of Kanauj and Prithvi Ráyá of Ajmír. Benares and the north-western part of that kingdom became the possession of the Rájás of Kanauj, while Lakshmana Sinha, or Lakamír[f], last of the Voidya Rájás, seized on Gaur and Bahar.

The family of Ghor, who originally possessed the mountainous district of Khorásán, south-east of Herát, was raised to distinction by the successful wars of Ghiyásu-d-dín Mohammed of Ghor; who had succeeded to the government of his native country, at the death of his cousin Alá-ud-dín[g]. He conquered the greater part of Khorásán, and expelled the Khárizmians. Previous to this time, the chiefs of Ghor had connected themselves with the kings of Ghazní

(f) The Habíbu-s-Sair says, that when Mohammed Bakhtiár Khiljí, one of the nobles of Kutbu-d-dín Aibuk, first Mohammedan king of Dehlí, took possession of Gaur and Bengal, A.D. 1203, the Rájá Lakamír had been in possession of his throne seventy years. He had probably succeeded as a minor, and must have commenced reigning A.D. 1133. This will be found to agree exactly with Abul-Fazl's account of his era, from which the people of Bengal date their transactions. When Akbar issued the firman for establishing the Ilahí era, in Hij. 993, the era of Lakshmana Sinha was then in its 465th year, and must have consequently commenced Hij. 528, or A.D. 1133. Ferishta is therefore in error when he places the first Mohammedan conquest of Bengal in Hij. 587, A.D. 1191.

(g) On the authority of the Kholásatu-l-Akhbár.

by marriage; but, as several of the former had been put to death by the latter, a fierce enmity was produced between the families, and ended by the Ghorians establishing their authority over the possessions of Ghazní on the ruin of their rivals.

A.D. 1174. Hij. 570. Ghiyásu-d-dín, being firmly fixed in the government of Ghor, conferred the title of Shahábu-d-dín Mohammed Ghorí on his brother, and appointed him his Viceroy at Ghazní [h]. An army was conducted the following year into India, where Multán and Úcha were subdued. Having again marched his troops into that country, A.D. 1178, Shahábu-d-dín Mohammed Ghorí, by the route of the Sind desert, advanced to the confines of Gujarát; where he was opposed by Bhíma Deva Chálukya [i], lieutenant of his brother, the Rájá of Nahrwálah. The Mohammedans experienced a severe defeat on this occasion, and suffered many hardships in their retreat [k].

A.D. 1186. Khusrau II. last of the princes of the Ghazní family. The power of the Ghazní princes, who had for some time maintained a

(h) Habíbu-s-Sair.

(i) The Sanskrit inscriptions from Abú, *A.R.* XV. p. 290 and 301, declare Bhíma Deva to be of the Chálukya race, and not of the Bajhíla, as asserted by the Mirát Ahmadí.

(k) Ferishta.

semblance of sovereign authority in India, was now completely extinguished: Khusrau II. having been made a prisoner, surrendered Lahore to the Ghorian. Six years previous to this event, Shahábu-d-dín Mohammed Ghorí had invested this capital; but, being unable to take the place, concluded a peace with the feeble representative of the once powerful house of Ghazní: the latter having agreed to deliver up his son, as a hostage, that the articles of the treaty might be fulfilled. The terms of the treaty were not observed, however, and the Ghorian, again obliged to invest the town, failed in an attempt to capture it. Treachery at length secured to him what force was not able to effect; and the empire of Sabuktagín was transferred to Mohammed Ghorí.

A.D. 1187. Mohammed Ghorí defeated by Prithvi Ráyá, of Ajmír.

No Mohammedan rival remained to oppose the conquests of the Ghorian in India; and his thoughts were now bent on extending his possessions in that country. The Hindú rulers of Kanauj and Ajmír were the only authorities who had the means of defeating his pretensions; and such, when weighed against the arrogance of the champion of Islám, would be as nothing in the balance. Mohammed Ghorí conducted his troops towards Ajmír, by the route of Sirhind[l], which he captured. He then took Kohram and Samana[m]. The Rájá of Ajmír, at this time, was Prithvi Ráyá, whom the Táríkhi Alfí names Gola, though more correctly written Gohila, as such was the appellation of his tribe[n]. Having heard that the Mohammedans had taken those places, he advanced with an army of Rájpúts, to stop the march of the Ghorians. The parties soon after came to blows; but the right and left wings of the Mohammedans being broken, took to flight, and left their leader, with the centre, to maintain an unequal contest. Mohammed Ghorí, though forsaken by cowards, was himself undismayed; and, notwithstanding many of his friends continued urging him to leave the field of action, he turned a deaf ear to their intreaties, till unhorsed, and about to become a cap-

(l) Táríkhi Alfí and Tabakát Akbarí. Colonel Briggs's Ferishta makes the troops capture Behtenda, but they appear to have kept more to the east.

(m) Both these places are south from Sirhind, and immediately west from the Gogur River.

(n) Legendary history commonly names his tribe the Chohan; but the inscription from Hansi, dated A.D. 1168 (*A.R.* XV. p. 444), says—" He was an autumnal moon for an ornament to the firmament of the tribe of the Gohilanta." This is excellent authority, and proves that the name of Chohan was only adopted about the time.

tive. A fierce struggle here commenced between the Rájpúts and the Mohammedans, the former endeavouring to carry off the Sultán, while the others made desperate efforts to prevent them. Fortune at length favoured their exertions; and the troops of Ghor, having by one determined effort driven back the Hindús, released their leader. Mohammed Ghorí, who thus narrowly escaped from an untimely death, was mounted by his followers on horseback, and carried from the field of battle. He had not gone far when, becoming faint and weak from the loss of blood, they placed him in a covered litter, and immediately continued their flight, till far beyond the danger of pursuit; notwithstanding the Rájpúts made no effort to follow up their first success[o]. On arriving in the neighbourhood of Lahore[p], Mohammed Ghorí disgraced

(o) Táríkhi Alfí. Ferishta says, that he was pursued; but this author has blended two different battles into one; and so frequently mixes up his narrative with fabulous accounts, manufactured in India, that, though he may be considered on the whole a good historian, many of his assertions must not be implicitly relied on. Ferishta was only a compiler, and not always a judicious one. He could not have extensively studied the history of the country, or the bearing of facts, and is very contradictory in his dates at different places.

(p) Colonel Briggs's Ferishta has Ghor, but he did not reside there, as appears.

the officers who had deserted him; and, having compelled them to hang about their necks their horses' mouth-bags, filled with grass, sent them into the city with this badge of infamy. During this year the Sultán remained at Lahore, to repair the disasters of defeat, and then marched to Ghazní.

The disgrace of defeat weighed so heavily on the mind of Mohammed Ghorí, that for several years he remained inactive; and, sorrowful for the event, was so vexed with those who had caused it, that he would not permit any of the disgraced nobles to approach him, or pay their respects. Having at length, however, assembled an army, without permitting any one to be privy in his counsel, he marched for Peshâwar. At this place an old man of Ghor came out to meet him; and, after having performed the usual salutations and respect proper to be observed before sovereigns, the sage requested to know what were his intentions; for, though there were many speculations regarding them, no one knew with certainty whither he was going. Mohammed Ghorí informed him, that, ever since his defeat by the Hindús, he had neither slept soundly nor indulged in pleasure; and, though little might be trusted to the troops of Ghor, he nevertheless felt confident that God would aid him in consulting the interests of the true faith, by conducting an army into India[q]. To this the sage replied — "Please God, your wishes will be so accomplished by our kinsmen, that your heart will be delighted: but let me advise you to forget their past offences, and so honour them with your confidence, that they may serve you with zeal, and omit nothing which may contribute to success." This good advice was followed; the disgraced nobles were called to the presence of their leader; to him they excused themselves, saying — "Though we know what our master suffered for the past, we had yet no remedy to offer; and prayed to God that he would again invade Hindústán, to give us an opportunity of wiping away the stain on our character. Thank Heaven, the time has now arrived when, by a victory over the idolaters, we may hope to have our wishes accomplished, and the load of sorrow, which has weighed down our hearts, removed[r]!" They were all again received into favour, and honoured with proofs of their master's regard.

Defeat of Prithvi Ráyá, the Prince of Ajmír.

After having passed the Indus, the Ghorians advanced by the route of the Panjáb to the neighbourhood of Dehlí;

(q) Táríkhi Alfí.

(r) Taríkhi Alfí.

while the Hindús, under Prithvi Ráyá, prepared to oppose them. The former were yet distant two stages from the camp of the enemy, when their leader made a feint retreat in the direction of Sirhind. Prithvi Ráyá, elated by his former success, and imagining the invaders were panic-struck, pursued the flying foe; who thus retreated, four or five stages, without indicating a wish to engage their pursuers. The Rájpúts sent the Mohammedans a message of defiance, telling them — "Like thieves, who enter the dwellings of men, and fear punishment, you fly before us; but it is now fit you stand a battle: fly not, therefore, if you respect the honour of your government." To this an answer was returned by the latter, that they, mistrusting their own prowess against that of their pursuers, were obliged to fly. The retreat had been thus continued, till the former reached the town of Naraini, since called Tiraurí[s], situated between Kurnal and Thánesur, on the banks of the Chittung river[t]. Here both armies encamped; the Mohammedans occupying the western and the Rájpúts the eastern bank. The latter, with

(s) Ferishta. This place is fourteen miles south of Thánesur, and is inserted in Mr. Elphinstone's map of Kábúl.

(t) Ferishta calls it the Sursutty (Saraswati) River, which is not far distant, and has erred through his ignorance of geography.

their leader, had been lulled into fatal security by the well-dissembled fears of the other; and Shahábu-d-dín Mohammed Ghorí, perceiving he had thus accomplished the object of his retreat, made seven thousand cavalry pass the river, during the night, with orders to attack the enemy's camp at daybreak. His instructions were attended to; the Mohammedans assaulted the Hindús, and took them by surprise; Prithvi Ráyá, in the first moment of panic, endeavouring to escape on horseback, was prevented by his followers, but, having subsequently mounted his elephant, bravely led on the Rájpúts; and the contest was maintained till nightfall, when victory declared for the Ghorians. Many of the Hindús were slain; and Prithvi Ráyá was made captive. This proud Rájpút chief, when brought into the presence of the Sultán, refused to do him homage, by bowing his head before him; but one of the Mohammedan attendants, indignant at the insult offered to his master, seized the fallen monarch, and bent his forehead to the earth[u]. On being asked by the Ghorian, how he would have treated him, had it been his own fate to become a captive, Prithvi Ráyá replied, that he had

(u) Táríkhi Alfí.

prepared golden fetters with which he intended to load his prisoner, had he himself been conqueror; but now that the day was his enemy's he was ready to bear whatever might be inflicted on him. He also advised the Ghorian, that, if his desire was to seize on Hindústán, he ought to proceed without delay to do so, as there was no one remaining who possessed power to oppose him; but, that if gold was the thing he fought for, he would present him with as much as his soul might covet. The former replied, that the conquest of the country, not the possession of gold, was his object in conducting his soldiers into India; and, having carried Prithvi Ráyá along with him, he advanced against Ajmír, which contained the treasure of the Hindú Prince. Ajmír, with several other strongholds in that quarter, was subsequently captured; and the Sultán, soon after having returned to Ghazní, appointed Kutbu-d-dín Aibuk, one of the royal slaves, his deputy in India.

Rájpút accounts of Prithvi Ráyá, and the causes of his defeat.

The war which Shahábu-d-dín Mohammed Ghorí waged with Prithvi Ráyá, for the monarchy of India, is alike celebrated among the Mohammedans and Rájpúts; but, in the legendary history of the latter, the exploits of this greatest among their heroes are embellished with all the poetical exaggeration that could alone render this subject pleasing to a people, whose vanity was gratified to hear their household bards sing the actions of their ancestors. There is nothing improbable, or highly coloured, in the Mohammedan narrative of this transaction, given on the authority before quoted; and, though it differs considerably from that given by Ferishta, it seems on the whole more consistent and authentic than the account of that author. No doubt exists of this action having been fought at Tiraurí; but, according to some authorities, the troops of Ghor, before they offered battle, had retreated westward of Lahore. With regard to the motives which induced the Ghorian to invade India, we learn, from the Mohammedans, that a desire to support the interests of Islám, and a wish to wipe away the disgrace of former defeat, were the only ones: though the Hindú legends would lead us to suppose that, in a war between the rulers of Kanauj and Ajmír, the former, when the losing party, determined to betray his country, and leagued with the invader. It certainly appears that Prithvi Ráyá was not supported in this war against the Ghorian by assistance from Jaya Chandra, of Kanauj; but the supineness of the former, on this occasion, may be with more reason ascribed to his jealousy, as a rival candidate for the supreme monarchy of India, than to revenge; and there is no good foundation for the belief that his more favoured opponent had carried off his daughter or his mistress. The supreme monarchy of India had become vacant, as we have seen, by the death of Náráyan Pála, of Gaur; and those who set up their pretensions to the paramount title were the Princes of Ajmír and Kanauj. Jaya Chandra, who ruled the latter, was of the Rahtore tribe; and Prithvi Ráyá, though a member of the recently established tribe of Chohan, was more commonly styled a Gohila, after the parent stock. If we may believe the Rájpút legends, and in this particular they are not unworthy of credit, the former resolved to perform the Rájasúya[x] sacrifice, and seal his supremacy. Prithvi Ráyá, who considered he had a superior claim to the honour, absented himself from the ceremony; though most of the other Rájás paid their homage to the monarch of Kanauj. The former was represented there, in effigy, as the doorkeeper. His subsequent arrival, in disguise, at the court of Kanauj; his conquest of the affections of Jaya

(x) A sacrifice performed by a universal monarch, attended by all his tributary princes.

Chandra's daughter, her flight from her father's house, his apathy in every thing but love, and indifference to the affairs of his kingdom, even when the invader was at his door, are so many poetical inventions to adorn a tale, but do not suit the gravity of history: notwithstanding they have been adopted by the historian, Abul-Fazl. The manner of his death is also a subject of doubt; but the Mohammedan account, that he was slain by order of the Sultán, after this victory, is agreeable to their usual policy.

Defeat and death of Jaya Chandra, Rájá of Benares and Kanauj.

Though it be related, by Hindú legends, that, in the war between Shahábu-d-dín Mohammed Ghorí, and Prithvi Ráyá, Jaya Chandra had called in the invader, there is no evidence to support the truth of the assertion. Mohammedan authorities are quite silent regarding this matter; and we cannot suppose that the latter, who have been long accustomed to detail the events of their history, could have passed such unnoticed had it taken place. But, though not actively aiding the Mohammedans, Jaya Chandra, by having become a tame spectator to the downfall of his rival, had materially aided them in subduing India; and soon after he had cause to repent of such indifference to his country's cause. Success only serves as a stimulus to ambition, or to

render its possessor more daring; and Mohammed Ghorí, who had accomplished the ruin of the Prince of Ajmír, and possessed his country, resolved to destroy the power of his rival. After the defeat of Prithvi Ráyá, the troops of Ghór, who marched for Ghazní, had wintered the following year in Pesháwar; and Kutbu-d-dín Aibuk, Viceroy of India, having in the mean time subdued many of the cities in this country, seized the inhabitants, and sent them as slaves to his master. The Rájá of Kanauj, now the greatest sovereign in Hindústán, prepared to revenge this wanton cruelty, and commenced hostilities against the Mohammedan possessions, with seven hundred war elephants, and one hundred thousand cavalry. On hearing
A.D. 1194. of this movement, the Sultán immediately returned to India, and effected a junction with the troops of the Viceroy. The united armies of Ghór advanced to the banks of the Jumna; where, between Chandwar and Etawah, they were met by the Hindús. Here an action was fought, in which the latter were defeated, and Jaya Chandra slain [y]. The death of the latter was not known till after the battle, when his body was recognized by his followers; who identified it by means of the golden studs

(y) Táríkhi Alfí and Ferishta.

with which his teeth, on account of extreme age, had been fixed in their sockets. Of the seven hundred elephants, which had been brought against the Mohammedans, ninety were taken; among which a remarkable white elephant is mentioned, that refused to make obeisance to the Sultán, and had almost killed the rider, who endeavoured to force the animal into compliance. A knowledge that the Rájás of Kanauj, like the monarchs of Siam, retained white elephants in their service, combined with other facts, leads to this opinion, that the former observed the Buddhist religion [z], and worshipped these animals.

Country subdued to the confines of China.

Shahábu-d-dín Mohammed Ghorí entered Benares after this battle, where he loaded four thousand camels with jewels, fine clothes, and rarities of every description, and sent them to Ghazní. At this time many other cities of India were captured, and the country subdued as far as the confines of China [a].

(z) The Jaina and Buddhist systems of faith were of old very little removed from each other; and the differences which now justify a division appear to be of modern origin.

(a) (Táríkhi Alfí.) Mr. Wilford, in his essay on Vikramáditya and Sáliváhana (*A.R.* IX. p. 203), has committed a remarkable anachronism, by ascribing the conquest of Kakha Ráj, or Cachar, with Rangamatti, or Kausumba, to Mahmúd of Ghazní, in A.D. 1017.

A.D. 1195. Conquests of Kutbu-d-dín Aibuk.

Soon after the defeat and death of the Rájá of Benares, Mohammed Ghorí returned to Ghazní; and the viceroy of India, having fought several battles, extended the Mohammedan possessions in his absence. He defeated the army of Bhíma Deva, of Nahrwálah; ravaged Gujarát and Ajmír; entered the province of Agra; laid siege to the hill fortress of Biana [b], north of the river Chambul; where, having heard that his master had left

December, A.D. 1196.

Ghazní, in the month of Muharram Hij. 592 [c], and was advancing into India, he abandoned the siege, and went to meet him at Hansí. The united armies, having again marched against Biana, took it; and Mohammed Ghorí subsequently laid siege to Gwalior. The Rájá of this place had defended the fortress for nearly twelve months, when the disturbed state of Khorásán, and the hostile incursions of the Saljúk Turkmáns, recalled the Sultán to Ghazní. Having left his general, Bahá-ud-dín Toghrul, to continue the siege of Gwalior,

January, A.D. 1197.

he marched from India, during the month of Saffar, in the following year of the Hijra. Gwalior still held out for some time against the Mohammedans; but the Rájá, tired of their persevering efforts to take it, sent at

(b) Ferishta. (c) Táríkhi Alfí.

length a messenger to the Viceroy, Kutbu-d-dín Aibuk, and instructed him to tell the latter, that, though he would not deliver up the fortress to Bahá-ud-dín Toghrul, he was willing to give the other possession of it, and would pay a tribute to his master. On this the Viceroy marched against Gwalior, to the great annoyance of Bahá-ud-dín Toghrul, who resolved to resist this interference; when his death happily relieved the former from all anxiety regarding this matter. The Rájá was subsequently reinstated in power at Gwalior[d].

Attempt to recover Ajmír by the Rájá of Nahrwálah.

The Supreme Rájá of Nahrwálah, Bhíma Deva Chalúkya, assisted by his feudatories, Prahladana and Dara Versha[e], the rulers of Chandravati, assisted by the Rájá of Nagore, made an effort to wrest Ajmír from the Mohammedans. The troops of the latter were, at this time, dispersed over the provinces; but Kutbu-d-dín Aibuk, with the few soldiers he could collect, marched to oppose them, and

(d) On the united authority of the Táríkhi Alfí and Ferishta.

(e) These are called Wallin and Darabarz by Ferishta; and are mentioned in the Inscrip. XVI. and XVIII. from Abú, translated by Mr. Wilson, *A.R.* vol. XVI. The magnificent ruins of Chandravati, situated on the western face of the Aravalli Mountains of Rájputana, were visited not long since by Sir Charles Colville, and several other gentlemen. This ancient city is only fourteen miles east of Abú.

was defeated. In this action the Viceroy was severely wounded, and carried to Ajmír; which was now besieged by the allied army of Hindús. When intelligence of these movements was received at Ghazní, reinforcements were immediately sent to the assistance of the Viceroy. Ajmír was maintained against the besiegers till the arrival of the troops from Ghazní; when the enemy, retiring, were pursued into the district of Sirohí. At this time, the rulers of Chandravati, who were encamped near Abú, resolved to defend the passes into Gujarát; and the Viceroy, hearing of this, attacked and defeated them with great slaughter. On this occasion vast spoils were obtained by the Mohammedans, who now advanced into Gujarát, and captured Nahrwálah. The Viceroy, soon after retracing his steps to Dehlí, took the forts of Badaún, Kalpí, and Kálinjar[f], having thus reduced the country as far as the junction of the Jumna and the Ganges.

Conquests by Mohammed Bakhtiár Khiljí, in Awud and Bahar.

Mohammed Bakhtiár Khiljí, who commanded a division of troops under the Viceroy, was at this time sent across the Ganges, to possess the province of Awud[g], which he reduced. Here he obtained much spoil; and,

(f) Ferishta. (g) Commonly called Oude in the maps.

having rendered hmiself formidable by increasing his military force, excited the envy of the other commanders who were serving under the Viceroy. Soon after, this general appears to have conquered the northern part of Bahar, or Mithila; and his enemies had become so jealous of his success, that they left no method untried of prejudicing the mind of Kutbu-d-dín Aibuk against him. The Viceroy yielded so far to their clamour as to enter, at one time, into a design of murdering Mohammed Bakhtiár Khiljí; but, having been persuaded by some of his intimates to commute this sentence, he determined that his servant should decide his fate, in single combat, against a fierce white elephant[h]. The latter was successful, and rose in the estimation of his master, who subsequently conferred on
A.D. 1203. him many favours. Mohammed Bakhtiár Khiljí was again sent into Bahar; the south-eastern part of which, or Magadha, was subdued, and Gaor, its capital city, taken. The Rájá of South Bahar, at this time, was Lakamír, or Lakshmana Sinha[i], last of the Voidya monarchs. He had reigned over the country

(h) The same elephant, no doubt, that was taken from the Rájá of Benares.

(i) These facts have been strangely confounded by Mr. Wilford, in his essay of Vikramáditya and Sáliváhana, *A.R.* IX., p. 190; and

for seventy or eighty years, and was renowned for his equity and liberality. When the Mohammedan general took Gaor, the Hindú monarch escaped; and the former, not long after, declared himself independent of the Viceroy, by reading the *khutba* in his own name.

A.D. 1206. Death of Mohammed Ghorí, and establishment of the Dehlí empire.

After the Gakkars had, in the beginning of this year, murdered Shahab-ud-dín Mohammed Ghorí, Kutbu-d-dín Aibuk was left undisputed master of all the Indian possessions that belonged to the former, excepting Bahar and Bengal, which owned the authority of Mohammed Bakhtiár Khiljí. From this date the first Mohammedan empire of Dehlí may be said to commence; and was sucessively ruled by different families of Afghâns, till the establishment of the Moghul dynasty by the celebrated Báber.

and Mr. Wilson, in following him, has committed a similar mistake in his comments on the Abú inscriptions, *A.R.* XVI., p. 326. The Laka, or Lagam Mír, of Mírkhond, author of the Habíbu-s-Sair, has been considered the same with Lakha Múl Deo, of Gujarát; but the Chalúkya Rájá of Nahrwâlah, and the Voidya monarch of Gaor, had no connexion with each other; and Gujarát was never invaded by Mohammed Bakhtiár Khiljí, as supposed by Wilford.

A.

PERSIAN MANUSCRIPTS, BELONGING TO THE TRANSLATOR, WHICH HAVE BEEN REFERRED TO, AS AUTHORITIES FOR THE FACTS OF THE HISTORICAL INTRODUCTION, OR MAY BE HEREAFTER CITED IN THE ANNOTATIONS.

حبيب السير Habíbu-s-Sair, compiled by Mír Khawand Sháh, otherwise named Mírkhond, in the end of the fifteenth century. I possess only the second volume, which is neatly written, and does not appear to have been copied in India.

تاريخ الفي Táríkhi Alfí, or the history of one thousand years, by Mullah Ahmad, the son of Nasr Allah of Nineveh. This general history of Mohammedan transactions was compiled at Agra, in Hij. 995, A.D. 1587, by order of Mohammed Jalál-ud-dín Akbar, Emperor of Dehlí. It is one of the general works used by Ferishta in compiling his general history of India. The second and third volumes of the work are in my possession, and were taken from a copy which once belonged to the library of Khuld Manzal Bahádur Sháh, the eldest son of Aurangzíb.

طبقات اكبري Tabakát Akbarí, by Nizámu-d-dín Ahmad Bakhshí, the son of Mohammed Mokim, of Hirát. It is an excellent general history of India, composed during the reign of Akbar, about Hij. 991, A.D. 1583. The plan of this work appears to have suggested to Ferishta the idea of his general history of India; and this author has borrowed from it largely. Nizám-ud-dín Ahmad was Bakhshí, or military paymaster, of the troops in Gujarát, and is frequently mentioned by the author of the Mirát Ahmadí. My copy of the work was written in Hij. 1071, A.D. 1660.

اكبر نامه Akbar Námah and Ayín Akbarí, by the learned Shaikh Abul Fazl, the renowned minister of the Emperor Akbar. My copy is complete in three volumes, and was copied, Hij. 1044, A.D. 1634.

تاريخ فرشته Táríkhi Ferishta, the history of Ferishta, which has been well translated by Colonel Briggs. The Persian copy to which I have occasionally referred is one which was lithographed at Bombay.

تذكرة الملوك Tazkarat-ul-Mulúk, or a memoir of Kings, by Rafi-ud-dín Ibrahím Shírází, of Bíjápúr. The author lived in the time of Ibrahím Ádil Sháh II. of Bíjápúr, and commenced to write about the time that Ferishta finished his history, or A.D. 1608. This work is a memoir of the author's own times, from A.D. 1559 to A.D. 1636, and is very rare.

جهانگير نامه Jahángír Námah, a history of the Emperor Jahángír of Dehlí, written by Motamad Khán. This work was used by Colonel Dow in composing the second volume of his Indian history.

تاريخ شاه جهان Táríkhi Sháh-Jahán, by Mírzá Amína. This history of the Emperor Sháh-Jahán, the father of Aurangzíb, afforded materials for his life in Colonel Dow's second volume.

تاريخ خافي خان Táríki Khafí Khán, sometimes called the Muntakhab-ul-Lubáb, an excellent history of India, from the time of Báber, written by Mohammed Háshim, commonly entitled Kháfi Khán. I only possess the second volume, containing the reign of Aurangzíb.

فتوحات عالمگيري Fatúhát Álamgírí, or victories of Aurangzíb, written by Shrídás, a Nágar Bráhman of Gujarát. The author was a spectator of the occurrences he details: and was in the service of the Shaikh-ul-islám, the son of Abd-ul-Wahháb Ahmadábádí. This work is very rare, and was copied at Nahrwálah Patan, in Hij. 1163, A.D. 1749.

مآثر الامرا Maásir-ul-Omará, or biography of the Nobles, by Samsámu-d-daulah Sháh Nawáz Khán. Two copies of this work are in my possession.

دستور العمل شاهنشاهي Dastúr-ul-Amal Sháhinsháhí, or the imperial regulations and political divisions of Hindústán and the Dekhan, compiled by Munshí Thakor Lál.

هفت اقليم Haft Iklím, a geographical and biographical treatise, composed by Amín Ahmad Razí.

With regard to the system of orthography followed in this translation, it is necessary to say a few words. Most of the consonants are to be pronounced as in English. The lisping ث is expressed by *s*, instead of *th*, adopted by some oriental orthographers; ج by *j*; چ by *ch*, as in the word church; خ by *kh*, a guttural, and pronounced like the Greek χ, or the German *ch*, as in the Scotch word *loch*; طت by *t*; ظض ذ by *z*; ص س by *s*, &c. In spelling the vowels, (´) Fat'ha, has been expressed by *a*; for (ˏ) Kisra, *i*, as in the Italian; for Zamma, or Pesh, (ʾ), *u* or *o*, according to what the pronunciation seems to require. The spelling of some names, familiarized by time to the English ear, and not far wide of the proper pronunciation, has been retained.

PREFACE

TO THE

MIRÁT AHMADÍ[a],

OR

MIRROR OF AHMAD;

A HISTORY OF GUJARÁT.

According to the inevitable will of destiny—"truly he is appointed vicegerent on earth, from the presence of him who is lord of every country, and who giveth to whomsoever he chooseth,"—it has been decreed, that Abú-Nasr Mujáhidu-d-dín Ahmad Sháh[b] should bear the ensigns of Royalty, and the seal of the Khiláfat. Being adorned with the signet of Prophecy, and bearing the exalted title of Kiblah of the world, and Kaba of the universe, the same is a king great as Jamshíd[c], and an emperor, whose court is exalted as the sky. He is styled protector of the glorious religion, such being recorded by the power and will of God, (granting nobility and conferring favour) and has bestowed on the world both ease and comfort.

[a] مراة احمدي [b] ابونصر مجاهدالدين احمد شاه [c] جمشيد

Moreover, the glad tidings of the clemency, kindness, and justice, of this mighty king, (who cherishes his servants and consumes his enemies) having spread abroad into the four quarters of Hindústán, let all subjects and vassals observe the usual obedience, and perform the customary services, giving thanks for such great presents, as are the blessings of this fortunate, prosperous, and tranquil age; and, praying continually that the state may remain stedfast, let them not oppose or resist the sublime decrees, that are to be honoured like those of fate.

And let this be known to governors, and keepers of the royal records, that, in past time, and after the passage of Aurangzíb Álamgír Pádsháh[d] from this transitory world, there happened to be confusion in the settlement and arrangement of the countries of Hindústán; and, because of the discord and innovation of that time, both trouble and perplexity began to spread themselves over the four quarters of that country; while ease, satisfaction, and security, necessarily and inconveniently disappeared. It being the will of God, that confusion should daily increase, and that there should be a cor-

[d] اورنگ زیب عالمگیر پادشاه

rupt negligence, both in the business of the treasury and administration, an anxious desire to mutiny arose in every heart; and, ambition being produced in every mind, each Názim[e] of a province grew disobedient and refractory, and became independent.

Wherefore business generally, and the important concerns of civil government, being thus impeded, fell into neglect and arrears; while the ordinances and regulations concerning such matters being lost and gradually forgotten, the treasuries and magazines became empty, as the hands of the poor. With respect to the Súbah of Ahmadábád[f] Gujarát[g], after Hámid Khán[h], in the year of the Hijra 1137, A.D. 1724-25, had put to death Shujáat Khán Bahádur[i], the deputy of Mobárizu-l-Mulk[k] in that province, he usurped the government lands and arrears of revenue; and, seeking to get rid of the servants and assignments, gradually obtained the volumes of the records, from the Register Office, where they had been accumulating for years. In this manner the revenue exchequer became useless. Other governors, perceiving this, retained the management of the province in their

[e] ناظم [f] احمدآباد [g] گجرات [h] حامد خان

[i] شجاعت خان بهادر [k] مبارزالملک

own hands, without the assistance of a minister; and, as there was neither inquiry nor question made from court concerning this, the collector-generalship of Gujarát, once the most important of any in Hindústán, was thus in a manner set aside. Nothing, at present, remains but the name and the remembrance of the office; and, as the affairs of the revenue court had been ended, the keepers of the records were scattered here and there, looking after their own affairs, or searching for employment; and the usual yearly records of the districts ceased altogether. Moreover, the volumes of the current business passed for the most part into the possession of Hámid Khán; and such as remained behind were entirely disregarded and neglected.

Truly, according to the saying, "times change with men," the period of the latter part of Mohammed Sháh's[1] reign will be explained by the blessing of God.

The writer of these pages, being appointed revenue administrator of the province, in the first year of Ahmad Sháh's reign, Hij. 1161, A.D. 1747-8, saw nothing to be done in this appointment; and, having ascertained that the

[1] محمد شاه

records, like the office of the administrator, were only known by name, he made diligent search and inquiry regarding the affairs of the Súbahs, Cities, Sirkars, Parganahs, and Towns, whilst registering the village lands and payment, the present revenue and assessment; and being, moreover, guided in these matters by the advice of Mittha Laal, of the Kait Tribe, who became his assistant, and had kept the provincial accounts, as did his father and forefathers, he thus collected the whole in the form of a book. He employed himself in correcting and arranging this, and, having brought it to a conclusion, named it the *Mirát Ahmadí*, or a History of the Province of Gujarát. It was also his intention to send one copy to the record office of the province, and the other to the Imperial Court; there being no such register known, on account of those accidents which have been mentioned. But, while anxious to forward the latter copy through Jáwíd Khán Nawáb[m], who was then the Emperor's Lieutenant and Minister, (and regarded this your servant,) it happened that unkind heaven took away the Nawáb's life; so the strong wish, then existing, that this book should be made

[m] نواب جاوید خان

perfect, became void; and, on hearing of this distressing event, the correction was deferred and delayed.

Doubtless, if this book, which is useful in other matters besides those of the province, be equal to what I wish it, and be presented at the Imperial Court, and be honoured by the inspection of the revenue accountants, (who collect gold, and whose sight hath the virtues of the philosophers' stone,) it must obtain a thousand thanks.

And amongst its uses there is one, that it points out the origin of the Fazlí Era, and in what it differs from the Hijra, of which none, in their researches, have hitherto found out the enigma, or true signification. While writing this book, the author was anxious to ascertain, from the annalists and accountants of this country, when it commenced; but, though he sought for explanation and information among the revenue writers of the government exchequer, no one could solve the difficulty. And, though he found neither mention nor record of it in the histories of former kings, the same became obvious and intelligible, after much labour and consideration; and, having discovered, through his poor understanding, all that regards this innovation, and the time when it came into use, and in what it differs from the Hijra, he laid down the method and rule for finding it, and annexed it to this volume. If it were God's pleasure, that the author's life should be spared, and sufficient leisure left him, amidst the anarchy of this province, he resolved to detail its commencement in a separate work, and leave it as a memorial of him in the present record office.

But what leisure and quiet can be obtained, for the completion of such things, in these perverse and unsettled times?—and where is the man who can thoroughly understand this, or one so perfect as to here appreciate perfection?—for truly painful is the labour of him who would attain perfection: according to the saying, "Perfection comes in the decline of things, and then the time of failure is complete."

Agreeably to these words, which are full of truth, "perfect yourselves in learning, that you may be honoured by the world: for he who is imperfect has no value in my sight." And be ye joyous, satisfied, and thankful, until the time when things be made manifest, from behind the curtain that conceals them.

But as the book, just mentioned, contained an account of the landholders and governors of these parts, from the time of Akbar's[n] conquest, along with the affairs of the revenue administration and taxes, the author's intimate friends, being aware of its preparation, frequently intreated him to separate the historical and revenue matters, into distinct volumes, for these reasons: First, that the above book was too voluminous and ponderous, as is the case with records, and that it was not proper to make known to every one the business of the treasury and revenue, or the regulations of government; and, secondly, that the affairs and condition of the landholders, from the first appearance of the Mohammedans in these provinces, with those of the rulers of the Dehlí[o] government, to the present time, ought not to be combined with the business of the revenue and administration. They said, moreover, that the historical portion, with only a small branch of the other, should be written as such works usually are, in order that men may profit thereby, and that, contemplating with awe the things which have passed, one might more easily learn and remember precept by example.

Though these pages possess not such excellence as to be accounted any thing among the

[n] اكبر [o] ديهلي

crowd of books, the author has complied with the wishes of those friends, to the best of his ability; and, after allowing ten years to elapse without finishing it, he at length changed the introduction, from what was originally intended, and brought it to a conclusion, in the year of the Hijra 1170, A.D. 1756, being the fourth year of the Azízu-d-dín Álamgír[p] II.; which was a period of great anxiety, and a time of constant contest, as will be here explained. The preface too, which detailed the state of the first transcript, has now become the commencement of the present work.

It must not be concealed, that, in what relates to the Rájás, who preceded the dominion of the Mohammedans, and also in what regards the rulers of the province, under the Patan government of Dehlí, prior to the Gujarát kings, the information was not wholly to be depended on: but such parts of the history as seemed well authenticated have been here abridged. The account of the several transactions which took place, during the individual reigns of the Gujarát kings, is selected from the *Mirát Sikandarí*[q], a history of that sovereignty written after its

[p] عزيزالدين عالمگير

[q] مراة سکندري

termination, in Hijra 1020,* A.D. 1611. The history of the period commencing with Akbar's conquest of the country, and ending with the tenth year of Aurangzíb's reign, along with what relates to the governors of the province, has been extracted from the *Akbar-Námah*[r], the *Jahángír-Námah*[s], and *Pádsháh-Námah*[t]. But, as no written record of the transactions after the tenth year of Aurangzíb's reign was procurable, the account of these, up to the present time, is given on such authentic information as could be obtained from the old men of that period.

And now regarding the author of the work. When he had attained his ninth year, in the beginning of the reign of Bahádur-Sháh[u] Khuld-Manzil, corresponding with the Hijra, year 1120, A.D. 1708, having come from Burhán-

r اکبر نامه   s جهانگیر نامه   t پادشاه نامه

u بهادرشاه خلد منزل

* In the original the date is 1120, but is an evident error of the copyist's; as the author says, in another place, that it was written forty years after the destruction of the Gujarát monarchy, which took place in Hij. 980. The author of the Mirát Sikandarí moreover mentions himself as being concerned in Gujarát transactions which preceded the death of Akbar.

púr into this country, he soon after began to write, in an abridged form, whatever made a strong impression on his mind; and selected all that was authenticated by trustworthy chronicles, concerning the governors of the province. The original intention being to detail the past condition, the several transactions and misfortunes, the desolation and confusion of this country, such gave rise to the production of the *Mirát Ahmadí*: though a description of the whole transactions would have been too long and troublesome, yet, had it been his intention to write such a work, the author might have accomplished it; but, as he has only chosen to detail a portion of these, with the years and months of their occurrence, he must be excused where his information failed him. The summary also of those things he witnessed has been written with care and attention.

But, previous to commencing with his design, it is necessary to say something of the state, extent, and revenue, of the province in former times; whilst he trusts, that, if the learned reader discovers mistakes or errors, which are unavoidable, he will amend and correct them.

SECTION I.

CHAPTER I.

PRELIMINARY OBSERVATIONS OF THE STATE OF GUJARÁT.

It must be known to discriminating and inquiring men that the country of Gujarát, which is one of the principal provinces in Hindústán, is in the second climate. It has a temperate atmosphere, generally ; but, in places on the sea coast, the air is variable.

The soil generally is sandy, and produces all kinds of wheat in abundance: though the greater part is cultivated with *bajrí*, which is the usual food of the horses in Kach[x], and even of a great part of the population there. In former times, good wheat was not to be obtained, but it is now generally procurable. In some of the districts, the fruits of the autumnal and spring crops, being blended together, are cultivated at such seasons, either by irrigation or the natural rains.

کچہ [x]

The fields and villages, for the most part, are surrounded by hedges of the prickly pear; by which they are completely fortified in the course of time. Many fruit and other trees, such as the *amba* and *khirní*, cover the face of the country, from the neighbourhood of Patan[y] to the town of Baroda[z], being a distance of a hundred koss. Here also we find cucumbers and *nashpatis* of a good quality, with melons of different kinds; which, when sown in the beds of rivers, are produced of an excellent quality and abundance, both during the cold and hot seasons. Such, however, are not procurable in Sorath. There are likewise different kinds of odoriferous herbs, fruits, and vegetables, used in these parts, whose names would occupy too much space in detailing them.

The houses are all built of burnt bricks, and are roofed with teak wood and tiles. In Sorath, however, they use stone instead of bricks.

The Kach horses possess activity; and are so well proportioned in their make as to bear a comparison with those of Arabia and Irák. The cattle of Gujarát, that run well in draught, are of a very white colour and handsome form. The panthers are incomparable hunters; and the

[y] پتن

[z] برودہ

buffaloes of this quarter are also very well made. Large elephants were formerly hunted in the territories of Rajpípalah[a], but, the passage in the mountains being now closed up, they are no longer found.

In respect to warlike instruments, the swords of Sirohí[b] are celebrated every where, and there are no better reeds than such as are procured in this country; so that they are carried to Hindústán, Persia, and other countries, for the manufacture of arrows.

Rings, like those of Yemen, necklaces, and cups, with handles for knives and daggers, are manufactured at Khambáyat, from cornelian of different colours; and these, with a variety of ivory instruments, when carried into the neighbouring countries, are exchanged for other commodities. Cloths also, like those of Persia, Arabia, Abyssinia, Constantinople, and Europe, are made and coloured here.

Another article of produce is salt. In all the places near the sea-shore, there are enclosed fields, called, in Hindí, *kiyarí*; which are filled, during the cold season, from reservoirs of salt water near them; and, the salt, when concreted there, is collected. But that procured at

[a] راج پیپله   [b] سروهي

the port of Khambáyat[c], resembles coarse sand; and, possessing a considerable degree of bitterness of taste, has the virtue of recruiting the strength of debilitated persons. The black salt, named black stone, and which is called *sanchal* in Hindí, is made at the above seaport by boiling a grass, called *morand*, in the manner usually followed in procuring *murdar sang**. This salt is then carried into the neighbouring countries both by sea and land. There is yet another kind, procured from the saline pits at the town of Junjwárah[d], in the *parganah* of Bíramgám[e]; and similar salt, when obtained from the water of the wells, is of a white colour and good quality, resembling bits of sugar. It is carried by the merchants into Málwa[f], and other places; and all the revenue collected therefrom is included in the settlement of the above-mentioned *parganah*.

Another article of manufacture here is paper. Although the Daulatábád and Kashmír paper be fine and beautiful, it is not equal to what is made at Ahmadábád, either in point of whiteness or purity. Several different kinds are produced; all of which are faulty in being pene-

[c] کهمبایت [d] جنجواره [e] بیرمگام [f] مالوه

* This is a vitreous oxide of lead.

trated with innumerable small holes, caused by the particles of sand, from this sandy country, which adhere to it during its manufacture, being rubbed off in the process of polishing. Notwithstanding this, it is much prized for its whiteness, and is carried, in exchange for other commodities, to the cities of India, and Arabia, and to Constantinople.

The teak wood here is only used for the ceilings and pillars of dwelling houses, or the building of ships ; but the black wood, which in quality and appearance resembles ebony, is used in the construction of bullock carriages and other things.

In the mountainous country, about Ídur[g], there is a quarry of white stone, which is procurable in no other part. The lime made from this is used in stucco work ; for the walls or terraces of buildings; and for fine edifices, pleasure-houses, and mausoleums. If employed in plastering, it takes so fine a polish as to reflect the light as a looking-glass. When, in the reign of Firdaus-Ashiáni-Sháh Jahán[h], the royal buildings of the citadel of Sháhjahánábád (Dehlí) were repaired, the lime made from this stone was taken from Gujarát, by the King's

[g] ايدر

[h] فردوس آشياني شاه جهان

order, and used in their construction. The mausoleums of the Mohammedan saints, the temples of the Hindús, and other public works (an account of which will be detailed hereafter,) are erected with this lime; as are also numerous canals, water reservoirs, wells, and other like buildings.

Though the water of the wells is salt, yet, were all the other good things of this province made a subject of praise, another volume would be requisite: for it must be noticed, that travellers from all quarters have heard of this country being proverbially good above all others.

In the present time, the settlement of the province is accomplished by five thousand cavalry, mustered by the Názim; in addition to those of the Faujdárs and other vassals, provided no addition be requisite for other services, than those belonging to the usual business of the province.

With regard to the extent and revenue of this country, in the reign of Sultán Muzaffir[i] III., who was the last of the Gujarát kings, and during the administration of Itimád Khán[k], in the Hijra year 979, corresponding with the

[i] سلطان مظفر [k] اعتماد خان

year of the Hindú era of Vikramáditya 1627,* and with A.D. 1571, the whole collection† from the government lands, and those assigned in Jágír, was 5,84,0050,000, or five *arabs*‡, eighty-four *krores*, and fifty thousand Gujarát *tankchas*;

* This era begins 56 years before the Christian era, and that number must be subtracted from it to make them correspond.

† The province of Gujarát, when most flourishing under its own Mohammedan kings, consisted of twenty-five *sirkars*, or districts; many of which had been conquered from the neighbouring provinces. The whole of the revenue, at that time, amounted to five *arabs*, eighty-four *krores*, and fifty thousand *tankchas*, equal to 2,336,002,000 *dams*. When the country was conquered by Akbar, a new political distribution of the districts took place; and Gujarát then consisted of nine *sirkars*. It is curious to contrast the original revenue of the province, when independent, with what it afterwards became, under the emperors of Dehlí. The statements which are given on the authority of Gladwin's translation of the Ayín Akbarí, Frazer's Life of Nádir Sháh, and the Dastúr-ul-Amal of the empire, by Thakor Lál, are as follow:

Revenue of Gujarát when independent,

Consisting of	25	Sirkars	2,336,020,000	dams.
Akbar's reign	9	do.	26,738,1619	
Jahángír's do.	9	do.	50,0000,000	
Aurangzíb's do.	9	do.	60,7849,135	
Mohammed Sháh's	9	do.	48,7344,000	

The above exhibits the revenue greatest in the time of Aurangzíb, and least in that of Akbar; a prince who did not exact too much from the people.

‡ According to the Indian computation, one hundred thousand rupees form a *lak*, one hundred laks one *krore*, one hundred krores one *arab*, one hundred arabs one *kharrab*, one hundred kharrabs one *sank*.

there being then two laks and three thousand horsemen mustered in the kingdom. There were, in those days, a hundred *tankchas* to a rupee, and the same is now reckoned at forty dams; so that the whole amount would, at the present time, be equal to five *krores* and forty-seven *laks* * of rupees. A sum also of twenty-five *laks* of *hoons*, and one *krore* of *ibrahímís*, that were two parts greater, being altogether nearly equal to five *krores* and sixty-two *laks* of rupees, was collected annually from the kings of the Dekhan[l], the European and Arab ports, and from other quarters as hereafter detailed.

Sultán Bahádur[m], after capturing the fort of Chitore[n], in the year of the Hijra 955†, A.D. 1548, fled from the emperor Nasíru-d-dín Mohammed Humáyún Pádsháh[o]. On this occasion he took refuge, on board of ship, at the port of Díu[p], (where there is a strong fortification surrounded by the sea,) and was fraudulently killed by the Europeans. At this period

[l] دکهن [m] سلطان بهادر [n] جتور

[o] نصيرالدين محمد همايون پادشاه [p] ديو

* The amount ought to be five *krores* and eighty-four *laks* of rupees.

† There is here a mistake. It was taken in the month of Ramazan A. H. 941; March, A.D. 1535.

the Europeans took possession of the above-mentioned harbour, as will be explained in the reign of that prince: and the kingdom of Gujarát soon after going to decay, the tribute from the ports was no longer paid.

During such time as the power and sovereignty of the Gujarát monarchy continued to increase, the several sirkars, and ports, which were then made subject to the government by conquest, were attached as parts of the country. In this manner twenty-five sirkars were obtained, and are named as follow:

Sirkar*
- " Júdhpúr[q].
- " Jalore[r] (in Rajputana).
- " Nagore[s] † (in Rajputana).
- " Bassai[t] (Bassein).
- " Manbai[u] (Bombay).
- " Damman[x] (Damaun).
- " Rám Nagar[y].
- " Dúngarpúr[z].

[q] جودهپور [r] جالور [s] ناگور [t] بسي [u] منبي
[x] دمن [y] رام نگر [z] دونگرپور

* A *sirkar*, or district, is called *tauman* تومان west of the Indus. Every *súbah*, or province, is divided into so many districts, or *sirkars*, and these again subdivided into *mahls* or *parganahs*.

† Nagore, which is eighty miles N.W. of Ajmír, is now subject to Júdhpúr.

Sirkar Bánswárah[a].
" Sirohi[b].
" Kach[c].
" Somnát[d].
" Dand-Rajpúrí[e] (in the Konkan).
" Ahmadábád[f].
" Baroda[g].
" Bhroch[h].
" Nadote[i].
" Súrat[k] (Surat).
" Chámpánír[l].
" Patan[m].
" Sorath[n] *.
" Navánagar[o].
" Godhrah[p].
" Múlhír[q] (in Khandesh).
" Nadarbár[r] (Nandarbar in ditto).

The personal establishment of Sultán Muzaffir III. and others, at this time, consisted of

[a] بانسواره [b] سروهي [c] کچهه [d] سومنات
[e] دندراجپوري [f] احمدآباد [g] بروده [h] بهروچ
[i] نادوت [k] سورت [l] چاماپانير [m] پتن [n] سورتهه [o] نوانگر
[p] گودهره [q] ملهير [r] ندربار

* Sorath, or the ancient Sauráshtra, and the same as the Syrastra vicus of Ptolemy's geography, must not be confounded with Súrat, now usually called Surat in the maps. The former is in the most western side of Gujarát, and in that part now called Kahtiwar: and is said to encompass the mountains of Júnagarh to the distance of thirty miles. The fort of Mangrole, generally included in this district, is the Monoglossum Emporium of Ptolemy.

thirty thousand horsemen, with estates of thirty-two *mahls ;* of which the revenue amounted to ninety laks of rupees*, equal to ninety krores of Gujarát *tankchas* ; and was divided in the following manner :

	Horse.	Tankchas.
Sultán Muzaffir[s]	10,000	330,000,000
Itimád Khán Wazír[t]	9,000	300,000,000
Alagh Khán Habshí[u]	4,000	110,000,000
Jahjahár Khán[x]	2,500	60,000,000
Maliku-s-Sherk[y]†	2,500	40,000,000
Wajíhu-l-Mulk[z] and others	2,000	60,000,000
	30,000	900,000,000

s سلطان مظفر t اعتماد خان u الغخان حبشي

x جهجهار خان y ملك الشرق z وجيه الملك

* The traveller Mandelslo, who was in Gujarát in 1633, or forty five years after it became subject to Dehlí, says, that the whole revenue of Gujarát amounted heretofore to eighteen millions of gold *(Trav.* 48) not counting the customs of Baroda and Bhroch, which were nearly eight hundred thousand crowns. The traveller Thevenot, who followed him and was there in A.D. 1655, says, " it paid the Moghul 25,500,000 French livres ;" and these, calculated at tenpence half-penny would make £1,115,625 English money. *(Travels in the Indies,* Chap. xviii.) Thevenot's visit to India took place in the early part of Aurangzíb's reign, and the revenue, as stated by him, will be found to correspond very nearly with the amount of it given, in a former note, on native authority : for, assuming the medium value of a rupee at 2s. then 60,7849,135 dams = 15,196,228 rupees = £1,519,622.

† The copyist of the original manuscript has evidently misconceived the name of the person here intended. In the Tazkarat-ul-

Fifteen *krores* and fifty *laks* of Gujarát *tankchas*, equal to fifteen *laks* and fifty thousand rupees of revenue, were obtained from the customs and other taxes of the city of Ahmadábád: of which total there were the following items:

	Tankchas.
The cultivation of the lands in the environs . .	5,000,000
Taxes on vegetables . .	100,000,000
Tax on coinage . . .	30,000,000
	13,5,000,000.

making up the sum of thirteen *krores* and fifty *laks* of *tankchas*.

Connected with the police department, the following sums were realized:

	Rupees.
From the office of the Kotwál .	15,000
〃 the Pán market . . .	50,000
〃 the sale of cattle and horses .	35,000
〃 the sale of lac . . .	5,000
〃 the manufacture of wires .	10,000
〃 the opium market . . .	5,000
〃 the silk market . . .	18,000
〃 the tax on porterage . .	5,000
〃 the tax on private messengers .	1,500
〃 the fines on false weights .	5,000

ul-Mulúk, written by Rafí-ud-dín-Shírází, contemporary with the characters above mentioned, Malik Arslán Imádu-l-Mulk, ملک ارسلان عماد الملک who must be the person here meant, is also noticed. There will be occasion, in a future note, to refer to the original passage.

	Rupees.
From the tax on shops	15,000
〃 the revenue of the 12 Purahs of the city . . .	3,500
〃 the collections of the city gate	13,000
〃 the other Purahs . .	14,000
〃 the tax on confections and other things	5,000
	200,000

The whole amounting to the sum of two *krores* of *tankchas*, or two *laks* of rupees, as above.

The revenue of the parganahs, that were fixed as a provision for the Sultán and others, altogether amounted to the sum of forty *laks* and fifty thousand rupees; being in detail as follows:

	Villages.	Rupees.
Parganah Pitlád[a] . .	276	2,000,000
〃 Khambáyat[b] . .	6	450,000
〃 Múndah[c], the Jágír of Jahjahár Khán[d]	84	500,000
〃 Mahmúdábád[e] . .	85	700,000
〃 Nariád[f]	36	400,000
	487	40,50,000

Of the amount received from Khambáyat, as inserted above, there were 50,000 rupees from the cultivation of the towns of Dhowan[g], Mahmúdpúr[h], &c. and 400,000 (four *laks*) from the collections of the city, tax on supplies, port duties, &c.

[a] پتلاد [b] کهمبایت [c] مونده [d] جهجهارخان
[e] محموداباد [f] نریاد [g] دهوان [h] محمود پور

Regarding the *bandars*, or ports, they were twenty-three in number; of which the port of Khambáyat, being registered separately, there were five other places belonging to Gujarát, viz.

1	Bandar	of	Bhroch[i].
2	"	"	Súrat[k].
3	"	"	Ghoga[l].
4	"	"	Khandár[m] *.
5	"	"	Ránír[n].

which, being put on one side from the total collection of 34,000,000, (thirty-four *laks* of rupees) left a revenue from the remaining twenty-two parts —

In the Sirkar of			Mahls.
"	"	Sorath[o]	
"	"	Bandar† Únah[p] . .	2
"	"	Diú . . .	1
"	"	Púrbandar . .	1
"	"	Màhwah[q] . . .	1
"	"	Patín Diú . .	1
"	"	Manglúr[r] ‡ . .	2

[i] بهروچ [k] سورت [l] گهوگه [m] کهندار

[n] رانیر [o] سورته [p] اونه [q] مهوه [r] منگلور

* Mentioned in Mandelslo's Travels, p. 16.

† The port of Únah is situated inland, on a river, and E.S.E. of Diú Point. This and the six following ports belong to the coast of Kahtiwar.

‡ This place, the Monoglossum Emporium of Ptolemy, though spelt Manglúr by the Mohammedan writers, is always called Mangrole by the natives. In Mandelslo's Travels it is spelt Mangerol, and is said to be famous for the great quantities of linen cloths made there.

			Mahls.
In the Sirkar of			
〃	〃	Bandar Taláchah [s]	4
〃	〃	Nágesar [t]	1
〃	〃	Goriya [u]	1
〃	〃	Dúngar [x]	1
〃	〃	Singhánúr [y]	1
〃	〃	Chiklí [z]	1
			17

amounting to fourteen *laks* of rupees.

The parts held in *jágír* by the nobles were as follow.

The *jágír* of Ikhtiyáru-l-Mulk[a], who served the State with ten thousand regular cavalry, consisting of the

			Towns.	Rupees.
Parganah of Ahmadnagar [b]			44	400,000
〃	〃	Paránti [c]	84	500,000
〃	〃	Jalore [d]	19	200,000
〃	〃	Hursúr [e]	84	300,000
〃	〃	Múrásah [f]	162	800,000
〃	〃	Mehkar[g], containing two hundred and forty-five towns, out of which, however, there were fifty held in Enám by the Rájá of Ídur, and fifty by the Rájá of Dúngarpúr, leaving balance	145	200,000
〃	〃	Píplúd [h]	36	300,000,

[s] تلاچه [t] ناگیسر [u] گوریا [x] دونگر

[y] سنگهانور [z] چکلي [a] اختيار الملك [b] احمدنگر

[c] پرانتي [d] جالور [e] حرسور [f] موراسه [g] مهکر [h] پیپلود

	Towns.		Rupees.
The Parganah of Khutnál [i] and Mamúrábád [k]	44	.	400,000
" " Bírpúr [l] . .	165	.	400,000
" " Bihal [m]	138		1,000,000
	921		4,500,000

Thus forming a total of eleven parganahs, giving an assignment of revenue for forty-five *krores* of Gujarát *tankchas*, or forty-five *laks* of rupees.

The *jágírs* of Sayyid Míran[n], and Sayyid Hámed[o], who were the children of Sayyid Mubárik Khán[p], and served the State with four thousand cavalry, consisted of

	Towns.		Tankchas.
The Parganah of Dholka[q]	615	.	160,000,000

sixteen *krores* of *tankchas*, or sixteen *laks* of rupees.

The *jágírs* of Shír Khán Faoládí, with seven thousand horse; of Hasan Jamál[r], with five thousand, with the assignment to the Shahzádah for five thousand horse, and of the Rájpúts for three thousand, consisted of

	Kasbah.	Towns.	Tankchas.
City of Patan, its cultivation, internal dues, and police taxes			160,000
Parganah of Patan[s] . . .		419	2,650,000
" " Barnagar[t] . .		13	8,500,000
" " Bísalnagar[u] .	1		45,000

[i] کهتنال [k] معموراباد [l] بیرپور [m] بهل

[n] سید میرن [o] سیدحامد [p] سید مبارک خان

[q] دهولقه [r] حسن جمال [s] پتن [t] برنکر [u] بیسلنگر

			Towns.	Tankchas.
Parganah	of	Bíjapúr[x]	98	617,000
"	"	Khirálú[y]	110	580,000
"	"	Pálanpúr[z]	180	525,000
"	"	Dísa[a]	23	285,000
"	"	Jalore[b]	400	2,600,000
"	"	Karhí[c]	299	2,800,000
				18,762,000

The whole collection of ten parganahs.

When the current value of the *tankcha* in the Patan parganah was less than of Gujarát generally, but was fixed in Jhaláwár[d] and Karhí at the same rate as that of Ahmadábád, the whole collection was one *arab* and sixteen *krores* of *tankchas;* being equal to one *krore* and sixteen *laks* of rupees.

The *jágírs* of Rustam Khán[e] and Jangíz Khán[f], the sons of Imád-ul-Mulk, who served the State with twenty-five thousand cavalry, and had charge of five *tahnahs*[g], each *tahnah* having five thousand horse, consisted of twenty-seven *mahls*, or parganahs, yielding a revenue of two *krores* and twenty-five thousand *mahmúdís* and *changízís**; which, according to

[x] بیجاپور [y] کهرالو [z] پالنپور [a] دیس [b] جالور [c] کرحي
[d] جهلاوار [e] رستم خان [f] جنگیزخان [g] تهانه

* These *changízís* are what the traveller Mandelslo calls (page 68) *Ropaias chagam;* which were of very good silver, and worth half a crown French money.

the current value of the Ahmadábád *tankcha*, at that time, was equal to one *arúb*, sixty-two *krores*, and fifty thousand *tankchas*, or one *krore*, sixty-two *laks*, and five hundred rupees. —Rs. 1,6200,500.

	Mahl.	Towns.	Changízís.
Of which sum the Sirkar of the port of Súrat, including port duties, provision-tax, and the rent of the cultivated land in the neighbourhood, yielded . .	1	993	500,000

Also the Sirkar of

	Mahl.	Towns.	Changízís.
Baroda[h], and the cultivation of its environs,	1		500,000
Parganah, and country round Baroda .		208	3,800,000
Dubhúe[i]		44	800,000
Shenúr[k] *		46	500,000
Bahádurpúr[l]		27	200,000
Saowankhírah[m]		82	200,000
		407	6,000,000

The above, consisting of seven *mahls*, or parganahs, and four hundred and seven towns, yielding a revenue of sixty *laks* of *changízís*.

Also Sirkar Bhroch[n]—

	Towns.	Changízís.
Parganah of Bhroch, and neighbourhood, not including the port . .	161	3000,000
" " Hansút[o] . . .	36	400,000

[h] برودہ [i] دبہوی [k] شینور [l] بہادرپور
[m] سونکہیرہ [n] بہروچ [o] حانسوت

* This place is called Sinnore in the maps. It is situated immediately on the Nerbuddah.

	Towns.	Changízís.
Parganah of Dejbárah[p]	12	150,000
〃 〃 Goralbárah[q]* . .	12	200,000
〃 〃 Úrpár[r]†	106	1200,000
〃 〃 Chármándwí[s] . . .	1	50,000
〃 〃 Kulah[t] . . .	36	400,000
〃 〃 Jambúsír[u] . . .	56	800,000
〃 〃 Oklasír[x] . . .	55	600,000
〃 〃 Atlísar[y] . . .	36	200,000
〃 〃 Tarkísár[z]	12	100,000
〃 〃 Ámod[a] and Makbúlábád[b] . .	36	400,000
	559	7,500,000

Being in all twelve *mahls*, or parganahs, five hundred and fifty-nine towns, yielding a revenue of seventy-five *laks* of *changízís*.

Also Sirkar Chámpánír[c]—

	Towns.
Sirkar Chámpánír, Parganah Chámpánír, and country adjacent . .	87

p ديجباره q گورلباره r اورپار s چارماندوي

t كله u جمبوسير x اوكلسير y اتليسر

z تركيسر a آمود b مقبول اباد c چانپانير

* I have some doubt regarding the place here intended. In the original manuscript the name is written Goralbárah, and is probably the same as Korul on the Nerbuddah, in Arrowsmith's map.

† The Oolpar of the maps. This change of the letter *r* and *l* is common in the names of places in India.

	Towns.
Sáolí [d] *	54
Dahwad [e]	100
Hálol [f]	34
Taimúrahbásnah [g]	106
Rájod [h]	25
Jhálod [i]	17
	423

Being in all eight *mahls*, or parganahs, four hundred and twenty-three villages, yielding a revenue of fifteen *laks* of *changízís*.

The *jágír* of Nasiru-l-Mulk†, who served the State with twelve thousand horse, consisted of

		Changízís.
Parganah	Nadarbár	25,00,000
"	Sultánpúr	15,00,000
"	Hissabeh and Nerrada	10,00,000

[d] ساولي [e] دحود [f] حالول
[g] تيموره باسنه [h] راجود [i] جهالود

* The name of this place, which is spelt with a French nasal in Sanúlee, is pronounced as here written.

† The places assigned for this *jágír* belong to the province of Khándesh. Sidí Alí ben Husein, who, as admiral of the great Ottoman Emperor Suleimán I. was ordered to carry a fleet down the Persian Gulf, to cruize against the Portuguese in the seas of India, makes mention of this Nasiru-l-Mulk, in the Mirátu-l-Mamálik, or Mirror of Countries. Mr. von Hammer of Vienna has given some extracts from the book, in Vol. ii. of the Bombay Literary Transactions. Sidí Alí ben Husein was in Gujarát about the end of A.D. 1554, and notices the death of Nasiru-l-Mulk soon after. As this event happened in the reign of Ahmad Sháh II., who was the predecessor of Muzaffir III., the author of the Mirát Ahmadí errs in including his *jágír* here, while professing to give the political divisions of the country in the reign of the latter.

Amounting in all to three *mahls*, yielding a revenue of fifty *laks* of *changízís*, and which are equal to twenty-five *krores* of *tankchas*, or twenty-five *laks* of rupees.

Moreover, Bohrjí, zamíndár of Baglánah[k], possessed the forts of Múlhír and Sahler; and performed service with three thousand horse.

([k]) Baglánah, the western and mountainous district of Khándesh, is divided from Sangamnír by the Chandú range of Ghauts. Mulher and Salher are two forts belonging to this part, which may lay claim to some antiquity. It was governed in former times by Hindú Rájás of its own, who, in A.D. 1370, were obliged to pay tribute to Malik Rájá Farúkí, the founder of the Mohammedan Kháns of Khándesh. The title of the Rájá who paid tribute was Bohrjí; and we find two descendants similarly designated, in A.D. 1529, during the reign of Bahádur Sháh of Gujarát. At a subsequent period, one of the family was incorporated among the nobles of Dehlí by Aurangzíb; and, regarding his ancestors, the Maásiru-l-Omará, or Memoirs of the Nobles, has the following passage:
بهرجي زميندار بكلانه از هزار و چهارصد سال مرزباني اين ديار
بآبا و اجداد او تعلق داشته اينها خودرا از راجه جيچند راتهور
كه راجه قنوج بود ميكيرند و هركه حاكم اين ملك بود بهرجي
نامند در سوالف ايام صاحب سكه بودند و چون ميان دكن و
كجرات واقع شده بهر طرف كه نيرو بيشتر ميديدند اطاعت كونه
ميكردند از مدتي پيشكشي كجرات شده واليان خانديش بنابر
قرب جوار دستبردي مي نمودند در نهصد وهشتاد كه ملك
كجرات بحوضه تصرف عرش آشياني در آمد و عرصه دلكشاي بندر
مبارك سورت مهبط رايات پادشاهي كشت بهرحي بملازمت
رسيده ميرزا شرف الدين حسين نيزبه پادشاه‌را كه طغيان ورزيده

The *jágír* of the Kamilu-l-Mulk[1] consisted of the Sirkar of Godhrah, containing twelve *mahls*

بغزيمت دكن عبورش در اين حدود افتاده مقيد نكاهداشته بود
از نظر كذراند و مورد نوازش كشت " The ancestors of Bohrjí, the zamíndár of Baglánah, having held the dominion of this country for fourteen hundred years, claim their descent from Jeychand Rathore, who was Rájá of Kanauj; and each of them, while ruling, obtain the name of Bohrjí. They had the power formerly of coining money, and, as the country was between Gujarát and the Dekhan, bore a nominal allegiance to each alternately, according to the preponderance of power on either side. Of old, while they paid tribute to Gujarát, the rulers of Khándesh, who were in their immediate neighbourhood, continued to plunder them. On the former country becoming subject to Arsh Áshiání (Akbar) in Hij. 980, A.D. 1572, Bohrjí came and paid his respects to him at Súrat; and, as the emperor's brother-in-law Mírzá Sharfu-d-dín Husain, who had rebelled, was passing through the country of Baglánah on his way to the Dekhan, Bohrjí seized and delivered him up to Akbar, who rewarded him accordingly." Though the authority of the Maásiru-l-Omará, like many other Mohammedan books, is here completely at fault with regard to the chronology of Hindú history; yet the claims made by this family to descent, from the Rájás of Kanauj, would seem authentic: as the present family of Júdhpúr Rathores trace the same connexion. Jaya Chandra, or Jey Chand, when defeated, in A.D. 1193, by Kutbu-d-dín Aibuk, was drowned in crossing the Ganges.

(1) It is impossible to determine the proper name of the individual here noticed under the title of Kamilu-l-Mulk. There is no one mentioned, in the history of Muzaffir III, by this appellation; and, at that time, this part of the country appears to have been included in the *jágír* of Rustam Khán; who was, according to some accounts, the nephew of Malik Arslán Imádu-l-Mulk, or his slave, according to others.

or parganahs, out of which the revenue of two mahls was settled on the zamíndár of Súth and Chattárál Kúlí, for the services they performed. Deducting these, there remain ten *mahls ;* yielding a revenue of fifty *laks* of *changízís*, being about twenty *laks* of rupees ; or being, in detail—

		Towns.	Changízís.
Parganah	Godhrah	171	2000,000
"	Sehra	24	1500,000
"	Míral	42	400,000
"	Samdah, called sometimes Nasirábád	42	800,000
"	Dodah	36	200,000
"	Ambábád	42	200,000
"	Jhálod	84	700,000
"	Morwah	24	10,00,000
"	Kaddhánah	24	200,000
"	Dahmod (m)	12	200,000
		501	7200,000

Being, in all, ten mahls, five hundred and one villages, yielding a revenue of seventy-two *laks* of *changízís*.

The *jágír* of Ghaznaví Khán, son of Malik Khánjí Jalori, who served the State

(m) In Gladwin's translation of the Ayín Akbarí, this place is written Dhamnúd. The name does not appear on the map, but the parganah meant must be near the sources of the Mahye River, as all the others lie between these and the Vindhya range of mountains, N.W. of the Nerbuddah River.

with seven thousand horse, amounted, as separately detailed, to the sum of ten *krores* of *tankchas*, or ten *laks* of rupees—

	Towns.	Rupees.
The mint of Jalore, consisting of eleven *mahls*, and Talúka Júdhpúr, from which the *talpat* [n] tax was taken . .	600	300,070
From the government lands, of which the fourth part belonged to the zamíndárs serving Ghaznaví Khán .	..	200,005
From the Talúka of Nagore, the fort of which, after being several years ruined, was restored, at the request of Malik Khanjí, by the Sultán, where half the lands of the Parganahs belonged to the *wultuns* of the Rájpúts, serving under Gháznaví, with two thousand horse	..	255,000
From the Talúka of Mírtah, in the Sirkar of Nagore, of which half the Parganah belonged to the zamíndárs enjoying the fourth part of the revenue; and who, under Ghaznaví Khán, with two thousand horse, were to assist the king of Ahmadábád, in case of war, with six thousand horse . .	..	200,000
		955,145

Thus amounting in all to nine *laks*, fifty-five thousand one hundred and forty-five rupees.

(n) *Tulput*, or *talpat*, lands that pay a full rent into the public treasury of the paramount authority. The term is used in contradistinction to the usufructuary inheritance of the soil called *wultun*.

Moreover, Rai Jey Sing, the zamíndár of Rájpípalah, who served the State with three thousand horse and one thousand foot, was excused the payment of the tribute.

The *jágírs* of Fat'h Khán(o), Rustam Khán, and others of the Balúchi tribe, who served the State with fourteen thousand horse, consisted of the

			Mahmúdis (p).
Parganah	of	Rádhanpúr	1500,000
"	"	Summí	600,000
"	"	Múnjpúr	800,000
"	"	Kakre	700,000
"	"	Tírwarrah	800,000
"	"	Morwarah	400,000
"	"	Santhalpúr	300,000
"	"	Thartád	1500,000
"	"	Múrbí	1000,000
			76,00,000

(o) The Turkish Admiral, already quoted, notices Fat'h Khán; but designates him by the name of his tribe. In five days we came to the town of Patan, where we visited the tomb of the ancient Shaikh Nizámi. Here Shír Khán and Músa Khán were collecting troops, and preparing for war with Bolody (Bulúch) Khán of Rádhanpúr. (*Bombay Literary Transact.* vol. II., p. 9.)

(p) The traveller Mandelslo says (p. 66), that the *mahmúdís* are made at Súrat, of a very base alloy, are worth about twelve pence sterling, and go only at Súrat, Baroda, Broitschia, Cambaiya, and those parts. There were twenty-six *peyse* in his time to a *mahmúdí*, and fifty-four to a rupee.

Forming a total of nine *mahls,* or parganahs, which yielded a revenue of seventy-five *laks* of *mahmúdís,* being about equal to thirty *laks* of rupees.

Moreover, the Rájpút landholders retained the revenue of their hereditary estates, or *wultuns,* on performing service to the government, viz.—

	Horse.
Púnja Rahtore, the Ídur zamíndár, keeping up .	2,000
Rana Sahumul, zamíndár of Dúngarpúr, retaining .	1,000
Waghílah Sahlah, who, with the enjoyment of the whole *grás*[q] of Jhaláwár, retained .	1,000
Jam Sahna, who had four hundred *grássia* dependents in the province of Sorath .	4,000
Jahra Khangar[r], the zamíndár of Búhj, who possessed 1409 towns, served the government with	5,000

The *jágír* of Amín Khán, Fat'h Khán, and Tatar Khán Ghorí, who with nine thousand horse served the government, consisted of Talúka.

	Rupees.
Júnagarh, containing eighty-seven *mahls,* of which seventeen mahls, including the ports, being counted separately, there remain seventy *mahls;* of which ten parganahs and ten *kasbahs* yielded a collection of one *krore* of rupees, equal to one *krore* of *ibrahímís* and twenty-five *laks* of *húns*	10,000,000

(q) A term of Sanskrit origin, meaning a mouthful of grass, which is now figuratively used to express a feudal feof, or possession; the feoffee, or possessor, is named *grassia.*

(r) This is the second among the ancestors of the present Rao of Kach. He obtained power A.D. 1549.

And, though there was no proper government, such was collected to the time of Sultán Bahádur.

Moreover, the whole number of bandars[s] amounted to eighty-four; from which, deducting the twenty-three belonging to Gujarát, and the sirkar of Sorath, which were accounted for separately, there remained sixty-one, of which the collection amounted to one *krore* of *ibrahímís*.

Regarding the port of Diú, and the *kasbahs* in possession of Malik Riyáz, and Malik Toghán, these were attached to the country of Sorath, and thus named—

Bandar Diú,
" Bhím,
" Madhapúr,
" Kajbin;

	Ibrahímís.
being in all four *mahls*, yielding a revenue of two *laks*	2,000,000

From the bandar of Damman, a dependency of Sorath, where there were seven hundred towns, a collection was made annually, amounting to forty-three *laks* of rupees,

	Ibrahímís.
Equal to forty-five *laks* of *ibrahímís*	45,00,000

([s]) Though the word *bandar* usually means a port, it also bears the signification of a trading town or mart; and in this sense it must be here understood; as many of the bandars hereafter enumerated are in foreign countries; to which commercial agents were appointed from Gujarát, or between which and the latter a trading intercourse was kept up.

The ports of the Europeans, being in all twenty-five *mahls*, yielding a revenue of

	Ibrahímís.
Twenty laks of Ibrahímís	20,00,000

The names of these were—

Bandar Chaiwal[t].
″ Dabúl.
″ Belâwal.
″ Bassai (Bassein).
″ Danda[u].
″ Panwelly.
″ Akassi.
″ Sorab.
″ Kallian.
″ Bhímry (near Bombay).
″ Dand-Rájpúrí.
″ Goba[x].
″ Manbai (Bombay).
″ Kharríkot.
″ Káhilan.

(t) The author of the Mirát Ahmadí spells this name as here written; and the traveller Barthema calls it Cevul. He visited Bisnagar, the capital of Narsingha, now called Bíjnagar, or Amagúndy, and touched at this fort, in the end of the fifteenth century. This place, which is now abandoned, is on the coast of the Konkan, immediately south of Bombay, and is called Chaul in the maps.

(u) Revadanda, in the Konkan, situated close by Chewal. It formerly belonged to the Portuguese, who built a fort and churches there.

(x) This is Goa, which is called in Sanskrit Gova: and, as *b* and *v* are constantly permuted in that language, it is here corruptly spelt Goba.

Bandar Kokha[y].
〃 Dass.
〃 Midrút.
〃 Kalsí.
〃 Málábár.
〃 Maldeo.
〃 Dhaora.
〃 Nandar.
〃 Shashtí.
〃 Navánagar.

From the *bandars* of the Arabs and others, that were twenty-six *mahls*, there was a revenue of twenty-five *laks* of *ibrahímís*. Their names were—

Bandar Maskat.
〃 Ekraneh.
〃 Basrah (Bussora).
〃 Lochi.
〃 Lahrí (Larí Bunder, in Sind).
〃 Harmúz (Ormus, in the Persian Gulf).
〃 Sawah[z] (in Persia).
〃 Níkú.
〃 Dehnasrí (in Sina).
〃 Milgat.
〃 Makkína.
〃 Maltah (Malta ?).

(y) In the travels of Ibn Batúta, (translated by Professor Lee) who arrived in India A.D. 1332, and took ship at Kambaiya to go southward, there is the port of Kula beyond Goha mentioned, and may be the same as this.

(z) This is the town of Saiva in Persian Irák, between which and the coast of India there was formerly an extensive commercial intercourse.

Bandar Súl[a].
〃 Hodirwah.
〃 Púnamah.
〃 Badirjí Khán.
〃 Bidar (a city in the Dekhan).
〃 Purbhaí.
〃 Bindasin.
〃 Bídarchín.
〃 Mallakhah (Malacca).
〃 Bedrassa.
〃 Kalliyán[b].
〃 Dhar.
〃 Rákal.
〃 Java.

Regarding the English ports, there were four *mahls*, and those of the Dutch (Wullendey) two *mahls*, being together six *mahls*, paying a tribute of ten *laks* of *ibrahímís*.

In addition to the above, Nezen Sháh Bheres, Ádil Sháh Bíjapúrí, Imád Sháh Berárí, Kutb Sháh Gulkandaví, and Rájá Alí Khán Burhánpúrí, gave twenty-five *laks* of *húns* in tribute yearly.

Inasmuch as many may doubt the truth of what has been now related, let them compare it

(a) This is the Souly, or Swaldy, near Súrat, which was formerly the port of that city. Thevenot in his Travels (p. 27) says, that in consequence of the Customs being after Slater, no ship was allowed to go there, since the year 1660. The revenue of the Súrat Customs are stated by Thevenot at twelve laks of rupees.

(b) This is the Calliany of the Dekhan, and not the one near Bombay.

with what has been written in the *Táríkhi Sikandarí,* regarding the power and greatness, the possessions, and wealth, of the Sultáns and Nobles of Gujarát, and they may there inform themselves. If I had written even more than I have done, I should be justified: for of these things there is proof in the written account of the power of Malik Ayáz, the slave of the Sultán Mohammed Begarrah. The remains of superb buildings, such as forts, mosques, tanks, and wells, yet to be seen, also testify of these things; and though there be no mountains in the neighbourhood of the city of Ahmadábád, yet all the buildings are of stone brought from a distance.

The detail of the sirkars and tribute, copied from the registers of Múl-Chand (who with his forefathers was the keeper of the records to the Nizámat), has been inserted here; and, as no other list but this was obtainable, many names of ports and other places may be erroneous. It is a tradition, however, that Sikandar ben Bahlúl, the King of Dehlí, said, "the magnificence of the kings of Dehlí consists of wheat and barley, whilst that of the King of Gujarát, who has eighty-four ports under him, has its foundation on coral and pearls[c]."

([c]) The power and wealth of this kingdom must have been at one time very great. Mandelslo, in his Travels, tells us "that there

A survey of the extent and boundaries of the province was made when taken possession of by Akbar; and embraced its súbahs, sirkars, parganahs, and towns. It was then ascertained that, from Bánswárah and Málwa, on the east, to Dwarka or Jiggut, on the west, this province was two hundred and ninety *kroh* long. Its breadth was found to be three hundred *kroh*, measuring in the following manner: from the city of Ahmadábád north to Birgaon, in the sirkar of Jalore, and súbah of Ajmír, one hundred and ten *kroh;* from the city south to the port of Súrat, one hundred and ten *kroh;* and thence to the passage of the mountains, at Khanapúr, situated on the borders of Khándesh and Baglánah, a distance of eighty *kroh*.

there is a vast trade driven in many commodities all over the kingdom of Guzuratta: but particularly in cotton and linen cloths, which are in fairness and fineness equal to those of Holland; as also in several silk stuffs, as *coutoons*, which are of several colours, satins, *taffatas, cummerbunds, ornis*, of gold and silk, which women commonly make use of to cover their faces withal, *brocades*, tapestry, or *alkatifs, chitringis,* or streaked carpets to lay over chests and cabinets, quilted coverlets of silk or cotton, which they call *geodries*, (Guddree) or *nalis, tents, periutos*, or *neuhar*, which they make use of instead of couches, *cadels* or bedsteads, cabinets of *lacque*, chess-boards of tortoise-shell, seals, beads, chains, buttons, and rings of ivory, amber, rock-crystal, and agate." (Travels of Mandelslo, translated into English by John Davies, p 66.)

At this time there were twenty-five sirkars belonging to Gujarát, as before detailed, nine of which, being conquests by the Gujarát kings from other súbahs, were afterwards attached to their original countries. This arrangement was effected during the provincial government of Shahábu-d-dín Ahmad Khán, A. Hij. 986.; A.D. 1578, by an order from the Emperor; and the names of these sirkars were—

Sirkar	Júdhpúr.	
"	Jalore.	
"	Nagore, united to the súbah of Ajmír.	
"	Múlhír	attached to Khándesh.
"	Nadarbár	
"	Bassein	parts of the Tul-Konkan, given over to the Europeans.
"	Manbai	
"	Damman	
"	Dand-Rájpúrí	made the possession of the Nizám Sháhí and government of Ahmadnagar.

Of the remaining sixteen sirkars, which belonged to the Dehlí government, ten were entered in the imperial registers; but, as the sirkar of Súrat had been assigned over to the revenue writers, nine sirkars only are entered in the collection from the súbah of Gujarát, namely—

	Mahls.
Sirkar Ahmadábád	33
" Bhroch	14

		Mahls.
Sirkar	Patan	17
"	Baroda	4
"	Nadote	12
"	Chámpánír	13
"	Godhrah	11
"	Sorath	63
"	Navánagar, called also Islámnagar	17
		184

The latter, during the reign of Sháh Álam I., was seized on by the Jam, a zamíndár of that part; and is now in his possession.

The whole number of sirkars, arranged as above, contained one hundred and eighty-four *mahls*, including cities and *parganahs*, in which there were fifteen ports and 10,465 towns, exclusive of those possessed by the zamíndárs, and not inserted in the revenue records. The fields belonging to these were, in the time of Rájá Todar Mal, measured by Akbar's order, and found to contain 12,360,594 *bígahs* and nine *biswahs*; out of which there were 8,374,498 *bígahs* [d] and three *biswahs* fit for cultivation. The remainder consisted of waste land.

The sirkars of Sorath, Godhrah, and Islámnagar, which, with forty-nine *mahls* of other sirkars, were not measured, do not appear in the revenue registers.

([d]) In Gladwin's translation of the Ayín Akbarí, the measurement is put down at 8,024,153 bígahs.

The sirkars not included in the revenue assessment, and belonging to zamíndárs, paid the *peshkash* (tribute), when enforced, to the governors of the province. These were,

Sirkar Dúngarpúr
" Bánswárah
" Kach, called Suleimán-Nagar
" Sirohí
" Somnáth
" Rám Nagar

of which the *peshkash* had been settled, however, on the revenue writers at the port of Súrat. Though the above, in former times, were not dependent on the Díwánship of the province, the collection therefrom, including the sirkar of Súrat, with the remissions and deductions on the public increase, amounted to 799,645,213 dams, even to the reign of Mohammed Sháh.

Twenty *krores*, eighty-two *laks*, six hundred and forty-two *dams* (20,8200,642) of the above sum were fixed for the imperial use and royal expenses. A sum, also, of 2,2000,000 *dams* was set aside for the Nizámat, and personal jágírs of the Sirdárs : so that, without the tribute from the zamíndárs, there was the sum of twenty-four *laks* of rupees belonging to the Názim. The remainder was settled to pay the Omarás, Mansabdárs, and other servants.

Nearly one *krore* and twenty *laks* of *dams*, collected from fifty thousand *bígahs* of land and one hundred and three villages, with one *lak* and forty thousand rupees, in money, were variously given away, as rewards and pensions to religious orders and establishments, agreeably to instructions from the government.

The whole annual revenue, at present, is one *krore*, twenty-three *laks*, and fifty thousand rupees, whilst the whole annual expence amounts to one *krore* of rupees. In former times, however, the surplus revenue payable to government amounted to sixty laks of rupees, not including the *peshkash* paid to the Sirkar, and to the Názim or provincial governor.

CHAPTER II.

THE BEGINNING OF THE KINGDOM OF GUJARÁT, UNDER ITS RÁJÁS; AND THE FOUNDATION OF THE CITY OF PATAN, SOMETIMES NAMED ANHILWÁRAH, OR NAHRWÁLAH.

In ancient times, the country of Gujarát was possessed by the Rájpúts and Kúlies; when every chief, being independent of another, was a person of power in his own domain. The army of Rájá Phúr [e], (Porus), however, then Deva Rájá of Kanauj, and greatest of all the Rájas of Hindústán, was annually sent to collect the tribute; and, after having done so, returned to the capital.

One of the Rájá's slaves, named Sáwant Singh, having committed some fault, was put to death;

(e) Gladwin's translation of the Ayín Akbarí has here Rájá Sirry Bhordeo: but, on referring to the original text, I find that the name is Phordeo, preceded by the Sanskrit *Srí,* श्री meaning prosperous. The name of Phúr, or Porus, would appear to have been a general title. Alexander the Great, after crossing the river Hydaspes, entered the territories of the brave Porus: but the possessions of the other Porus, called by the Macedonians the Coward, lay between the rivers Acesines and Hydraotes; and from this we may infer, that this word is a title and not a name. I am not much inclined to rely on the etymology, which would trace the origin of this word to the name of a comparatively modern tribe of Rájpúts, called the *Powars;* but consider it has been applied, in a general way, to designate the Sovereign of the eastern country; and is derived from the Sanskrit *Púrva,* meaning Eastern. It is here so applied, I would say; and that there was once a connexion between Kanauj and Gujarát is evident from what Abú Zeid al-Hasan of Siraf, the Arabian traveller, in the middle of the ninth century, says of the Indians, "who have devotees and doctors known by the name of Bramins. They have poets also who compose verses, stuffed with flattery, in praise of their kings. Astrologers they have, philosophers, soothsayers, and men who observe the flight of birds, particularly at Kanuge, a great city in the kingdom of Gozar." By the last, Gujar, or Gujarát, is meant; though spelt Gozar, in the above extract from Renaudot's Travellers.

and, as his house was plundered at the same time, his wife, while pregnant, fled towards Gujarát. On her journey to this country, she bore a son; who, being discovered in the wilderness by Rájá Síl Deva [f], was carried to Palanpúr, and there brought up by him. This boy, on arriving at man's estate, became so fond of evil company, that, soon following the ways of his companions, he turned highwayman and robber. Having, at length, seized on some treasure on its way from Gujarát to Kanauj, he was, from that time, blessed with the smiles of fortune, and established his power and independence. Soon after he became intimate with a marketman named Champa, who weaned him from his evil propensities; and, having now assumed the title of Ban-Ráj, or Bansráj, he laid the foundation of the city of Patan, and made it the seat of his government. This occurred five years after he had first become independent[g]; and from that

(f) This is a title, and not a name, of the then ruling Rájá. Thus the famous Bhoja is called Saila Dhara (see *A.R.* IX. p. 137); and, according to Wilford, this Saila Deva, or Síl Deva, was a most holy man, mentioned by Masúdi, who wrote about A.D. 947. (*A.R.* IX. p. 181-2.)

(g) An interesting commentary on these traditions, written by Mr. Wilford, will be found in *A. R.* IX. p. 185-87. According to Wilford, Bansrájá is a corruption of *Vana Rájá*, or king of the forest,

time, until the foundation of the good city of Ahmadábád, Patan continued to be the royal residence and the capital of Gujarát.

When Ban Ráj had resolved on founding the city of Patan, he went in search of a site favourably situated for the amusement of the chase; and, having at length met a shepherd, was informed by him where a suitable place might be found. The shepherd, whose name was Anhil, stipulated that the city should be named after him; saying at the same time, that he had there seen a hare beat a dog by her exertion and agility. The ground was selected; and when a population had collected, received the name of Anhilwárah. This became known by degrees under the name of Nahrwálah; which, when the population increased, and the town became a place of note, was changed to Patan: for, in the Hindí language, they call a favoured town and a royal residence Patan. The era of the foundation is 802 of Vikramáditya, corresponding to A. Hij. 130, A.D. 747, or, as some say, to A. Hij. 202, A.D. 817.

Three royal races of Hindús have successively ruled over this country, namely the Cháwurah[h],

forest, who was found in the wilderness, A.D. 696; and at fifty years of age built Nahrwálah, A.D. 746.

(h) Though I prefer reading the name of this tribe *Cháwura*, as

Solankhí [i], and Baghílah races. According to the Ayín Akbarí, the total number of individuals belonging to the tribes who held power amounted to twenty-three, and these retained possession of the country for five hundred and seventy-five years previous to the period when Gujarát became subject to the Mohammedans.

Of the Cháwura race there were seven individuals; one of whom, Ban Ráj, who first established the principality, appears to have

as being the well known designation of one of the thirty-six royal races of Rájpúts, yet the original text of the Ayín Akbarí has plainly Jáwudán جاودان, and that of the Mirát Ahmadí, Jáwudáh جاوداه The transition from Jáwudáh جاوداه to the name چاوره Cháwura becomes very easy on the obvious principles of Persian writing and Indian pronunciation; for the Arabic *j* ج being permutable with the Persian and Sanskrit *ch*, (چ, च) whilst the Arabic *d*, pronounced hard in the Indian dialects, assumes the sound of the Sanskrit *d*, ड pronounced like *r*, Jáwudáh, from the mouth of an Arab, becomes Cháwura by the pronunciation of a Hindú.

(i) The Solankhí is the same Rájpút tribe as that named Chálukya, in Sanskrit. Several of the Chálukya tribe were the founders of Hindú States, in the south of India, about the beginning of the eleventh century; and there is an inscription, by one of this race, on the pillar of an old Hindú temple, within the fort of Bíjapúr, announcing a grant of land to the Brahmins, in the year 1114 of the Sáliváhana era, A.D. 1192. The Rájá who gives this grant is named Chálukya Malla Deva: the same, probably, as the Rakshamalla Deva of the Curugode inscription, dating Sáliváhana 1103, A.D. 1181, and which has been translated (*A.R.* IX. p. 425.)

lived sixty years, and the others ruled as follow :—

Ban Ráj	60
Jog Ráj	35
Khím, or Bhím Ráj	25
Rájá Pithú	29
Rájá Bijy Singh[k]	25
Rájá Ráwat Singh	15
Rájá Sáwant, or Sámant Singh .	7

The Cháwura tribe ruled one hundred and ninety-six years ; after which the power passed into the hands of the Solankhí tribe in this manner. Sáwant Singh Cháwura gave his only daughter in marriage to one of the Solankhí tribe ; and she becoming pregnant died in child-birth. The child, however, being cut from her womb, was preserved ; and, as the moon was then in her 19th mansion, called *Múl* in Hindí, the boy received the name of Múl-Ráj. Sáwant Singh brought up the boy as his own ; and having, in a drunken fit, named him his heir, afterwards denied he had done so. At the death of Sáwant Singh, Múl Ráj found an opportunity to possess himself of the government ; and from him descended ten individuals, who

(k) The names are here written after the provincial manner of pronouncing them ; but the correct Sanskrit designation would be Rájá Vijaya Sinha.

reigned two hundred and fifty years and six months:

	Years.	Months.
Múl Ráj[l]	56	
Jomúnd[m]	12	4
Bílba		7
Dúrla, the brother of Jamúnd[n] . .	8	
Rájá Bhím Deo	42	
Rájá Kiran	31	
Sid Ráj Jey Singh	50	
Kúnwara Pál	30	6
Ají Pál, who poisoned his master and seized his power	3	1
Lakhú Múl Deo, who was descended from the brother of Bhím Deo	20	
	253	6

(l) The individuals of this family are enumerated in an inscription, from the temples of Abú, which has been translated by Mr. H. Wilson, *A. R.* XV. p. 288.

(m) These three names are corruptions of the more correct Sanskrit designations, *Chamunda, Vallabha,* and *Dúrlabha.* Mr. Wilford says that Bílba, being a weak man and blind, was succeeded by the two sons of his brother, Dúrlabha and Bhíma Rájá, in A.D. 1025. (*A. R.* IX. p. 288.)

(n) Dúrla, or more properly Dúrlabha, who was the nephew of Vallabha, according to Wilford, abdicated the throne of Patan, in Samvat 1079, or A.D. 1023, (see *A. R.* I. p. 223); and, if the length of his reign be there correct, it began A.D. 1011. He it is said visited Múnja, but, as Mahmúd of Ghazní invaded Gujarát, A.D. 1026, and Jamúnd was there reigning, the above period must be erroneous, as fixed by Major Tod for his pilgrimage to Gaya, and his interview with Múnja. Dúrlabha, according to the Kumára Pála Charitra, quoted by Major Tod, (*A. R.* I. p. 222) abdicated the throne in favour of his son,

Bhíma.

In the reign of Jamúnd, A. Hij. 416 (o), A.D. 1025-6, Sultán Mahmúd Ghaznaví marched for Somnáth by way of Multán ; when, having in-

Bhíma. This was twelve years after the conquest of Gujarát by Mahmúd of Ghazní, an event which happened in A.D. 1026, though erroneously placed by Major Tod on Hindú authority in A.D. 1011. Dúrlabha, after abdicating, made a pilgrimage to Gaya ; and, if we allow twelve years for his reign, he must have done so in A.D. 1038 ; or, if he reigned only eight years, A.D. 1034. Wilford, as quoted in a former note, has not erred considerably in fixing the beginning of his reign A.D. 1025 ; and if Dúrlabha was the brother of Jamúnd, Vallabha was probably the same as Dábishlím, the anchorite. The conjecture that he was so derives some support from the acknowledged shortness of his reign, and the fact that both he and Dábishlím became blind.

(o) This is the true date of Mahmúd's expedition to India, during which he captured the celebrated temple of Somnáth : though Ferishta, in his History, erroneously places the commencement of this march in the month of Shabán of A. Hij. 415, or A.D. 1024. It was during this last mentioned year that Mahmúd led an army to the Oxus, and settled the affairs of Máwará-n-Nahr, or Transoxiana. From thence he returned to Ghazní, and wintered there. Nizámu-d-dín Ahmad, the author of the Tabakát Akbarí, after placing the expedition to Transoxiana, in Hij. 415, says : و از انجا مراجعت نموده بغزنین آمد و زمستان در غزنین گذرانید و بمقتضای عادت خویش بآن لشکر بجانب هندستان بقصد تسخیر سومنات کشید "From thence returning to Ghizneen, he spent the winter there, and carried that same army into Hindústán, with the intention of capturing Somnáth." As the winter of A. Hij. 415 fell in the end of A.D. 1024 and the three first months of A.D. 1025, Mahmúd could not have marched for Hindústán before the end of March in that year ; and, as he was still further obliged to delay his intended expedition to India, in order to avoid the rainy season of

vaded the territories of Nahrwálah Patan, Rájá Jamúnd quitted that city, and fled. Mahmúd, after capturing Nahrwálah, made the necessary preparations for his army to march on Somnáth; and, in the month of Zú-l-kadah of the same year, accomplished the conquest of that place. Having afterwards received intelligence that Rájá Jamúnd, the ruler of Nahrwálah, had at this time taken refuge in a certain fort [p], distant forty-five farsangs, Mahmúd resolved on capturing it. He accordingly marched against this place, which, on his arrival, was discovered to be a fortification surrounded by deep water on every side. Two divers were brought to him; and, being asked regarding the depth of the water, replied that, although a passage might be effected at a certain place, yet should the flood-tide come in while making the attempt, all of them must perish. Sultán Mahmúd, after confidently intreating the divine

of that country, which commenced in June, he did not begin his march for Somnáth till the tenth of Shabán, in Hij. 416, or the seventh of October, 1025. He reached Multán about the middle of Ramazán, or the tenth of November following; and did not arrive at Somnáth before the month Zú-l-hijjah, A. Hij. 416, or the end of January, A.D. 1026. Khondamír's History of the Habíbu-s-Sair is my authority for these dates, and is fully supported by the account in the Tabakát Akbarí.

(p) This fort is called Gundaba by Ferishta.

favour, advanced through the water with his cavalry, and safely landed them below the walls of the fortification. Rájá Jamúnd Solankhí, observing this, quickly took to flight: and the army of Islám, after obtaining an enormous booty, put the people of the garrison to the sword. The author of the Rauzatu-s-Saffá has given a curious account of this transaction.

CHAPTER III.

THE CAPTURE OF SOMNÁTH BY SULTÁN MAHMÚD GHAZNAVÍ.

It has been generally reported that Sultán Mahmúd, after capturing Somnáth, wished to remain several years in that quarter; as the country, being open and extensive, pleased him. There were then wonderful mines in that part, yielding pure gold[q]; and all the precious stones of Hindústán were the produce of the mines of

(q) The sands of several rivers in Gujarát are mixed with gold dust. I have also heard that specimens of gold ore were sent to Bombay, by the late Rao of Kach, with a view of ascertaining whether the gold could be separated from the matrix. It is, therefore, probable that Mahmúd heard of such mines, and this is further confirmed by Captain McMurdo's testimony, in his remarks on Kahtiwar, (*Bombay Trans*. I. p. 264) that the chief of Ají had rings and ornaments made of his native gold.

Sirándíb, (Ceylon) which was then a dependancy of that country[r]. The nobles, however, represented, that if Somnáth was made his capital, it would be too distant from Khorásán; and the Sultán, now adopting the resolution of returning, said it would be necessary to appoint some one who would regulate and retain the country for him. The king's ministers told him that the only option left was to give it in charge to some one among the people of the country: and, as the Sultán had at this time consulted his intimates and friends, some of them said that none of the royal tribe of this country equalled Dábishlím[s] in his ancestry, both by the father and mother's side: and, as one of that family was

(r) It would appear, from the Mahá-Vansí of Ceylon, or the historical book describing the lineage of Buddha, that the island was then a dependency of India; and, it was not until the year A.D. 1290, that the king Vijayabáhu recovered his independence, and shook off the Indian yoke. (See Upham's *History of Buddhaism*, p. 31.)

(s) This word, written by the Mohammedan historians Dábishlím, would appear to have been an honorary title, and not the name of an individual. It is derived from two Sanskrit words, *Deva* देव and *Síla* शील meaning the meditative king; and, as the people, in the south of India, would put it in the objective instead of the nominative case, they would say Devasílam, instead of Devasíla, just as they use Vaishnavam for Vaishnava, meaning the sect of Vishnu. The corruption of Devasílam to Dábishlím is then easily made. This Deva Síla, or the anchorite,

was

yet remaining who had been employed in studying philosophy and mortifying the flesh, it would be well that the Sultán gave the government to him. Others, who were averse to this proposal, made it appear that Dábishlím, the anchorite, was an evil-disposed person, who had fallen under the displeasure of God; and that his seclusion from the world and devotion came not of his own choice, as he had taken refuge in a soli-

was an intriguing Rájpút of Somnáth, as would appear; who, by deceiving Mahmúd with flattery and large promises, obtained the sovereignty of Somnáth, to which he had no just right. The words of the original text of Ferishta, though not fully translated by Colonel Briggs, are:— سلطان با بعضي از اهالي سومنات در اين باب سخن كرده جمعي از ايشان گفتند كه هيچ طايفه از اهالي اين ديار در حسب و نسب بدابشليمان نميرسد و امروز از آن دودمان يكي در لباس براهمه در اينجا برياضت مشغول است اگر سلطان اين مملكت را بدو مسلم دارد مناسب است "The Sultán, after speaking to several of the people of Somnáth, was informed by them that there was no family in that part of equal rank with the race of Dábishlím; and, as there was one of such remaining who, in the dress of a Bráhman, was now leading an abstinent life, it would be well if the Sultán entrusted him with the government." The other Dábishlím, or the king, was probably the lawful ruler of the country; but was an inferior to, and distinct from the Rájá of Nahrwálah, who is called Parm Deva by the Tabakát Akbarí and Ferishta. Parama Deva is said to have been the greatest of all the Rájás of Hindústán, as implied by his title, which means in Sanskrit Supreme Lord. Colonel Briggs has mistaken the word Parama Deva, and makes it Brahma Dew in his translation.

tary retreat, with a view of saving his life, after his brothers had several before times confined him. They also informed him that there was another Dábishlím, related to the former; and, as he was very wise and learned, all the Bráhmans had great faith in his wisdom. The same was now reigning over a certain country; and it would be therefore better that the Sultán, appointing him to the government, ordered a firman to be written in his name, permitting him to rule over this country, according to the right he would be thereby invested with. It was also said that this Dábishlím was so upright and trustworthy, that, having once taken upon himself the payment of tribute, he would, notwithstanding the length of the way, send the same annually to Ghazní. To this the Sultán replied, that, would this Dábishlím come and make such a request, he might consent to grant it: but wherefore should he confer so large a territory on one who, if he wished to be named to the sovereignty, had not even done a service, or paid him so much courtesy. Dábishlím the anchorite was then sent for; and, having obtained the government of the country, became bound to pay tribute: saying, at the same time, "Whatever your Highness commands, I will obey, and will send to Ghazní all the gold and jewels obtained from the mines of Hindústán. There is one of my kinsmen, however, another Dábishlím, who is very hostile to me; and, as several battles have taken place between us, he will, doubtless, advance against me on knowing your Highness has departed; and, as I am not yet firmly seated in my power, or have confidence in myself, I must be subdued, and he gain possession of my country. But if the Sultán," said he, "would now march against him, and defend me against his evil designs, I will send to Ghazní a yearly tribute, equivalent to that of Khorásán and Kábúl." The Sultán consented to his proposal; and, when he turned his arms against that country, the people of Somnáth upbraided Dábishlím the anchorite, saying, "You have done wrong to instigate the Sultán to a religious war; yet the Almighty delights in preserving the honour of the good whom he favours; and such a one will not be injured by your designs or calumnies."

On these words being reported to the Sultán, he was much annoyed; but, having marched to that quarter, was pleased not to forget or forgive them. In fine, having taken Dábishlím the king, he gave him in charge to Dábishlím the anchorite, who represented "that it was customary for the kings of this country, when there is an enemy in their power, to prepare for him a dark dwelling below their own royal seat; where, causing him to be seated on a throne, and kept closely confined, only a hole is to be left open, through which he may receive his daily food. In this manner," said he, "the king, who is in possession of the throne, treats his adversary during such time as he may reign. But, as I cannot just now confine him, it would be better and more convenient if your Highness would carry him to Ghazní, and send him back to me, after I have taken possession of and arranged the country, so as to become quite settled. I can then imprison him, in the manner just mentioned; and to have my requests granted is nothing wonderful or uncommon from your Highness."

The Sultán now resolved on departure, and sounded the march for returning home. Succeeding this, Dábishlím the anchorite seated himself on the throne of Somnáth; and, by forwarding rich gifts and presents, continued to please the nobles of Ghazní by all manner of good offices, till the time came for making a request that his enemy might be delivered up. The Sultán hesitated delivering a blameless person into the hands of his enemy: but, as Dábishlím the anchorite,. through liberal distribution of presents to the courtiers, had gained their support, all of them represented it was not necessary to have compassion on a Pagan idolater. They also said that the Sultán, having entered into a compact, ought not to break his promise; since by such opposition Dábishlím the anchorite would lose the country. The Sultán at length delivered up Dábishlím the king to the servants of the other Dábishlím, writing at the same time to the kings[t] of Hind, that they must escort him to the neighbourhood of Somnáth. On the former approaching Somnáth, Dábishlím the anchorite gave orders to get ready the prison which had been made for him under the throne. As it was, moreover, a custom with the kings of this country to advance one stage and meet an enemy, when approaching the royal residence, in order that they might make him run before their horses, carrying on his head the royal goblet and ewer to the precincts of the palace, the anchorite Dábishlím therefore came forth: and, there being some delay in the other's approach, determined on following the chase. After having pursued the sport in every direction, till the heat of the day became very great, the

(t) The petty Rájpút princes, on the banks of the Indus, who were Zamíndárs, with the title of Ráwal, are here meant.

whole army received an order to halt; when Dábishlím the anchorite, having taken up his station under a tree, covered his face with a red handkerchief and went to sleep. There happened to be many beasts of prey in that jungle, who had both sharp claws and beaks; and one of these, while on the wing, having mistaken the red cloth for a piece of flesh, descended and carried it away in its claws. Dábishlím, from the blow of its beak, became blind of an eye on this occasion; and hence arose a great tumult in the army. In the mean time, the other Dábishlím arrived. When the royal attendants saw that the anchorite of that name had a personal blemish, and that there was no one worthy or fit for the sovereignty but the former, all of them agreed he must be king; and made their obeisance to him accordingly. Having also advised his opponents to submit, they placed the goblet and ewer, which had been prepared for him, on the head of Dábishlím the anchorite; and, after making him run before them to the palace, confined him in the prison he had himself made[u].

(u) The account of Mahmúd's conquest of Somnáth, as given by the Habíbu-s-Sair, is similar to what has been above detailed. The author of that History informs us that the place was named after the idol Somnáth, and quotes the words of Shaikh Farídu-d-

dín

CHAPTER IV.

THE SOVEREIGNTY OF THE BAGHÍLAH RACE AT NAHRWÁLAH; AND THE EDIFICES ERECTED BY SIDDHA RÁJÁ SOLANKHÍ JEY SINGH.

WHEN the sovereignty of Nahrwálah came to Bhím-Deo Baghílah, Sultán Moizzu-d-dín Sám, generally known by the name of Shahábu-d-dín, while acting as the lieutenant of his brother, led

dín Attár, to prove that this image was identified with the idol Lát, one of those worshipped by the ancient Arabs, in the Máh Kadah, or temple of the moon at Mekka. Farídu-d-dín Attár says:
لشکر محمود اندر سومنات یافتند ي بت که نامش بود لات
"The army of Mahmúd found in Somnáth the idol whose name was Lát." The appellation given to it among the Hindús was Somnáth, or Regent of the Moon; this being derived from the Sanskrit words, *Soma*, the Moon, and *Náth*, Lord or Master. It is very possible, however, that it was similar to the Arabian idol Lát, which Herodotus mentions under the name of Alilat, or, as it would be written in Arabic, الالاهة signifying the Lord above. The Habíbu-s-Sair gives the story of Dábishlím's exemplary punishment in these words:— دابشلیم مرتاض در حکومت سومنات استقلال یافته بعد از چند سال رسولان نزد سلطان فرستاد و خصم خودرا طلب نمود سلطان نخست در فرستادن آن جوان متردد کشته اخر الامر بنابر اغواي بعضي از امرا آن دابشلیمرا حواله فرستادکان دابشلیم مرتاض نمود وچون ایشان اورا بحدود سومنات رسانیدند دابشلیم مرتاض فرمود تا زندان معهودرا ترتیب کردند و بنابر آن قاعده که

an army to Úcha, in A. Hij. 570, A.D. 1174; and, having afterwards obtained the sovereignty of Ghazní, in A. Hij. 574, A.D. 1178, he again returned, and took that country from the Infidels.

در میان ایشان متعارف بود باستقبال آن جوان از شهر بیرون آمده خواست که طشت و آفتابهٔ خاصه‌را بر سرش نهاده اورا در رکاب خویش بدواند وبدان زندان رساند در اثنایي راه بشکار اشتغال نموده آنمقدار بهر جانب تاخت که حرارت هوا بروي استیلا یافت چنانچه بعد از آن در سایهٔ درختي باستراحت مشغول شده رومالي سرخ بر رو پوشید در اینحال بتقدیر ایزد متعال طایر سخت چنکال آن رومال‌را کوشت خیال کرده وازهوا درآمده چنک در آن رومال بمثابهٔ زد که اثر ناخن او بچشم دابشلیم مرتاض رسیده کور شد و چون اعیان هندوستان معیوبان‌را اطاعت نمي‌نمایند شورشي درمیان لشکریان افتاد در اینضمن آن دابشلیم دررسید و همه بر سلطنتش اتفاق کرده همان طشت وابریق‌را بر سر دابشلیم مرتاض نهادند و تا زندان معهود دوانیدند اخرش دابشلیم مرتاض بدانچه در بارهٔ آن جوان اندیشیده بود کرفتار کردید

Dábishlím the anchorite, having obtained absolute dominion in the principality of Somnáth, sent ambassadors, some years afterwards, to request his enemy might be given up. The Sultán at first refused to comply; but, at length, through the instigation of the nobles, gave him in charge to the agents of the anchorite Dábishlím. They having brought him to the neighbourhood of Somnáth, Dábishlím the anchorite ordered that his enemy's appointed prison should be made ready, and, having according to established custom come out from the city to meet him, resolved to make him run at his stirrup, carrying the royal goblet and ewer on his head while they conducted him to the prison. But Dábishlím, having engaged himself in hunting while on the road, continued the pursuit till the air became oppressively hot; and, having

At this time, also, having subdued the sinners of Multán, he resolved to go into Gujarát, by way of Rájásthán (the sandy desert). Bhím Deo Baghílah opposed and defeated him in battle; after which the Sultán had much difficulty in reaching Ghazní.

Succeeding this, Kutbu-d-dín Aibuk, having constituted Dehlí the capital of the country, in the 589th year of the Hijra, A.D. 1193, brought an army to Nahrwálah Patan, and revenged the Sultán's defeat on Bhím Deo[x].

Moreover, Rájá Siddha Rájá Jey Singh Solankhí, having obtained the sovereignty of Nahrwálah, conquered the country as far as Málwa and Burhánpúr. At this time he founded the ports of Bhroch and Dubhúe, constructed many other buildings, such as the re-

having then sought repose under the shade of a tree, covered his face with a red handkerchief. At this time, by the will of the Almighty, some bird with sharp claws mistook the handkerchief for beef; and, descending, struck it in such a way that its claws entered the anchorite's eyes, by which he became blind. As the nobles of Hindústán do not submit to any one defective in his members, a great tumult on this occasion arose among the troops; but the other Dábishlím arriving in the mean time, all agreed on making him king; and, having placed the goblet and ewer on the head of the anchorite, they in this manner conducted him to the prison which had been appointed. The anchorite Dábishlím thus obtained the lot which he had prepared for the other.

(x) This defeat of Bhím Deo happened in the year after the Hijra 591, A.D. 1194, according to Ferishta, p. 179.

servoir of Sahsar Ling[y], at Patan, and several others at Bíramgám ; and, having caused several water reservoirs to be dug in the country of Sorath, built them up with stone. The above-named Rájá also built the idol temple of Rudra Mála[z], in the city of Sidhpúr, which he had rendered habitable ; and the same temple is famous throughout the world.

The Rájá, on signifying his intention of building the above-mentioned temple, requested the astrologers, it is said, to appoint a fortunate hour ; and they at this time predicted the destruction of the building by Alá-ud-dín Khiljí,

(y) Sahsar Ling, in Sanskrit, signifies the thousand Lingas ; the symbols of Mahádeva, or Siva. As this Rájá dedicated so many edifices to this god, he was a zealous follower, as appears, of Sivaite worship. His successor, however, encouraged the heterodox sect of Jaina.

(z) According to an inscription in my possession, the Rudra Mála, a temple dedicated to Mahádeva, was built in Samvat 1202, A.D. 1146. According to Captain Tod, and the *Kumára Pála Charitra,* he reigned from Samvat 1150 to 1201, or A.D. 1094 to 1145 ; but my inscription extends his reign to Samvat 1202, or A.D. 1146. He was contemporary with Nara Verma, of the Pramara race, who was the grandson of Bhoja Rájá, sovereign of Dhárá in Málwa ; which Nara Verma, according to the copper-plate grant translated by Mr. Colebrooke (*A. R.* vol. 1. p. 230), died Samvat 1190, A.D. 1134. The conquest of Málwa, as above noticed, was made by this Siddha Rájá from Nara Verma. Assuming, then, that Siddha Rájá began to reign, as would appear evident, in A.D. 1094, and continued to do so until 1146,

who was to be sovereign of Dehlí, as plainly perceivable from the revolution of the heavenly bodies. The Rájá, confiding in the words of the astrologers, wished to make a treaty with the Sultán just noticed, by sending letters to him: but to these the latter replied, saying, "If, by means of this treaty we have entered on, I do not neglect the injunctions of the law, I will certainly fulfil it[a]." In short, that great man, having soon afterwards obtained the sovereignty of Dehlí, sent an army to these parts, and fulfilled the obligations of the law, by converting the temple into a mujid with minars. But, besides the above-mentioned temple, there are many other celebrated ones,

1146, A.D., he would have reigned fifty-two years, or two years longer than the length of his reign assigned by the *Mirát Ahmadí*. Kumára Pála, who succeeded him, reigned thirty years; therefore, the end of his reign would fall in A.D. 1176; and we know he was converted by Hímáchárya Jati, his Pradhán (see *Bombay Transact*. 1. p. 183) in A.D. 1174. Ají Pál, his successor, is said to have reigned three years; therefore, it terminated A.D. 1179, to which, if we add the twenty years of Lakhú Múl-Deo, we have A.D. 1199 for the end of his and beginning of Bhím Deo's power, previous to which he had acted as the lieutenant of his cousin Lakhú.

([a]) There is here the usual quantity of error, which may be found mixed up with most historical traditions. Alá-ud-dín Khiljí did convert the temple into a mosque, but not till a century and a half after the death of Siddha Rájá Jey Singh.

which, with wells built of stone, were completed by this Rájá.

Regarding the transfer of the sovereignty from the Solankhí family to the tribe of Baghílah, it happened in this manner. As Lakhú Múl-Deo Solankhí had no child fit for the sovereignty, it became the property of the Baghílahs, of whom there were six persons who held power one hundred and twenty-six years and one month, viz.—

	Years.	Months.
Anwal Múl Deo . . .	12	5
Rájá Bísal Deo[b], who colonized the town of Bísalnagar . .	34	6
Rájá Bhím Deo . . .	12	0
Rájá Arjund Deo . . .	10	0
Rájá Sárang Deo . . .	21	0
Rájá Karan[c]	6	2
	126	1

([b]) This is the Versala Deva of the Abú inscription, No. 22, (*A.R.* XVI. p. 311,) who was governor or ruler of Chandravati, with eighteen hundred *mandals*, or districts, and ought not to be included among the Rájás of Nahrwálah. He was subject to the then reigning lord paramount Sáranga Deva, who lived at Anahilla Pata, or Nahrwálah. Both Bhím Deva and Sáranga Deva were of the Jain faith. The inscriptions of the last date A.D. 1294.

([c]) There is a Rájá Kiran, or Parran, called a descendant of the ancient Rájás of Gujarát, who is mentioned A.D. 1356.

CHAPTER V.

THE TRIUMPH OF THE FAITH, AND ESTABLISHMENT OF THE MOHAMMEDAN RELIGION IN THE COUNTRY.

It being the will of God that the faith and laws of the Prophet should be made known, the sovereignty and power of the tribes already noticed came to an end, and were transferred to the supporters of our pure religion and illustrious law, in order that the light of the exalted faith might shine resplendent as the sun, amidst that dark region of infidelity ; and we, by publishing the words of truth, and obeying the commandments of that religion, forbidding us to do evil, might turn away the people from the terrible desert of error, and lead them on the high road of salvation.

In fine, the *khutba*, or public prayer, was read in the name of Sultán Alá-ud-dín, who was sovereign of Dehlí in the year of the Hijra 696, A D. 1296. At this time, an army was sent into Gujarát, under the command of Alif Khán, (who is called, by the people of Gujarát, Alp Khán[d],) and Nusrat Khán Jalesrí; and they having plundered the country about Nahrwálah, Rájá Karan Baghílah, who was the last of the Rájás, gave them battle. Not being able, how-

([d]) According to Ferishta, this expedition was undertaken A. Hij. 697, A.D. 1297; and Almás Beg Alif Khán is called the king's brother. Raí Kurrun, the then reigning prince of Nahrwálah, fled to Rám Deo, the Rájá of Deogarh, in the Dekhan. Colonel Briggs, in his Translation of Ferishta, mistakes the Alif Khán for Alp Khán. The last, whose name was Malik Sanjar, was brother-in-law to Alá-ud-dín. According to Colonel Briggs's translation of Ferishta, he obtained the title of Rúka Khán on the accession of Alá-ud-dín to the throne; but is there afterwards named Alif Khán. My copy of the original text of Ferishta is correct, with regard to his title; and agrees with that of the Tabakát Akbarí. The words of the former are: چنانچه الماس بیک را الفخان و ملک نصرت جالیسري را نصرتخان و ملک هزبر الدین را ظفرخان و سنجر حسریوره یعني برادرزن را که امیر مجلس او بود الپخان خواند "Wherefore he called Almás Beg by the title of Alif Khán; Malik Nusrat Jalesrí by that of Nusrat Khán; and named Malik Hizabru-d-dín, and Malik Sanjar, who was his wife's brother, and president of his council, by the respective titles of Zafir Khán and Alp Khán." The Táríkhi Alfí of Múlá Ahmad of Nineveh also says: بتاریخ نوزدهم شهر ذي حجه سنه خمس وتسعین و ستمایه الماس بیک که الفخان خطاب یافت با ظفرخان و سي چهل هزار سوار بدفع اولاد سلطان جلال الدین خلجي نامزد شدند "On the 19th of Zú-l-hijjah, Hij. 695, A.D. 1295, Almás Beg, who obtained the title of Alif Khán, was appointed, along with Zafir Khán and thirty or forty thousand cavalry, to expel the children of Sultán Jalálu-d-dín Fíroz Khiljí."

ever, to make a stand against them, the Rájá fled to Deogarh, in the Dekhan, while his women, daughters, treasure, and elephants, fell into the hands of the victors. The two commanders plundered the rich merchants of Kambay; and, having destroyed the idol of Somnáth, which had been again set up after the time of Mahmúd of Ghazní, sent all the effects and women of Rájá Karan to Dehlí, and presented them to the Sultán. The daughter of Rájá Karan, who was named Dewalde, having arrived at Dehlí, Khizr Khán, the son of Alá-ud-dín Khiljí, became enamoured of her beauty; and the circumstance being made known to his father, the latter gave her in marriage to his son, whilst he himself formed an unlawful connexion with the mother of the damsel. Amír Khusrao of Dehlí, in his poem of the loves of Khizr Khán and Dewalde, a book celebrated throughout the world, tells us that Alif Khán took care of Dewalde in her infancy; and, having brought her up with his own family, afterwards married her, in compliance with the Sultán's orders, to Khizr Khán. The following stanzas are extracted from the above-mentioned poem :—

"Dewalde Rání, incomparable among the beauties of Hindústán, was named Dewalde, in the Hindí language, by her mother and father; as the first syllable in the name of that *peri* was Dew, (an angel in Hindí,) the Magic of Hind guarded her from the Devil (Dew, in Persian). On reflection, therefore, I have changed the name from Hindí to Persian; and, by dropping one letter, have converted Dewal into Dawal. The plural of *dawal* is *daolat'há* (possessions), and in this her history, many such are embodied. As the Rání is possessed of wealth and affections, I have made her name Dawal Rání; with which, when the name of her husband became united, the heaven received exaltation in the shadow of both. The name of this book is the Ashukí-Bahr, or the advantage of love between Dawal Rání and Khizr Khán."

After the conquest of Nahrwálah, and the defeat of Rájá Karan Baghílah, Alif Khán was commissioned to govern the country; and from this time, the rulers of the province were appointed by the Sultáns of Dehlí. Alif Khán, moreover, built the Friday mosque of white marble, which remains at the present time, and the pillars of the same work of his, as known to the common people, are so numerous, that one often makes a mistake in counting them. They also relate that it was once an idol temple converted to a mosque; but it is, in short, a wonderful and noble building, which was then in the centre of the city, though now distant from the part inhabited.

Regarding the greatness and extent of the buildings in the city of Patan during former times, there are yet many visible signs ; for, from the present inhabited part to the distance of three coss, the bricks and rubbish, strewed in the jungle, give testimony of these ; whilst round towers and ramparts, in different places, indicate where once extended the city. Certainly, in the course of ages, there have been many changes ; and, by degrees, the vestiges of many former edifices have been obliterated.

During the period the Rájás held power, so much marble was brought from Ajmír and other places, for building the Hindú temples, that on digging it is now found in abundance. All the marble which has been used at Ahmadábád and other places came from the same place.

In short, Alif Khán governed Gujarát, on the part of Alá-ud-dín Khiljí, for the space of twenty years ; but, being recalled towards the latter part of that king's reign, because of the enmity and accusation of Malik Náib, the eunuch, and then Wazír, was unjustly put to death[e]. Khizr Khán, being accused along with

(e) The author of the Mirát Ahmadí here confounds the names of Alif Khán and Alp Khán. The person put to death was Alp Khán

Khán

him, was imprisoned in the fortress of Gwalior ; succeeding which, the Sultán, after reigning twenty-one years, died of the dropsy, in the 717th year of the Hij., A.D. 1317. Some say that Malik Náib caused the Sultán to be poisoned ; and, that having set aside Khizr Khán's right to the sovereignty, he placed a young boy, Shahábu-d-dín[f], on the throne, in whose name, wielding the power and authority of the State, he deprived Khizr Khán of sight. After things continuing in this state for a month and five days, several of the nobles belonging to the former government put Malik Náib to death.

CHAPTER VI.

THE REIGN OF SULTÁN KUTBU-D-DÍN MUBÁRAK SHÁH, SON OF ALÁ-UD DÍN KHILJÍ.

The nobles and other grandees having released from prison the Sultán's son, Kutbu-d-dín Mubárak Sháh, then in his eighteenth year, seated him on the throne.

Khán Malik Sanjar, brother-in-law to the king; and, as Alif Khán Almás Beg died after the siege of Rentumbhore, A. Hij. 699, A.D. 1299, according to Ferishta, he could not have been twenty years Governor of the province. This confusion has arisen from the similarity of the names, and from Alp Khán having succeeded Alif Khán in Gujarát.

(f) His titles were Shahábu-d-dín Omar Khiljí.

At the time when Alá-ud-dín recalled Alif Khán from the government of Gujarát, he put him to death: after which there happened to be great disorder in the affairs of the government; and, as both mutiny and sedition occurred in the country, rebels rose up in every direction. But Sultán Kutbu-d-dín Mubárak Sháh, on commencing his reign, sent Malik Kamilu-d-dín to allay these disturbances; and this commander, having entered Gujarát, obtained the honour of martyrdom in a war with the Infidels; after which the disturbances of the country increased. At length Ainu-l-Mulúk Multáni was deputed on this important business; and, accompanied by an army, made a settlement of the province in the manner he thought best calculated to bring it to a state of repose.

After these disturbances had been put down, the Sultán sent Malik Dínar, his father-in-law, with the title of Zafir Khán, as Governor of Gujarát, who, after being employed three or four months, completely settled the province, and sent large sums of money to the Royal Treasury. But the above-mentioned Khán, who was without a fault, and the chief support of the State, was recalled from Gujarát and put to death. At the same time, Hissámu-d-dín, brother of Khusrao Khán, who had found favour in the eyes of the Sultán, obtained the equipage formerly belonging to Zafir Khán, and was sent into Gujarát. On his arrival there, the Hindú tribe of Parmár[g], to which both brothers belonged, assembled, and wished to excite him to rebellion. The other commanders who accompanied him discovered his evil designs, and, imprisoning him, sent him to the Sultán. Succeeding this, Malik Wají-ud-dín Koreshí, a brave and active officer, was sent into Gujarát, in the place of Hissámu-d-dín ; and the same brought the country into a peaceable state, after it had been disturbed by the former. At length, Wají-ud-dín was recalled, and obtained the title of Táju-l-Mulk.

Khusrao Khán, as before noticed, a Hindú of the Parmár tribe, and who was intimate with and possessed great power over the Sultán, was next appointed to Gujarát. Not being satisfied with this, however, he entertained improper desires of possessing the throne; and, collecting his own tribe around him, put the Sultán to death. Having afterwards usurped the government, he assumed the title of Nasiru-d-dín.

In short, the reign of Kutbu-d-dín Mubárak

(g) The Parmár, or Pramara tribe, is one of the thirty-six royal races of Rájpúts, and is the same tribe as that now called Powar. Colonel Briggs has mistaken the name, and reads Purwary, which is the appellation for a Hindú outcast.

Sháh lasted four years and four months. At the end of this time, Ghází Malik[h], a nobleman of the former dynasty, becoming acquainted with Khusrao Khán's evil deeds, and urged on by a nice sense of honour, collected an army, and made him a prisoner in war. He afterwards cut the traitor's body in pieces, and sent it to the capital. In consequence of their being none of Alá-ud-dín's posterity remaining, the nobles elevated Ghází Malik to the sovereignty, in the year of the Hijra 720, A.D. 1320. He having assumed the title of Ghiásu-d-dín Toghluk Sháh, appointed Táju-l-Mulk to the government of Gujarát, in order that he might bring the same into subjection. This took place about the latter part of his reign, of which only four years and a few months had passed away, when the roof of a summer-house falling in killed him, with six other persons.

CHAPTER VII.

THE REIGN OF SULTÁN MOHAMMED TOGHLUK SHÁH.

Sultán Mohammed Toghluk[i], the son of Ghiásu-d-dín Toghluk, was next seated on the

(h) Otherwise named Ghází Beg Toghluk.

(i) Sultán Mohammed Toghluk commenced reigning in A. Hij. 726, A.D. 1325-6. Several hundred gold mohurs and dínárs, belonging

throne. He was a king of quick understanding, who had acquired excellence in several branches of knowledge; and, entertaining thoughts of great extent, as mentioned in various historical books, he adopted extraordinary schemes of ambition.

In this reign, Malik Mukbil, the son of a musician [k], and who with the title of Khán Jehán, and Náibi Mukhtár, held the government of Gujarát, while marching by way of Baroda and Dubhúe, on his way to Dehlí with treasure and horses collected for the royal stables, was plundered by the chiefs of the Siddhas (Moghuls). At this time, Malik Mukbil fled to Nahrwálah; and the Sultán, on receiving intelligence of

belonging to this time, were dug up by some villagers of the Konkan, in the end of 1830, A.D. They are beautiful coins; two of which are in my possession, and were struck at Damman (Damaun), in the first and second years of the reign. The inscription within a circle, on one face of the dínár, is لا اله الا الله محمد رسول الله "There is no god but God, and Mohammed is the prophet of God;" around which the following is written:—
هذ الدينار الحضرت دهلي في سنه سبع و عشرين و سبعمايه
"This is a dínár of Dehlí, A. Hij. 727," (A.D. 1326-7.) On the reverse the following is written:— محمد تغلق شاه العبد الله الرحمن الرحيم ضرب دمن "Mohammed Toghluk Sháh, the servant of the most gracious and merciful God. Struck at Damman."

([k]) This is Lutchina the singer, mentioned by Ferishta, vol. 1. p. 434.

these transactions, became enraged, and brought an army into Gujarát. After tarrying in the country for two years, endeavouring to capture the fort of Girnal (Júnagarh), on which occasion Khengar, the Rájá of Kach, waited on him[1], the Sultán departed, and appointed Nizámu-l-Mulk to the government of Gujarát. At this very time, Sultán Mohammed Toghluk fell sick on the road, and the Angel of Death carried his soul to the world of eternity.

CHAPTER VIII.

THE REIGN OF FÍROZ SHÁH TOGHLUK III. OF DEHLÍ, WHO WAS THE COUSIN OF MOHAMMED TOGHLUK.

Sultán Fíroz Sháh was crowned King on the
March 23, 1351. 24th of Muharram, in the seven hundred and fifty-second year of the Hijra A.D. 1351,

(1) Nizámu-d-dín Ahmad, author of the Tabakát Akbarí, states the capture of Girnal was effected by Mohammed Toghluk, in A. Hij. 748, A.D. 1347; but Ferishta doubts his authority, and thinks it was not taken before the time of Mahmúd Bígarrah of Gujarát, in A. Hij. 837, A.D. 1469. As Khengar Rájá, the ancestor of the present Kach family, did not obtain power until A.D. 1549, or eighty years after, he could not have been contemporary with either. This, therefore, is an anachronism, and is at variance with what the author has before stated, that he was contemporary with the last of the Gujarát kings.

having been elected successor to Sultán Mohammed, by the unanimous voice of the Mohammedans, on account of his natural merit. He engaged himself in regulating the important affairs of State, and in protecting religion; and also obtained many victories. After the capture of Nágrakót, he visited Gujarát, when, having displaced Nizámu-l-Mulk, he appointed Zafir Khán [m] to the government. At the death of the latter, in A. Hij. 773, A.D. 1371 [n], his elder son, with the same title [o], was elevated to this dignity. At this time, Shamsu-d-dín Damghání represented to the Sultán, that he would give forty laks of tankchas, one hundred head of elephants, twenty-two hundred Arabian horses, and four hundred slaves, above the usual collection received from Gujarát. It was then settled that, if Shamsu-d-dín Anwar Khán, the deputy of Zafir Khán (Daria Khán), would consent to

(m) In a chronological table of mine, written at Baghdád, Gujarát is said to date as a kingdom from A. Hij. 773; this, or the first Zafir Khán, being erroneously supposed to be its founder.

(n) It was after the conquest of Nágrakót that Fíroz, according to Ferishta, marched against Jam Babúnia, or Bany, the chief of Sind. In his account of the Dehlí Kings (vol. 1. p. 455), this event is placed A. Hij. 762, A.D. 1360. In the following year he marched into Gujarát, and gave the government to Zafir Khán.

(o) Ferishta calls him Daria Khán.

such a payment, he would be preferred to another. But, as he would not consent to do so, Shamsu-d-dín Damghání was appointed; and the latter, when not able to fulfil his agreement, went into rebellion. The Sultán, having sent an army against him, caused him to be slain, and committed the government of Gujarát to Malik Mofarrah, who afterwards obtained the title of Farhatu-l-Mulk Rastí Khán. Sultán Fíroz Sháh III., who died A. Hij. 790, A.D. 1387, reigned thirty-eight years and nine months.

CHAPTER IX.

THE REIGN OF GHIÁSU-D-DÍN TOGHLUK II., WHO WAS GRANDSON OF FÍROZ, AND ALSO CALLED FÍROZ SHÁH IV.

On the death of Fíroz Sháh III., the king's servants seated his grandson, Ghiásu-d-dín, on the throne, and gave him the title of Fíroz Sháh IV. He was the son of the prince Fat'h Khán; and, being quite a youth, became addicted to indolence, giving himself up to pleasure and sensual amusements. As the people consequently suffered oppression, Malik Ruknu-d-dín, the Viceroy, put him to death, in A. Hij. 791,

A.D. 1387, and hung up his head in front of the *darbár*. His reign lasted six months and five days[p].

CHAPTER X.

THE REIGN OF SULTÁN ABÚBEKR SHÁH, GRANDSON OF FÍROZ III., AND THAT OF HIS UNCLE, MOHAMMED TOGHLUK II.

After the death of Fíroz Sháh IV., called otherwise Ghiásu-d-dín Toghluk, his cousin, Abúbekr Sháh (who was the son of Zafir Khán, third son of Fíroz III.), was raised to the throne. He was made a prisoner by his uncle, Mohammed Toghluk II., and died, after having reigned one year and six months.

Mohammed Sháh Toghluk II. then obtained the sovereignty; and, as the people of Khambáyat complained against Farhatu-l-Mulk Rastí Khán, and sought for redress, he sent Mohammed Sháh Zafir Khán (son of Wají-ul-Mulk), as governor to Gujarát. Zafir Khán accordingly took his departure, to assume this office, on the 17th of Rabí-ul-awal, A. Hij. 793,

(p) This event happened the 21st Safar, A. Hij. 791, 18th of February, 1388, A.D.; and, as Fíroz Sháh III. died on the 3d of Ramazán, A. Hij. 790, 23d October, A.D. 1387, it would be about the time in lunar months.

(Feb. 21, A.D. 1391 ;) and his master, the Sultán, falling sick, died in A. Hij. 796, A.D. 1394, after a reign of six years and seven months.

SECTION II.

THE DYNASTY OF GUJARÁT KINGS.

CHAPTER I.

THE GOVERNMENT OF ZAFIR KHÁN, SON OF WAJÍ-UL-MULK, WITH THE FOUNDATION OF THE GUJARÁT METROPOLIS, AND THE REIGN OF THE GUJARÁT KINGS.

The original intention with which these pages were written was to explain the events that took place under the administration of the several governors, after the conquest of the country by Akbar, and to detail those accidents which led to the ruin of the province, and converted it from a flourishing condition into one of barrenness. Although several learned men of former times have left behind them histories of the Gujarát kings, such as the Táríkhi-Muzaffir Sháhí, subsequently the Hulwa Shírází, the poetical history called Ahmad Sháhí, the Táríkhi Mahmúd Sháhí (so called from Mahmúd Bígarrah), and the Táríkhi Bahádur Sháhí, all of which were written during the reigns of the different kings, yet none of them embrace the general history of the Gujarát dynasty. This may be found in the history named the Mirát Sikandarí, which was composed forty years after the destruction of the Gujarát monarchy; and, as it was necessary to explain and arrange the several occurrences which took place, from the period when the Rájás held dominion to the establishment of the Gujarát kings, a selection of whatever appeared most necessary to be known, regarding each reign, has been made from the last-mentioned work. Whosoever may wish to know their history more at length will find it in the book just mentioned.

The first among the ancestors of the Gujarát kings, who adopted the faith of Islám, was Wají-ul-Mulk. He belonged to the Tank tribe of Rájpúts, which is one of the Kshatriya branches claiming descent from Rámachandra, whom they worship as a god. What is related in other histories of Gujarát, regarding the conversion and appellation of the Tanks and Gohilas, need not be here noticed.

Sultán Mohammed Toghluk Sháh II., who obtained the sovereignty of Dehlí in the year of the Hij. 792, A.D. 1390, hearing of the rebellion and tyrannical administration of Malik Mofarrah (otherwise styled Farhatu-l-Mulk Rastí Khán), then forming the country of Gujarát, soon after conferred the title of Azím Humáyún on Zafir Khán, the son of Wají-ul-Mulk; and, granting him permission to use a red canopy, such as peculiarly distinguishes kings, sent him into Gujarát to punish Rastí Khán.

Feb. 7, A.D. 1391. On the 2d of Rabí-ul-awal, in A. Hij. 793(q), A.D. 1390-91, Azím Humáyún pitched his tents by the edge of the Howzikhas, at Dehlí; where the Sultán, on the 4th of the same month, coming to take leave of him, adopted his son, Tátár Khán, as one of his own children. Azím Humáyún, after marching several stages, received intelligence of a son being born to Tátár Khán, whom they named Ahmad; and, when he arrived by successive stages at the town of Nagore, was there met by the people from Khambáyat, who complained of being oppressed by Rastí Khán. Azím Humáyún, after giving them every encouragement, marched to the city of Patan, where, having encamped, he forwarded the Sultán's letter, enjoining Rastí

(q) As the 1st of Muharram in that year was on the 9th of December, 1390, the 1st of Rabí-ul-awal was the 5th of February, 1391.

Khán to submit; but, no proper answer being returned, the latter advanced to give him battle. In the engagement which took place between them, at the town of Kambhú, a dependancy of the sirkar of Patan, Zafir Khán Azím Humáyún was victorious; and Farhatu-l-Mulk Rastí Khán was slain. Succeeding this, the former returned to Patan, in A. Hij. 794, A.D. 1391-92; where he enforced his authority, by conciliating the cultivators and other subjects. He also founded a town on the spot where the victory took place, naming it Jítpúr; and, continuing to labour in the service of the true God, after having plundered the temple of Somnáth, established the Mohammedan religion in many places. Subsequently, having taken possession of all the cities of Gujarát, he befriended those who had been oppressed by Farhatu-l-Mulk Rastí Khán, so that the chiefs and common people were pleased with him.

On the death of Sultán Mohammed Toghluk II., happening in the year of the Hijra 796, A.D. 1393-94, the affairs of the Dehlí empire were in a state of disturbance. About this time, Tátár Khán, the son of Zafir Khán Azím Humáyún, and prime minister to Nasiru-d-dín Mohammed Sháh, the son of Mohammed Toghluk II., being defeated by Mullú Ikbál Khán, fled to his father in Gujarát[r]. Intelligence was then also received that Amír Taimúr Kúrkán had encamped in the neighbourhood of Dehlí; and, as the country was in a helpless condition, many people fled from Dehlí and came into Gujarát. Soon after this period, Nasiru-d-dín Mohammed Sháh, having fled from Dehlí, came into Gujarát; but, having nothing to look for in this part, turned towards Málwa[s].

(r) Tátár Khán appears to have fled to his father in Gujarát, sometime about the middle of A. Hij. 800; which, beginning 24th September, A.D. 1397, would place it somewhere about April or May 1398, A.D. According to Ferishta, on the faith of Dehlí histories, which are here the best guides, Tátár Khán fled to Gujarát, when Mullú Ikbál Khán laid siege to Pamput, of which Tátár Khán was governor, on the part of Nasiru-d-dín Nusrut Sháh (not Nasiru-d-dín Mohammed), the brother to Ghiásu-d-dín Fíroz Sháh IV. At this time, Tátár Khán marched to Dehlí, and was defeated there. These events happened after Pír Mohammed Jehángír, grandson of Taimúr, passed the Indus; and which he effected soon after the 1st of Muharram, A. Hij. 800, or the 14th September, A.D. 1397. According to the Rauzatu-s-Saffá, Taimúr, on hearing of Pír Mohammed's having arrived at the Indus, left the banks of the Oxus, to invade India, in Rajab A. Hij. 800, or March, A.D. 1398.

(s) The first passage of the Indus was effected by Pír Mohammed Jehángír, grandson of Taimúr, soon after the 1st of Muharram, A. Hij. 800, or the 24th September, 1397. Subsequent to this, Taimúr became acquainted with the event, and set out from Samarkand to invade India, in Rajab, A. Hij. 800, March 1398. He arrived at the Indus, and passed that river on the 12th of Muharram, 801, or the 13th September, A.D. 1398, and did not reach

Amír Taimúr Kúrkán, having marched back to Samarkand, Mullú Ikbál Khán again became master of Dehlí. Tátár Khán, at this time, advised his father to take revenge of this chief, and to expel him from the capital; saying they had a large army, which was well equipped, and that the throne was the property of no one. But Zafir Khán, having foresight of things, did not agree with his son for several reasons; and having, after much wrangling, withdrawn himself from authority, gave up the attendants and ensigns of authority in Gujarát to the latter, and then retired into solitude.

The more true account, however, is this: that Tátár Khán, having imprisoned his father, assumed the title of Mohammed Sháh, and commenced his reign at the town of Yessáwal, in the month of Jumádi-ul-awal, A. Hij. 806. In the same week he commenced a religious war against the Infidels of Nadote([t]), where, having

reach Dehlí till the 5th of Jumádi-ul-awal, Hij. 801, or the 13th January, 1399, about which time Sultán Mohammed Toghluk, according to the Dehlí histories, fled to Gujarát, and, not being well received, went to Diláwár Khán in Málwa.

([t]) The author of the Tabakát Akbarí says he marched against Nadote, the 1st Shabán 806, on the 13th February, 1404 A.D.; and if his death took place then, the information agrees with the accounts given in that history, that his father, Zafir Khán, died in the beginning of A. Hij. 813, after reigning six years, seven

 months,

slain many, he resolved on marching to Dehlí. Ikbál Khán, hearing of this, became alarmed; when unexpectedly, in the month of Shabán in

months, and twenty days. Ferishta, in his history of Gujarát, has placed Tátár Khán's usurpation in A. Hij. 807, and the death of his father, Zafir Khán, in A. Hij. 814; but has evidently erred on both occasions. The author of the Táríkhi Alfí says, in one place, that, in A. Hij. 807, the intelligence was received at Dehlí, that Tátár Khán had usurped the government of Gujarát, after imprisoning his father; and, when on his way to Dehlí with an army, was soon after poisoned by Shams Khán. In a subsequent passage, however, the author says that these events took place in A. Hij. 806, and the following are his words:— و در گجرات ظفرخان بحکم سلطان محمد پسر سلطان فیروز شاه حاکم شد و در خمس و تسعین و سبعمایه در گجرات مستقل شده بایدر لشکر کشیده از حاکم پیشکش بسیار گرفت و در ثمان و تسعین و سبعمایه بپاي قلعه هندوانه لشکر کشیده و یکسال و چند ماه آن قلعه‌را محاصره نموده و پیشکش گرفته مال بر حاکم انجا مقرر کرد و باجمیر و دندوانه وسانیر تاخته براه دبواره وجلواره بگجرات مراجعت نمود و در رمضان ثمانمایه بنهرواله رسید و تاتارخان پسر او که تا غایت در دهلي بود از ملو اقبالخان بر گریخته باز ملحق گشت و پدر و پسر یکبار دیگر لشکر کشیدند و پیشکش بسیار گرفته مراجعت نمودند و سلطان محمود حاکم دهلي چون از صاحبقران شکست یافت بگجرات گریخت لیکن از انکه ظفرخان با او خوب سلوک نکرد او بجانب مالوه رفت و در ثلث و ثمانمایه باز لشکر گجرات بایدر رفت و ایدر بتصرف ظفرخان در آمد و در اربع وثمانمایه بجانب سومنات رفته بندر دیورا بتصرف در آورد و در سنه ست و ثمانمایه تاتارخان پسر ظفرخان پدر خودرا بي اختیار کرده و حاکم گجرات

the same year, Sultán Mohammed Sháh Tátár Khán, having fallen sick, several ingenious physicians were employed to cure him, but all to no

شده سکّه و خطبه بنام خویشتن کرده خودرا محمد شاه نامید
الغرض ابتداي سلطنت گجرات از این وقت باشد بعد از این محمد
شاه با لشکر بسیار متوجه دهلي شده تا قصبهٔ سنور آمد و در انجا
بزهریا باجل طبعي درگذشت و در اینصورت ظفرخان که در قلعه
بهروچ بود ایلغار کرده و باردو آمده و حاکم بالاستقلال شده تا سنه
عشر و ثمانمایه حکومت کرد و چون گجرات‌را بسکه و خطبه وچتر
و دورباش و دیکر اسباب پادشاهي زیب و زینتي نداده بود در
سال مذکور همه‌را ترتیب داده خودرا مظفر شاه نام کرده قدم بر
سریر سلطنت نهاد Zafir Khán became governor of Gujarát by order of Sultán Mohammed, the son of Sultán Fíroz Sháh III. In the year of the Hijra 795, A.D. 1392-3, having gone into Gujarát, he carried an army against Ídur, and levied a large tribute from the governor of that part. In A. Hij. 798, A.D. 1395-6, he led a force against the fort of Hindwánah, where, after a siege of one year and some months, he levied a tribute, confirming the possession of the place to the person then ruling there. From thence he hastened to Ajmír, Dindwanah, and Sanír; and, returning to Gujarát by way of Dubwárah and Julwárah, he arrived at Nahrwálah during the month of Ramazán, Hij. 800, A.D. 1397-8. At this time his son, Tátár Khán, who had been for the most part at Dehlí, having fled from Mullú Ikbál Khán, joined his father; and they together, after again levying a large tribute with an army, returned to Nahrwálah. As Sultán Mahmúd was at this time defeated by Taimúr, he fled into Gujarát; but, not being well received there by Zafir Khán, went from thence to Málwa. Again, in the year of the Hijra 803, A D. 1400, an army went against Ídur, at which time Zafir Khán subdued the place;

purpose. The people of Gujarát, however, think it well established that the cause of the before-mentioned Sultán's death was, that, when he paid no regard to the support of his father's honour, and became covetous of worldly greatness, several of the companions and intimates of Zafir Khán poisoned him; and sometimes they say that this was effected at the instigation of his father, Zafir Khán. In fine, the body of Sultán Mohammed, being brought to Patan, was buried there, and honoured as that of a martyr.

After this, Zafir Khán went to the camp, where all the nobles and government servants submitted to his authority; and it is a current tradition that Zafir Khán continued to weep for his son until the day of his death.

place; and, having in the year of the Hijra 804, A.D. 1401-2, gone against Somnath, he obtained possession of the port of Díú. His son, Tátár Khán, having usurped the government of Gujarát, in the year of the Hijra 806, A.D. 1403-4, and having caused the *khutba* to be read in his name, assumed the title of Mohammed Sháh. In short, the commencement of the Gujarát kingdom is from this date. After this, Mohammed Sháh, having marched towards Dehlí with a large army, arrived at the town of Sinúr, where he died, either through poison or a natural cause. Wherefore Zafir Khán, who was then at Bhroch, having returned with an army, became ruler of the country, possessing absolute power till the year of the Hijra 810, A.D. 1407-8, when he assumed the ensigns of royalty in Gujarát, and, seating himself on the throne of that country, assumed the title of Muzaffir Sháh.

The disorders of the government increased among the descendants of Sultán Fíroz Sháh III. till there were none of them remaining; and Mullú Ikbál Khán being slain in the battle by Sayyid Khizr Khán, the nobles and other grandees represented to Zafir Khán that, as there was neither peace nor order in the affairs of Gujarát, and no one was at that time more suited for this important business of government than himself, he ought to establish a kingdom there. In compliance, therefore, with the request and wishes of his well-wishers, he commenced his reign at the station of Shírpúr [u], six years and seven months after the death of his son, Sultán Mohammed. This happened in A. Hij. 810, A.D. 1407-8; and Zafir Khán, having assumed the title of Muzaffir Sháh [x], struck

(u) In the Tabakát Akbarí it is written Bírpúr.

(x) Muzaffir Sháh appears to have marched into Málwa in the latter part of A.D. 1406, or beginning of 1407, being A. Hij. 809. Ibrahim Sháh Sharkí, of Júnpúr, who had spent the rains of A. Hij. 809, or those of A.D. 1406, at Kanauj, marched to Dehlí at their termination; when, in A. Hij. 810 (commencing the 8th of June, 1407), he heard of Muzaffir Sháh having defeated Húshing of Málwa. On his arrival at the Jumna, the Málwa histories say he arrived before Dhar, in the beginning of A. Hij. 810, or 8th of June, 1407; and, having soon after returned to Gujarát, he may have been formally crowned in the rains of that year. But it is a most obvious error for the author to state that he reigned six years and seven months from that date, as he contradicts his own statements, and must have meant that such was the length of his whole

coins in his own name, and appointed his grandson, Ahmad Sháh, to succeed him as his heir. He continued to dispense justice, to punish the wicked, and to protect the poor, till his grandson, Ahmad Sháh, poisoned him, in the year of the Hijra 813, A.D. 1410-11.

There are different accounts given regarding the manner of his death. The author of the *Mirát Sikandarí* considers this the more authentic, that the Kúlies, inhabiting the town of Yessáwal, having become disobedient, commenced to rob and plunder the highway. At which time, Sultán Ahmad Sháh, grandson of Zafir Khán, was sent with an army against them; and he being about to depart from Patan, encamped on the bank of the tank called Khání Sarwar, where he demanded of the divines whether it was consistent with religion and the law to take revenge on the person who had unjustly killed one's father. All of them answered in the affirmative, and gave a written decision, which the Sultán preserved. On this, unexpectedly returning to the city, he imprisoned his grandfather, Zafir Khán, and administered poison to him in a cup.

whole reign, from the death of his son. The author of the Tabakát Akbarí says, that the length of it from the death of his son was six years, seven months, and twenty days.

They also relate that Zafir Khán said to his grandson, "Oh, my child, you are in a great hurry; though if you had not done so, all I have was intended for you." To which the other replied, "that his time was come;" when Zafir Khán continued saying, "Hear these words of advice from me, that they may profit you: first, place no confidence in the person who has urged you to this proceeding, and put such a one to death; secondly, abstain from wine, since it is necessary that kings should do so; and, lastly, put to death Shaikh Malik and Shír Malik[y], as both of them are mutinous servants."

Having given him several other portions of advice, he tasted the bitter cup of death about the latter part of the month of Safar, in the year before mentioned, and was buried in the mausoleum, which stands within the citadel of Patan. He possessed power for the space of eighteen years, eight months, and fourteen days.

From the time that Muzaffir Sháh established the kingdom of Gujarát, in A. Hij. 810, A.D.

(y) Both these persons are mentioned in Ferishta's Gujarát history. The former was the son of Shaikh Malik Ahdím, of Bakkar; the other was Shír Kachí, both of whom soon after went into rebellion.

1407-8, until the latter part of the month of Safar, A. Hij. 980, A.D. 1572-73, being a period of somewhat less than one hundred and seventy lunar years, there were thirteen or fourteen kings, his descendants, who reigned over the country.

CHAPTER II.

THE REIGN OF AHMAD KHÁN, GRANDSON OF MUZAFFIR, AND ENTITLED AHMAD SHÁH.

It was an invariable practice for the Sultáns of Gujarát to call their children Khán, in addition to their name; and, when these succeeded to the government of the kingdom, they were styled Sultáns. On this account, Ahmad Khán, after the death of Muzaffir Sháh, in the month of Ramazán, A. Hij. 813, A.D. 1410, took the title of Sultán[z] Ahmad, when obtaining possession of the throne.

The 1st of Ramazán, Hij. 813, was 28th Dec., A.D. 1410.

At that time, Modúd[a], the cousin of the Sultán, son of his uncle Fíroz Khán, and governor of Baroda, having gained over the chiefs of that

([z]) In Ferishta's Gujarát history, the death of Muzaffir Sháh is placed A. Hij. 814, A.D. 1411; but, in his Málwa history, it occurs A. Hij. 813, A.D. 1410.

([a]) In Ferishta he is called Fíroz Khán.

part to his interests, excited a disturbance. After a battle with the army sent against him, he fled to the fort of Bhroch for refuge. Succeeding this occurrence, he had an interview with the Sultán; who, when returning from that part of the country, having reached the neighbourhood of Yessáwal, determined to extirpate Assa Bhíl, and to found the good city of Ahmadábád, being instigated to do so by Shaikh Ahmad Khattú Ganj Bakhsh.

In the year of the Hijra 814, A.D. 1411-12, he led an army against Ídur; when the Rájá, who had fled from thence, became ashamed of his actions[b], and, agreeing to pay a fixed tribute to the Sultán, was pardoned by him.

It must be known that in the time of Alá-ud-dín, the Mohammedan faith was introduced into the country, extending from Nahrwálah Patan, on the west, to Bhroch, on the east: but infidelity was still established in many places. These, however, became purified and enlightened by degrees, through the efforts of the Gujarát kings: and many of them acquired the light of the faith, through the labours of Ahmad Sháh. Wherefore, being desirous of carrying on a religious war against the infidels of Girnar, which

(b) From Ferishta it would appear that Rájá Ránwal had joined the rebellion of Modúd.

is a fort in the district of Sorath, he ordered an army to be sent against it in A. Hij. 817, A.D. 1414-15; when the Mandalik Rájá[c], giving the army battle, sustained a defeat, and took refuge in the fort of Baroda. From this time, it is said the fort of Júnagarh, in the neighbourhood of the mountain of Girnar, fell into the possession of the Sultán; but the Mohammedan faith was not extended over the whole of the country at the time; although the zamíndárs of that part, becoming dependent, paid the tribute.

Hij. 818. began 9th July, A.D. 1415. Subsequently to this, in the month of Jumádi-ul-awal, A. Hij. 818, A.D. 1415-16, he destroyed the Hindú temple of Sidhpúr, and, during the year 819, A.D. 1416-17, carried an army against the town of Dhar, in Málwa.

31st Oct. 1418. On the first of Zú-l-kadah, A. Hij. 821, A.D. 1418, having attacked the country about Songarh[d], he caused a mosque to be built in the fort there; 20th March, 1419. and on the 22d of Safar, 822, A.D. 1419, having appointed a kází and a preacher to the mosque, he there established the Mohammedan faith. In that same year he re-built the fortified wall at the town of Mangní, a dependancy of Songarh, and stationed a party

(c) The Rájá of a small circle. The original government of India was made up of these petty States.

(d) A fort on the borders of Khándesh.

of troops there for the protection of the country; but, in consequence of a letter[e] received from his uncle, Shams Khán Dindání, who was the ruler of Nagore, he soon after returned from thence. They also relate, that at this time, Shams Khán's four front teeth became elongated, from which he was called Dindání.

In the year of the Hijra 823, Ahmad Sháh, having returned to settle the boundaries of his own country, dispersed the refractory, and, destroying the Hindú temples, built mosques in their place.

([e]) In Ferishta's Gujarát, the letter is mentioned, and is said to have been written by Fíroz Khán, the son of Shams Khán, or the same Fíroz who, according to that authority, rebelled, instead of Modúd, as before mentioned. The cause of Ahmad Sháh's return was a combination of the Rájás of Ídur, Chámpánír, Mundalgarh, and Nadote; who, assisted by Sultán Húshing of Málwa, his son Ghazní Khán, and brother-in-law Nasír Khán Farúkí of Khándesh, were to invade Gujarát. Malik Nasír had taken Tálnír, in Khándesh, from his brother Malik Iftikhár, A. Hij. 820, A.D. 1417; and was assisted by his nephew, Ghazní Khán; after which the combined forces marched to Sultánpúr, N.E. of the Taptí. Ahmad Sháh had moved in that direction, the 31st October, 1418, A. Hij. 821, and, having built the mosque in March 1419, returned to Gujarát, during the rains of the year 822 of the Hijra; but, hearing of this combination, he marched soon after in that year against the rebels, or A.D. 1419. Having dispersed them in the rains of that year, he returned to the conquest of Málwa, in the cold season of Hijra 822, when Húshing, being defeated in battle, fled to Mandú. In the following year, Hijra 823, A.D. 1420, Ahmad Sháh returned to Gujarát, and concluded a peace with Húshing, in A. Hij. 824.

Having also founded forts in such places, he left garrisons in them, among which may be mentioned the fort at the town of Jinúr, in the Parganah of Barrah [f], and that of Seopúr. After this, he established the market-town of Dahmod, among the mountains: where he erected a fortification. After this, the fort of Karieh, built in A. Hij. 704, A.D. 1304, by order of Alp Khán, who governed the country for Alá-ud-dín Khiljí, was now repaired, and named Sultánábád.

A. Hij. 830, began Nov. 2, A.D. 1426. In the year of the Hijra 830, he again carried an army against Ídur; when the Rájá of that place fled before him. Sultán Ahmad followed him into the mountainous country, where he established the city of Ahmadnagar, situated ten coss from Idur, and on the banks of the river Channel called Sabarmatí: and, having enclosed it with a strong stone wall, made choice of it for a residence.

In the year Hijra 831, A.D. 1427, when the army were foraging, Púnja, the Rájá of Idur, left his ambush, and came upon the foragers. The commander of the foraging party took to flight, and his elephant was driven away by Púnja. The multitude, which had been dispersed, again collected, and went in pursuit of Púnja: when the opposing parties, having come

(f) A district on the seaside.

to a place where on one side of the road there was a high mountain, and on the other a deep pit, between which a single horseman could pass with difficulty, the elephant-driver took an opportunity of turning the elephant round to attack Púnja, whilst the army of Islám was in his rear. On this occasion, Púnja's horse having fallen into the pit, Púnja disappeared along with him; and the Sultán's troops recovered the elephant. Some days after, a woodcutter, who had cut off the Rájá's head, brought it to the audience tent of the Sultán.

For two succeeding years, the Sultán, being at leisure, did nothing but settle and take care of his country; and, by the advice of his ministers and military chiefs, made arrangements for the advantage of his army and government.

The nature of this arrangement was to pay the soldier one half of his subsistence by a grant of land, and the other by money; as he perceived that, if the whole was a money payment, it would not be adequate to the expense; whilst the soldier, without his necessary equipments, could have no solicitude about the management of the country. But, if the half was paid by an assignment of land, the soldier would thus obtain grass, wood, and other necessaries from his estate; and, by making improvements, both in cultivation and in building, would take an interest in the management and protection of the province. The other half, or money payment, would then come to him unsought or unlooked for; and the soldier, not burdened by debt, whether for future contingencies or present wants, would hesitate in spending more than his assigned estate, whilst he could not obtain his pay from the royal treasury till every thing necessary for an army had been supplied. This would also keep him from accumulating debts with interest; and would create for him an interest in his own domestics, that he himself might use the revenue of his landed property.

It was also usual to appoint men of power among the royal slaves; associated with whom was an accountant, who was legitimately descended: for, if both were of legitimate descent, they might become friends or connexions, and thus engage in treason; or, were both slaves, the same result was to be dreaded.

The officers of districts were, therefore, appointed in the manner just mentioned; and this practice was maintained to the end of Sultán Muzaffir's reign, who was the son of Mohammed Bígarrah. But, when the army became much increased during the reign of Sultán Bahádur, the ministers, condensing the details of revenue, farmed it on contract; so that many parts, formerly yielding one rupee, now produced ten; and many others seven, eight, or nine. In no place, almost, was there a less increase than from ten to twenty. After this, many changes were introduced; and, the overseer of the regulations having been dismissed from his office, mutiny and confusion were introduced into Gujarát, as will be explained in the proper place.

The Sultán continued to make annual expeditions, sometimes to ravage the country about Ídur, and sometimes to chastise Nasír Khán, the ruler of Assír, or Sultán Ahmad Báhmaní. He occasionally sent an army against Mewar; and, as victory always accompanied his standards, the army of Gujarát, which never sustained a defeat in his time, overcame the troops of Mandú, the Dekhan, Assír, and the infidels of Mewar. He died at Ahmadábád, in the 845th year of the Hijra, A.D. 1441; and was buried there in the tomb standing in the market-place, now called Manik, which is in front of the Jumaa Masjid.

He was born the 19th day of Zú-l-hijjah of the Hijra year 793; and, being twenty years of age when he mounted the throne, whilst his reign lasted thirty-two years, six months, and twenty-two days, must have died at the age of fifty-two.

He was a scholar of Kutbu-l-Masháikh Shaikh Rakamu-d-dín, and was second to none in being distinguished for justice, temperance, and liberality.

It is related that, when his son-in-law committed an unjust murder, through the pride and arrogance of youth, the Sultán confined him, and sent him to the kází. The latter satisfied the murdered man's heir with a fine of twenty-two gold mohurs, and carried him back to the Sultán, who said, "that, though the murdered man's heir was satisfied, he was not, and could not be so; as such a practice protected the evil-disposed who were wealthy, and, by causing such a one to be enamoured of power, would only make him more hardened in murderous acts. In such a case, retribution for the injury is better than a fine." He then ordered the murderer should be hanged in front of his own house; and, after allowing his body to remain there a night and a day, issued his commands for burying it. After such an example of punishment, none of the nobles or soldiers, during the Sultán's reign, were ever known to be engaged in any case of murder.

There is a story also told of him, that, one day, while enjoying the prospect from a pleasure-house on the banks of the river Sabarmatí, he perceived the water was disturbed, and that something black was rolling in it below. Orders were given for ascertaining what this might be; when it was discovered that a jar containing a dead body had been set adrift in the river. The Sultán commanded that all the potters of the city should be collected, in order to discover who had made the jar. One of them saying that he had sold it to the *mukaddam* of a certain town in the environs of Ahmadábád, this person was brought before the Sultán ; and it was then clearly ascertained that the *mukaddam*, having murdered a merchant, put the body in a jar, and set it adrift in the river. The order was consequently given to put the murderer to death. These were the only two murders that happened during this reign.

CHAPTER III.

THE REIGN OF SULTÁN MOHAMMED SHÁH I.

After the decease of Ahmad Sháh, his son Mohammed ascended the throne, in the year of the Hijra 845, A.D. 1441 ; but he giving himself up to pleasure and amusement, showed no solicitude about the affairs of his government. Being very liberal and profuse in his presents, this Sultán was named by the people Zir-Bakhsh. In that very year, he led an army against the Rájá of Ídur[g], who, having fled before him, lurked for some time among the hills; but, having soon after sent ambassadors to ask pardon for his faults, he was accordingly forgiven, and gave his daughter in marriage to the Sultán. From thence he carried an army into the district of Bágar (Wágar); and, after plundering the country, returned to his capital. In that same year, the holy Shaikh Ahmad Khattú Ganj Bakhsh died.

The Sultán, after ordering a mausoleum and mosque to be erected in the neighbourhood of the Shaikh's tomb, marched against the fort of

(g) This Rájá was a son of Púnja. Ferishta, in his original text, places this expedition in the first year of his reign; which commenced, he says, A. Hij. 846, A.D. 1441, or the year in which his father died; and adds that, after his return, he engaged in no war, until Hijra 853, A.D. 1449. In the following year, moreover, A. Hij. 854, A.D. 1450, he marched to Chámpánír. But, in Col. Briggs's translation, the year 853 after the Hijra is put down as the date of this last expedition. In the Tabakát Akbarí, it is said to have taken place A. Hij. 849, A.D. 1545; when he had a son born, called Mahmúd, but, in the Mirát Sikandarí, named Fat'h Khán. The latter history gives A. Hij. 849 for the date of the Ídur expedition. In the Tabakát Akbarí the Rájá of Ídur is named Bír, a corruption probably of the title Víra Rájá.

Chámpánír, in A. Hij. 854, A.D. 1450. When returning from this expedition, he fell sick at the town of Godhrah in the parganah of Sanaulí, and died afterwards at Ahmadábád, on the 20th
22d Feb. A.D. 1451. day of Muharram, A.Hij. 855, A.D. 1451, when he was buried under the vault of his father's mausoleum.

The length of this Sultán's reign was nine years and some months, though sometimes said to be seven years and four months. The manner of his death is also differently related, as may be found in the history called the *Mirát Sikandarí.*

CHAPTER IV.

THE REIGN OF JALÁL KHÁN, ENTITLED KUTBU-D-DÍN.

Sultán Kutbu-d-dín, son of Mohammed Sháh I., was residing at Nariád at the death of his father. He ascended the throne in the month of Muharram, A. Hij. 855, at the request of the ministers and nobles; and, as had been the custom of his ancestors, conferred honorary dresses and presents on the soldiers.

At this time, Mahmúd-Khiljí, king of Málwa,

leaving his capital, moved an army towards Gujarát, with the intention of subduing that country. After tarrying some time in the neighbourhood of Sultánpúr, Mahmúd Khiljí advanced by way of Baroda, where he plundered the neighbourhood; and, hearing that Kutbu-d-dín had encamped at Khánapúr, on the banks of the river Mahindrí, advanced on Ahmadábád by way of Kapparwanj. The armies met near the last town, when the king of Málwa [h], suffering a defeat, fled. This happened on Friday the first day of Safar, A. Hij. 856, A.D. 1452; and, on the first day of Zú-l-hijjah of that year, the saint Burhán-ud-dín Kutbu-l-Álam died.

A. Hij. 856, 22d Feb. A.D. 1452.

When Mahmúd Khiljí advanced to the confines of Gujarát, several writers of the civil department, it is said, who had been neglected by Sultán Kutbu-d-dín, went to the presence of the king of Málwa; and he, asking them for the paper containing the divided appropriation of property, in the country of Gujarát, perceived

(h) Mahmúd Khiljí had advanced in A. Hij. 854, A.D. 1450, to assist Rájá Gunzadas of Chámpánír, during its siege by the Gujarát army; and, in the following year, A. Hij. 855, determining to conquer the country, he advanced in the end of A.D. 1451, and was defeated, February, A.D. 1452. The Mahindrí river mentioned in the text is the Myhee of our maps, which falls into the Gulf of Kambay.

that one-third was assigned over to the military for services, the other was the government share, and the remainder was given in charity to Inamdárs and religious establishments. On this occasion, Mahmúd Khiljí observed that the conquest of Gujarát would be a difficult business, as it has an army always ready to defend it.

Kutbu-d-dín, thus victorious and prosperous, returned to Ahmadábád, and completed the mausoleum of the holy Ganj Bakhsh, which his father, Sultán Mahmúd, had founded. He also completed at that time several other celebrated works: such as the tank (reservoir of water), at Kankriyah, the garden called Nugínah, and the edifice called Ghattámandal.

The author of the *Mirát Sikandarí* says that, some years previous to the composition of his history, he had seen all these works; but, at the present, the only ones remaining are the reservoir at Kankriyah and the garden before-mentioned.

Sultán Kutbu-d-dín, having formed a confederacy with Mahmúd Khiljí of Málwa, in the year of the Hijra 861, A.D. 1456-7, advanced with an army against Rána Kúmbha, who had endeavoured to seize on the territory of Nagore; at which time, the former first conquered the fort of Abú. From thence he advanced to Kúmbhalmír, with the intention of taking it, but only plundered the neighbouring districts.

The Ráná at this time had gone to Chitore; and, the Sultán having also advanced in that direction, the former came out of Chitore, with forty thousand horsemen, and fought against him for fifty days. Ráná Kúmbha, being at length obliged to fly, took refuge in the fort of Chitore; and sending ambassadors to the Sultán to ask pardon, agreed to pay tribute, and stipulated to not again molest Nagore. The petition of the ambassadors was at last granted; and, the Sultán returning to his capital, Mahmúd Khiljí[i] went to Málwa.

The Ráná[k], soon after, having broken the treaty, advanced with an intention of plundering Nagore, of which Malik Shában Imádu-l-Mulk

(i) Ráná Kúmbha built the pillar of Chitore, between A.D. 1449 and A.D. 1459, according to the inscription on it. It was in honour of a victory over Mahmúd Khiljí.

(k) This Ráná Kúmbha was the son of Mokal, the Hindú king of Mewar, and of the Chohan tribe of Rájpúts. He was the fourth in descent from Arsí, who married the daughter of Rájá Ratten Sinha, who opposed Alá-ud-dín Khiljí of Dehlí. According to Ferishta's History of Málwa, he defeated Mahmúd Khiljí of Málwa, A. Hij. 859, A.D. 1454; when the latter, in the succeeding year, formed a treaty at Chámpánír with the king of Gujarát.

(the then Wazír) gaining intelligence, sent forward the Sultán post haste to Kúmbhalmír: and the Ráná, being apprized of this circumstance, returned to his own territory.

The Sultán a second time went with his army against Sirohí; and, after attacking and plundering the Ráná's country in that direction, returned to Gujarát, and died on the 6th of the
13th May, A.D. 1459. month of Rajab, A. Hij. 863, A.D. 1458-9. He was buried in the mausoleum of Sultán Ahmad, and by the side of his father. The length of his reign was eight years, six months, and sixteen days. There are other accounts given regarding the manner of the Sultán's death, which may be found in the *Mirát Sikandarí.*

CHAPTER V.

THE REIGN OF SULTÁN DÁOD, THE UNCLE OF KUTBU-D-DÍN.

On the third day after the death of the Sultán
May A.D. 1459. Kutbu-d-dín, and in Rajab, his uncle Dáod was seated on the throne, through the favour of the ministers and nobles. He soon after committed some improper acts; when

Imádu-l-Mulk, at the instigation of the nobles, set up Fat'h Khán, half-brother of Kutbu-d-dín, and who was then receiving his education under the instruction of Sháh Álam. The second flourish of the trumpets, which announced the entrance of the latter into the royal residence at the citadel, having reached the ears of Sultán Dáod, made him aware of what had happened; and he escaped by means of a window that overhung the banks of the river Sabarmatí. The length of his reign was only one month and seven days.

Sultán Dáod, after abdicating, went into the monastery of Shaikh Adhan Rúmí, where, entering among his disciples, he served their master, and became daily more distinguished amongst them; but soon after died there.

CHAPTER VI.

THE REIGN OF SULTÁN FAT'H KHÁN, ENTITLED MAHMÚD BÍGARRAH.

A. Hij. 863, 18th June, A.D. 1459.

Sultán Mahmúd was enthroned at Ahmadábád, on Sunday the 12th of Shabán, in the year of the Hijra, 863, A.D. 1459. Regarding his surname of Bígarrah, the people of Gujarát say that each of his mustachios, being large and twisted like a cow's horn, and such a cow being called Bígarrah, they thus obtained for him the name. Again it is said that the number two, in the Gujarát language, being called *bí*, and the name of a fort, *garrah*, the people called him Bígarrah, in consequence of the two fortifications of Júnagarh and Chámpánír having come into his possession.

The author of the *Mirát Sikandarí* says, that Sultán Mahmúd was the best of all the Gujarát kings, on account of his great justice and beneficence, his honouring and observing all the Mohammedan laws, and for the solidity of his judgment, whether in great or small matters. He obtained a great age, and was distinguished for strength, bravery, and liberality. He was also, it is said, a great eater.

After thirteen years, ten months, and three days, of his age had passed away, he began to reign; and, following the example of his ancestors, gave the soldiers gifts and presents. Some months from this date, several of the nobles, who were averse to the minister Imádu-l-Mulk, otherwise named Shabán, and were anxious to destroy both his rank and influence, calumniated him to the Sultán, and put him in chains. At night, the master of the elephants, named

Abdúlah, explained to Mahmúd Bígarrah that the minister was the friend of the government; and when the slaves of the palace had accidentally released Imádu-l-Mulk, the Sultán ordered that the perfidious nobles should be seized and their houses plundered. The nobles, on becoming acquainted with the king's intentions, prepared to defend themselves, and encamped with a force at Bhaddar. At this time the king ordered all the persons then in his service, amounting to five hundred, to assault them with the royal elephants. Wherefore they attacked the enemy, and, having dispersed the discontented nobles, punished those of them who were seized.

After this transaction, no one had an opportunity of disobeying during the whole of this king's reign; and, the conspirators having been put to death, five hundred and two persons, who obtained titles and dignified offices, received assignments of land for their support.

In a short time after this, a large army was collected, and tranquillity every where prevailed in the country. The Sultán also made it a rule that the assignments of land belonging to those who happened to fall in battle should be given to their sons; and, in the event of there being no son, that the half of the estate should be given to the daughter. When there was neither son nor daughter, he was in the practice of granting a pension to the relations or dependants, in order that they might not complain of their lot. On one occasion, some person told the Sultán that the son of a certain nobleman who had died was not worthy of possessing wealth. To whom the king replied, that wealth would make him worthy[1]; after which no one ventured to say a word on this subject.

The Sultán built several magnificent caravanseras and lodging-houses for travellers, and founded several colleges and mosques. He also ordered, that no one in his army should borrow money with interest; and established a distinct pay-office for such of the soldiers as were obliged to get in debt. By this means, a soldier could obtain an advance; for, as he said, if the Mohammedans live in debt, how is it possible they can fight?

All the fruit-trees in the open country, as well as those in the city, towns, and villages, were planted in the reign of this Sultán; who, if he ever knew of a shop or dwelling-house becoming empty, made inquiry after the causes, and ordered it to be inhabited.

(1) This anecdote deserves the notice of our Indian legislators, who, to better the Indian character, must give the people more places of trust.

In the eight hundred and sixty-sixth year of the Hijra, A.D. 1461-2, the Sultán advanced towards the Dekhan, having been requested to do so by Nizám Sháh Báhmaní, in consequence of Sultán Mahmúd Khiljí, the king of Málwa, having marched an army into that country[m]. Mahmúd Khiljí, on hearing that the king of Gujarát was advancing by way of Burhánpúr, desisted from the siege of Bídar, and returned towards his own territories. When the ambassadors of Nizám Sháh Báhmaní were on this occasion sent to the Sultán, they omitted nothing that could be deemed a compliment; and, having requested permission to depart, returned home. The king of Gujarát also returned to his capital.

After this, and in the year of the Hijra 871, A.D. 1466-67, being desirous of capturing Girnar and Júnagarh, in Gujarát, and to extirpate and destroy the Mandalik Rájá, or petty prince of Girnar, he made preparation accordingly,

([m]) Nizám Sháh Báhmaní, the son of Humáyún the Cruel, and then a child of eight years, had succeeded to the Dekhan throne under a Regency, of which his mother was head. Dissensions soon arising among the members of it, the king of Málwa was induced to advance into the Dekhan, where, having met the Dekhan troops three coss from Bídar, he gained a battle, and besieged the town, until relieved by the approach of Mahmúd Bígarrah, with eighty thousand horse.

ordering, it is said, the pay-office to carry along with it five krores of gold coin. He also ordered the commissary of stores to carry along with him eighteen hundred gilded handled swords, of Egyptian, Arabian, African, and Khorásánian manufacture, whose handles did not contain less than from four to five Gujarát sírs of gold ; and to take in addition three thousand eight hundred swords, whose handles, of Ahmadábád manufacture and of silver work, were of different weights ; with, moreover, seven hundred daggers and poniards, whose golden handles should be from three to two sírs and a half weight in gold. The Sultán at this time commanded the Master of the Horse to attend him in the expedition, with two thousand Arabian and Turkish horses, all of which, with the gold and arms, he distributed among the troops, during the period of the siege. Succeeding these things, he sent his victorious army to plunder the country of Sorath, where the soldiers obtained a large booty. The Rao Mandalik, or petty sovereign, having submitted, asked for favour, through means of ambassadors ; and the Sultán, thinking it advisable to desist from the siege of the fort for that year, returned to his own capital.

But, in the year of the Hijra 872, A.D. 1467-8,

having heard that the Rao Mandalik visited the temple of idolatry, and went there with all the ensigns of royalty, the Sultán became ashamed of royalty, and appointed forty thousand horse, with many elephants, to take away the royal umbrella and other kingly ensigns from him. The Rao Mandalik, on becoming acquainted with this, instantly forwarded the umbrella and other ensigns to the Sultán; and the gold and jewels obtained on this occasion were distributed among the king's musicians.

In the year of the Hijra 874, A.D. 1469-70, on indicating a desire to take the forts of Girnar and Júnagarh, the Sultán received an unexpected visit from the Rao Mandalik. On this occasion the Rájá addressed the Sultán, saying "that whatever he might command should be obeyed, and requested to know why he desired the destruction of his obedient subject, who had committed no fault." To this, the Sultán replied, "that there could be no greater fault than that of infidelity, and, if he was to expect tranquillity, he must acknowledge the unity of God, and secure to himself his country; for that, otherwise, he would extinguish him." The Mandalik Rájá, seeing such was the state of affairs, fled by night to his fort, and commenced a war, but soon after came and entreated for his life, as the garrison was starved into submission. The Sultán guaranteed his safety, on condition that he would receive the faith of Islám ; and the Rájá, having quitted the fort, delivered the keys to the Sultán, and uttered the confession of faith, in imitation of the conqueror. This conquest happened in the year of the Hijra 877, A.D. 1472-73[n].

Regarding the conversion of the Rájá to Mohammedanism, it is sometimes said that, having come to Ahmadábád with the Sultán, he became a follower of Hazrat Sháh Álam, as related in the Mirát Sikandarí, and that his tomb, situated near the road leading from the Kolápúr gate, is conspicuous on the right-hand side.

After this, Mahmúd Bígarrah called together the Sayyids and learned men of every quarter, in order to settle them in the country of Sorath ; and, having turned his thoughts to populating it, rebuilt a fort, and founded a noble palace there. The nobles also built dwelling-houses agreeably to order ; and in a little time there arose a city, almost equal to Ahmadábád, which was named Mustafábád. He also gave the

([n]) According to Ferishta, the conquest of Júnagarh and Girnar was effected in A. Hij. 875, or two years earlier ; and his authority for this date appears to be corroborated by the author of the Tabakát Akbarí.

Mandalik Rájá the title of Kháni Jehán, on whom he conferred a jágír; and having taken away the golden images from his idol temple, ordered that they should be distributed as a present among the soldiery.

After this, he hastened into Sind; and in the year of the Hijra 878, A.D. 1473-74, having made many prisoners in that quarter, brought them from thence to Júnagarh. In the same year, he conquered the island of Sankha-dhára[o], dependant on Jiggat, to which he was urged by a complaint from Múlá Mohammed Samarkandí, that the infidels of that quarter had captured a boat, in which was he with his whole family. The difficulties and dangers of that expedition have been detailed at length by the author of the Mirát Sikandarí, where the account may be found.

During the time of destroying the idols and temples of Jiggat, many rubies, pearls, and silken cloths, were obtained as booty; and the Sultán, having built a mosque there, gave the charge of Sankha-dhára to Malik Toghán, otherwise entitled Farhatu-l-Mulk.

(o) Sankha-dhára means the City of Shells; and, regarding Sankha-dwípa, which Mr. Wilford identifies with Africa, something will be found in *A. R.* vol. viii. p. 303. This island is now called Bate.

In the year of the Hijra 800, A.D. 1475-6, Hazrat Sháh Álam, the glory of the Saints, died; and his tomb, which exists in Rasúlábád, was built by the instructions of Táj Khán Narialí, one of the nobles of distinguished rank at court.

The Sultán having arrived at Mustafábád, September 16, A.D. 1475. or Júnagarh, on Friday, the 13th of Jumádá-ul-awal of the same year, heard that the people of Malabar had come with several *ghorábs* (small boats,) and were blockading the ports of Gujarát. He immediately ordered that several boats should be got ready for the punishment of the parties, and took his departure for the port of Goa; whence returning by the way of Khambáyat, he encamped at Sirkí, where he remained three days on a pilgrimage to the tomb of Shaikh Ahmad Khattú. At this place, having called together the children of the nobles and soldiers who had fallen in battle, or had died during the above expedition, he settled the jágírs on their sons. Where there were no sons, he conferred half the jágír on the daughters; and in case of there being neither sons nor daughters, he fixed the means of subsistence for the dependants. Immediately following this, he returned to Ahmadábád, where he continued inactive (with the exception of going once a year on a journey to Mustafábád for the purpose of hunting) until the time when he resolved on the capture of the fort of Chámpánír, which was in the possession of Rawal Tuppaí[p]. On the occasion of his journey thither, while hunting one day on the banks of the River Watruk, twelve coss south-east from Ahmadábád, he founded there the city of Mahmúdábád; and, having fortified a rising ground on the banks of the before-mentioned river, he ordered noble palaces to be built, of which the marks and remains are yet to be seen at the time of writing, being the year of the Hijra 1170, A.D. 1756.

After this, he pursued his intention of capturing the fort of Chámpánír, which submitted
Nov. 22, A.D. 1484. to him on the 2d of Zú-l-kadah, A. Hij. 889, A.D. 1484; and, being much pleased with the climate of the place, he established it as his capital, and ordered a mosque and a fort to be built, and having made it a great city, it was known by the name of Mahmúdábád

(p) Tuppa means the subdivision of a parganah, the same as a talúka, or district; and this Zamíndár, or Rájá, is so named from possessing the tuppas of the Chámpánír parganah. One of the Rájás is called Rawal Pati, in Colonel Miles's account of this fort; but the Tabakát Akbarí calls the one mentioned in the text Jey Sing, the son of Gangádás, who had become refractory, having been encouraged by Ghiásu-d-dín, of Málwa.

Chámpánír. The nobles and ministers, with the merchants and tradesmen, at length built houses for themselves, and several gardens ornamented the neighbourhood of this place. One of these gardens was known by the name of Halol.

In A. Hij. 891, A.D. 1486, he went to Mustafábád, and returned several times to Mahmúdábád.

After this, in the year Hij. 892, A.D. 1487, he committed the charge of the country about Sorath and Júnagarh to the prince, Khalíl Khán ; at which time some merchants, who had brought for sale four hundred Iráki and Turkí horses, from the countries of Khorásán, came to demand redress, saying, that having brought these along with several silken stuffs, they had been plundered in the neighbourhood of the mountains of Abú, by the Rájá of Sirohí, who had not even spared their old garments. The Sultán ordered that an account of the price of the horses and other articles should be made out, and commanded the merchants to be paid the money from the treasury, as he could receive the amount from the Rájá of Sirohí. The Sultán, having then marched towards Sirohí, sent a menacing order to the Rájá, and to this effect, that if he did not return the merchants' horses and their goods, the royal troops would be sent against him. The Rájá, on this being made known to him, asked for forgiveness, and complied with the order ; on which the Sultán returned to Mahmúdábád, where he amused himself for four years, going to Ahmadábád during the hot season of ripe melons, and returning again to Ahmadábád, after enjoying himself there for six months.

In the year of the Hijra 904[q], A.D. 1498, when Ádil Khán Farúkí, the ruler of Khándesh, neglected to send the usual tribute, a force was sent forward to that quarter ; but, immediately on the arrival of the Sultán at the banks of the Taptí River, Ádil Khán sent the tribute and made his excuses. The Sultán, consequently, sent back his army by the way of Nadarbár, and went in the direction of Tálnír, for the purpose of seeing its fort : whence returning to Nadarbár, he there joined his army, and went to Mahmúdábád (Chámpánír).

Having carried an army against Chaiwal, in the year of the Hijra 913, A.D. 1507, in order to destroy the Europeans, he effected his designs against the towns of Bassai (Bassein) and Manbai (Bombay) ; and returned to his own capital

(q) Ferishta places this A.D. 1498, or A. Hij. 905.

A. Hij. 914. 12th May, A.D. 1508. on the 11th of Muharram, A. Hij. 914[r], A.D. 1508.

([r]) There were several attacks made on the Portuguese in the Indian Sea. This was the first in which the assistance of the Turks was given. Ferishta calls the Turkish commander Amír Husn; and the Gujarát admiral was Malik Iyáz Sultání. The Turkish emperor was then Báyázíd II. A subsequent expedition was undertaken against them, aided by a Turkish fleet, in the reign of Suleimán II. of Constantinople. The admiral commanding the last was Sídí Ali Kátibi, who has written an account of the expedition, in the "Mirror of Countries," as translated, *Bombay Literary Transactions,* vol. ii. p. i. The expedition sailed from Bassora, A.D. 1553. The author of the Tabakát Akbarí mentions the first of these expeditions; but, by dating it A. Hij. 896, A.D. 1490, has erred in his chronology about seventeen years. That historian's account of the transaction is as follows:
در این سال فرنکیان در بنادر اسلام شور انکیختند سلطان متوجه بندر ماهیم کشت و چون بخطهٔ دون رسید خبر آوردند که ایاز غلام خاص از بندر دیو چند سلسله جهاز خاصه و ده جهاز رومي مستعد ساخته با فرنکیان بندر چیول جنک کرده فرنکي بسیار بقتل آورد ودرین جنک چهار صد رومي کشته شد و فرنکیان کریختند و یک جهاز بزرک ایشان که یک کرور متاع در ان بود بجهت انکه تیر چوب اورا بتوپ شکسته بودند دردریا غرق شد "In this year, the Europeans excited disturbances at the different Mohammedan ports. The Sultán (Mahmúd Bígarrah) went to Máhím; but, when he arrived at Dún, intelligence was brought him that Iyáz, one of the royal slaves, who from the port of Díú got ready for sea with several of the king's own and ten Turkish vessels, had engaged the Europeans off the harbour of Chaiwal, and slain many of them. In this battle four hundred Turks were killed, and the Europeans fled. Moreover, one of their large ships, containing property valued at a krore of rupees, sunk on this occasion, in

Subsequently to this, Álam Khán, who was the Sultán's grandson by his daughter, and whose father was the ruler of Assír and Burhánpúr, requested his mother to petition the king of Gujarát, representing that eight years had elapsed since the death of Ádil Khán I. son of Míran Mubárak Farúkí, who died without heirs; and that the nobles, who supported the claim of one of Malik Ráji's relations to the government, had given him the title of Ádil Khán[s]; while they, being in possession of the country, were predominant in his name. This petition further requested that the Sultán would place Álam Khán on the throne of his ancestors and protect his servant. The Sultán gave it his favourable attention; and, in the month of Rajab, advanced

consequence of one of her ribs being broken by a shot." In the Portuguese accounts of this transaction, it is stated that the Admiral, Don Lorenzo Almeida, was killed, and his ship taken, with the loss of one hundred and forty men.

(s) In the *Mirát Sikandarí*, as here, the grandson of Mahmúd Bígarrah is called Álam Khán, and the Pretender Ádil Khán; but in the Tabakát Akbarí the history of Nizámu-d-dín Ahmad, the grandson of the Sultán, is Ádil Khán, who finally succeeded as the second of that name; and the Pretender is styled Álam Khán. This last agrees with Ferishta's account of the Gujarát and Ahmadnagar kings. Álam Khán was the son of one of the Farúkí family born to the daughter of Ahmad Nizám Sháh of Ahmadnagar.

towards Nadarbár, for the purpose of supporting Álam Khán. Having arrived at Tálnír, after the Ídu-z-zohá, (the passover or sacrificial feast) he gave the title of Ádil Khán to Álam Khán, the son of Húsí Khán; and, presenting him with four elephants and three laks of tankchas, fixed him in the government of Assír and Burhánpúr. He also raised Malik Sarang Khiljí to the title of Khán Jehán, and presented him with the town of Bunnass, which is a dependancy of Sultánpúr and Nadarbár, and was his place of nativity. In the grant of this gift, he inserted the name of Ádil Khán, and likewise promoted several of the nobles about Court.

At length, Ádil Khán departed well pleased to Assír, and the Sultán returned to his capital; at which time Sayyid Mohammed Júnpúrí came to Ahmadábád, and laid claim to the miraculous power of the Imám Mehdí. The Pretender took up his abode in the mosque of Táj-Khán, son of Salar, which is near the Jumalpúr gate; where he began to assemble the people. On this account, the Ulamas and doctors issued a religious decree against him, ordering that he should be put to death; but the Sayyid took his departure for Patan, where he supported his ministry.

The Mohammedans of Pálanpúr became his followers; and there are now some of the Medhiví[t] sect to be found there.

Not long after this period, in the month of Zú-l-hijjah, of A. Hij. 916, A.D. 1510, the Sultán set out for Patan; and, as this was the last time he appeared in public, having collected together all the great men of the state, he told them that his life was near a close. On returning from Patan, he came to Ahmadábád in four days; when, having made a pilgrimage to the burial place of Shaikh Ahmad Khattú, he wept tears of repentance over his own tomb, which had been built at the foot of the Shaikh's mausoleum. Subsequently to this, having entered the city of Ahmadábád, he fell sick; and, continuing so for three months, sent for the prince, Khalíl Khán, from Baroda. After informing him of his approaching dissolution, he finally took his leave for another world, on Monday the 3d of Ramazán, in the year of the Hijra 917, A.D. 1511; and his remains were deposited in the mausoleum which exists at Sirkej.

A. Hij. 917, 3d Ramazán, 25th November, A.D. 1511.

(t) An account of the Medhiví sect, written by Lieutenant Col. Miles, will be found in the Transactions of the Bombay Literary Society, ii. p. 281. This impostor, according to that, was born A. Hij. 847, A.D. 1443.

Mahmúd Bígarrah, who was born in the month of Ramazán, A. Hij. 849, A.D. 1445, reigned fifty-four years, having attained sixty-seven years of age when he died.

CHAPTER VII.

THE REIGN OF KHALÍL KHÁN, ENTITLED MUZAFFIR SHÁH II., OR THE CLEMENT.

Khalíl Khán, having assumed the title of Muzaffir Sháh, mounted the throne, at Ahmadábád, on Friday the 17th of Ramazán, A. Hij. 917, A.D. 1511, being then in his twenty-seventh year. He distributed presents, according to every man's rank, after the manner of his ancestors; and those who had been his intimate friends, while he was prince, received titles. The noblemen of the late court had also their dignities increased, and additional villages were assigned for their support.

An ambassador from Sháh Ismael Safawí, king of Persia, whose name was Mír Ibrahím Khán, arrived in the month of Shawál; when a crowd of nobles went out to meet him by order of the king of Gujarát, and received him with every honour. The ambassador brought with him a cup of turquoise stone of great value, which, with a box full of jewels, many silken clothes, and thirty horses of Irák, sent by the king of Persia, he presented to the Sultán. The latter, after presenting the ambassador in return several costly dresses and princely presents, set out on a journey to Baroda, and named the district of that city Daulatábád.

About this time, intelligence was received that a battle had been fought on the plains of Mandú, between Sultáns Mahmúd and Mohammed[u] of Málwa; and that Sultán Mohammed, in order to take refuge with Sultán Muzaffir, had in the mean time encamped near Mahmúdábád Chámpánír. The Sultán ordered that he should be supplied with whatever he might require; and sent a message that, if it pleased God, he would advance with him to Málwa, after the end of the rainy season. The Málwa prince and his family came to live in the palace belonging to Ádil Khán, the son-in-law of the Sultán; which residence he inhabited till the time when he unexpectedly took his departure, without taking leave of the Sultán; as there was a great talk about what had happened between him and the followers of the Persian ambassador. The Sul-

(u) The latter is called Sáhib Khán in Ferishta.

tán was much annoyed at this, and sent an ambassador with presents to take leave of the prince; when, in the month of Shawál, of A. Hij. 917, A.D. 1511, it was represented to him that Sultán Mahmúd of Mandú, brother of the Prince Mohammed just mentioned, having heard that the latter was in Málwa, had collected a large army of Rájpúts, and, after opposing him in battle, had put him to flight. It was also said that Maidání[x], or Mídání Ráo, Sultán Mahmúd's chief man of business, had acquired such authority, as to leave nothing with the Sultán but the name of a king, and that infidelity was, consequently, spreading afresh in the cities of Málwa.

1st of Shawál, A. Hij. 917, was 22d December, A.D. 1511.

The Sultán of Gujarát, being now moved with zeal for the cause of the true faith, commenced his march for Málwa, in the above mentioned month. During the period of the army halting at the town of Godhrah, waiting the junction of other troops, the Sultán received intelligence that the Rájá of Ídur had become disobedient.

(x) This is the Mídání Ráo of Baber's Memoirs (p. 312). He was a Rájpút and an officer in the Málwa Government, who rose into power, under Sultán Mahmúd II. of Málwa; and who, after the capture of Mandú, by Muzaffir Sháh II. of Gujarát, held the districts of Chanderí and Gagrone. Baber says he took the former from Mídání Ráo, A. Hij. 934, A.D. 1528, at which time he was under Ráná Sanka of Chitore.

He consequently ordered the troops to march in that direction, and to destroy the buildings and temples of Ídur. This happened in the year of the Hijra 919, A.D. 1513. The Rájá, repenting of his conduct, caused the fixed tribute to be paid. After this, the Sultán returned to Godhrah; where he gave the prince, Sikandar Khán, an audience of leave, on his departure for Mahmúdábád Chámpánír, and he himself continued his march for Málwa. After arriving at the town of Dohad, he gave orders for the construction of a fortification there, when, continuing to advance, he received intelligence that Mídání Ráo had carried Sultán Mahmúd to Chanderí. On this occasion, the Sultán declared that it was not for the purpose of seizing the throne of Málwa from its prince that he carried his army there, but in order to drive Mídání Ráo and other infidels out of the country, by which he might reconcile the brothers to each other.

The Sultán, after hearing the praises of the edifices that existed in the hunting-park at Dhar, went to amuse himself there; and, having displayed intrepidity in the chase, returned to Ahmadábád.

In the year of the Hijra 920, A.D. 1514, it was represented that Rái-Mal, brother of Bhím Ráo, Rájá of Ídur, having expelled his brother's son,

Bhára Mal, from Ídur, was assisted by Ráná Sanka, Rájá of Chitore, and had obtained power there. At this the Sultán was displeased; saying, "that Bhím Ráo ruled Ídur by his authority, and what power could Ráná Sanka have to appoint Rái-Mal to Ídur?" Wherefore, Nizámu-l-Mulk, the Jágírdár of Ahmadnagar, received orders to expel Rái Mal from Ídur, and deliver over the country to Bhára-Mal. Rái Mal continued a warfare with the Sultán's troops, to the year of the Hijra 923, A.D. 1517, having been alternately victorious and defeated. In the mean time, the nobles of Málwa, such as Habíb Khán, dreading Mídání Ráo, fled from thence; and, waiting on the Sultán, represented to him the then state of Mandú, saying, "the Mohammedan religion had been banished from thence; that Mídání Ráo had caused many of the faithful to be slain, and would soon put to death or imprison Mahmúd, the king of Málwa." In consequence of this, the Sultán of Gujarát said, "that at the end of the rainy season he would advance into Málwa, in order to punish Mídání Ráo." At this time, Sultán Mahmúd of Málwa, perceiving the whole resources of this country were at the disposal of Mídání Ráo, and that he himself was strictly watched, found opportunity, one night, of mounting on one horse, whilst he placed his wife on another ; and having escaped to Gujarát, was on his arrival there congratulated by Sultán Muzaffir[y] ; who, after furnishing him with a tent, elephants, horses, and whatsoever else was proper for a king, advanced into Málwa, on Thursday the 4th of Zú-l-kadah, A. Hij. 923, A.D. 1517.

18th November, A.D. 1517.

29th November. On Tuesday the 15th of the same month, Sultán Muzaffir met Sultán Mahmúd of Málwa at the town of Deoláh ; and marching from thence by regular stages, the Sultán encamped with his army in the neighbourhood of Mandú, on Sunday the 23d of the same month ; when he commenced erecting his batteries. Mídání Ráo, after quitting the fort of Dhar, went to Ráná Sanka for succour ; and sent to tell the besieged that they must ask for a truce, by which a month's delay would be gained, and he in the mean time would bring the Ráná, with assistance.

7th December.

The Ráná, being bribed by means of several jewels and fine elephants, which Mídání Ráo had taken from Sultán Mahmúd of Málwa, was induced to send a large army as far as Sarangpúr. The Sultán, being made acquainted with this, and having discovered the treachery of the

(y) It appears from Ferishta that the king of Málwa was then at Gohand.

besieged, sent Ádil Khán Asírí Kawámu-l-Mulk, and Malik Sarang, with several other brave and intelligent men, in order to keep in check the Ráná; whilst he himself, ordering the assault to be made on the fort, captured it on Monday the 2d of Safar of A. Hij. 924, A.D. 1518. On this occasion, nineteen thousand Rájpúts, and fifty-seven officers of rank, whose names are detailed in the histories called Mirát Sikandarí and Muzaffir Sháhí, were slain. The departure of the Sultán, the entertainment given to him by the king of Málwa, and his visit to the fort, are also detailed in the above-mentioned histories.

In the following year of the Hijra 925, A.D. 1519, intelligence was received that a great battle had been fought between Ráná Sanka and the king of Málwa, and that the latter, after being wounded, had fallen into the hands of his enemies. The Sultán was much astonished on receiving the news of these events, and sent an army for the protection of Mandú. Ráná Sanka permitted Sultán Mahmúd of Málwa to return to Mandú, after his wounds were healed, and retained his son as a pledge.

Moreover, Ráná Sanka, hastening towards Ídur, in A. Hij. 926, A.D. 1520, made war on the Jágírdárs of Ahmadnagar and other places.

The Sultán's troops, then opposed to him, being defeated, the Ráná was enabled to advance as far as Barnagar and Bísalnagar, which he plundered; but, after hearing that the royal army had left Patan and Ahmadábád, in order to bring him to order, he returned to Chitore.

In the year of the Hijra 927, A.D. 1520–21,
1st Muharram, 12th December, A.D. 1520. and in the month of Muharram, Sultán Muzaffir sent an army of one hundred thousand horse with one hundred strings of elephants, under the command of his slave, Malik Ayáz Sultání, and twenty thousand cavalry, with twenty strings of elephants, in command of Kawámu-l-Mulk, in order that they might punish the Ráná for his audacity. These troops first advanced against Bágarh (Wágarh), and plundered the country, as the Rájá of that part had joined this mutinous coalition. The army, after killing many Hindús in this expedition, advanced against Ráná Sanka's country. About this time news of the Ráná's death arrived, and also of the death of Sultán Mahmúd Khiljí II.[z] who

([z]) This is quite an anachronism. Mahmúd Khiljí II., of Málwa, was put to death by the guards of Bahádur Sháh of Gujarát, A. Hij. 932, A.D. 1526; according to Ferishta's history of Málwa. In the same history and same year, Ráná Sanka is said to have died, and to have been succeeded by his son, Ráná Rattan Sing. Ráná Sanka is mentioned by Baber in A. Hij. 928, A.D. 1523, (see Memoirs, p. 287.)

had marched from Mandú, with the intention of assisting Sultán Muzaffir.

In the same year, a peace was patched up with the Ráná, in consequence of the hypocritical conduct of the officers commanding the troops, who now returned to Ahmadábád. The Sultán, in consequence of this, showed his displeasure with Malik Ayáz, by saying that he would go himself after the rains, and complete the business: whilst Malik Ayáz received permission to proceed to Sorath.

In A. Hij. 928, A.D. 1521-22, having prepared for an expedition, in order to punish the Ráná, he came to Ahmadábád; but the Ráná's son having, in the mean time, waited on the Sultán, with the promised elephants and tribute, the expedition was stopped.

In A. Hij. 931, A.D. 1524-25, the prince, Bahádur Khán, who was displeased with the smallness of his jágír, went to Dehlí, by way of Dúngarpúr, Chitore, and Mewat, in order that he might have a meeting with Sultán Ibrahím Sháh Lódí of Dehlí. At this time, the latter, who had opposed Zahíru-d-dín Bábar Pádsháh, on the plains of Pánipat, sent for Bahádur Khán, and received him with much honour and respect. When Sultán Ibrahím Lódí, and other people of Dehlí, became acquainted with the bravery and intrepidity of Bahádur, they were filled with jealousy. Bahádur Khán, aware of this circumstance, went towards Júnpúr, where, on his arrival, he heard Muzaffir was dead; and immediately set out on his journey for Gujarát.

Sultán Muzaffir was much vexed when he heard that Bahádur Khán had gone towards Bágarh in disgust; and indicated his anxiety to pacify him, and make him return; but the prince had previously abandoned the country. At this time, the Sultán fell sick; when, at length, in the year of the Hijra 932, A.D. 1525-26, having come on account of this very sickness from Mahmúdábád Chámpánír to Baroda, he proceeded by easy stages to Ahmadábád, and took up his residence there, in the palace which is called Ghattámandal. Men nowbegan to despair of his life; and the prince, Latíf Khán, through fear that his brother Sikandar Khán, heir to the throne, would not leave him alive, 1st Jumádá-s-sání, 15th March, A.D. 1526. departed for Baroda on the first of Jumádá-s-sání, where a crowd of followers accompanied him.

On the second of the same month, Sultán Muzaffir ordered that Sikandar Khán should be called to him, when he exhorted him to study the interests of his kingdom; and, after asking a blessing for great and poor, he departed this life on Friday the 22d of Jumádá-s-sání, of A. Hij. 932. He was buried in the mausoleum of Mahmúd Bígarrah, which stands at Sirkej, after he had reigned fourteen years and nine months.

This king was a follower of Sayyid Táhir, who is buried at Baroda. For piety and learning, clemency and intelligence, liberality and bravery, he had no equal of his time: and he is known by the name of the clement Muzaffir, on account of his many merciful acts. The author of the Mirát Sikandarí tells us that there were no drunkards in his time, and that good manners were agreeable to him. On account of his clemency, he was careless of punishing many things that required it; and such conduct was on the whole the cause of disturbances. As universally known, the Sultán once ordered part of the lands in the Parganah of Jhaláwár should not be sown, but left as waste, because the people in that part complained that in consequence of the many cultivated fields they had no pasturage for their cattle.

CHAPTER VIII.

THE REIGN OF SULTÁN SIKANDAR.

Sultán Sikandar, on the very day his father Muzaffir died, seated himself on the throne at

7th April, A.D. 1526. Ahmadábád; and on the 25th of Jumádá-s-sání of A. Hij. 932, undertook a journey to Mahmúdábád, where, having distributed presents in the manner of his ancestors, he commenced his reign. After conferring titles on all those who had served him while he was a prince, he gave away, as presents among his people, seventeen hundred horses.

The nobles belonging to the court of the late Muzaffir were much vexed at this proceeding; and Imádu-l-Mulk, otherwise named Khúsh-Kadam, the foster-brother of the king, and who was in hope of his being made his prime-minister, was greatly annoyed. The discontented nobles, being apprized of this circumstance, persuaded him that the king wished to cut him off. Imádu-l-Mulk, who was very powerful, now engaged in a conspiracy; and joined the discontented nobles with part of the troops that had been gained over by his promises. At this time, Latíf Khán, brother to the king, who set up his pretensions to the throne, held possession of the mountainous country about Sultánpúr and Nadarbár. He was assisted by Bhím Rájá, and kept up a correspondence with several of the nobles; wherefore Shirza Khán was appointed to expel him from these parts; but, he being killed in action, Nasír Khán was sent with a large army to succeed him.

When the conspiracy was completed, Imádu-l-Mulk, who, feigning sickness for some time, had confined himself to his house, wrapped up his head one day in the manner of a sick person, and waited on the king. He was accompanied by fifty horsemen; and finding a fit opportunity, while most of the king's attendants were absent, he entered the royal apartments. Having carried along with him Malik Páhár, and finding the Sultán asleep, that person murdered him, on a signal given by Imádu-l-Mulk. This
26th May, A.D. 1526. event happened on the 14th of Shabán of A. Hij. 932; and the Sultán was buried at Halol, which is two koss from Mahmúdábád Chámpánír.

Imádu-l-Mulk, having thus accomplished the important undertaking of Sikandar's murder, took from the harem a son of the late Muzaffir, then five or six years of age, and, after giving him the name of Sultán Mahmúd, seated him on his knee; but, distributing at the same time horses and honorary dresses among the soldiers and nobles, he conferred titles on them[a]. All the nobles, who thirsted after the blood of Imádu-l-Mulk, on account of this murder, retired

([a]) The author of the Mirát Ahmadí has not reckoned the child raised to the throne after the murder of Sikandar as one of the regular kings. In Colonel Briggs's Ferishta he is called Mahmúd Sháh II.

to their own jágírs; and, anxious to find the means of revenge, despatched messengers in haste to acquaint Bahádur Khán of these events, and urged his return.

The length of Sultán Sikandar's reign was two months and sixteen days.

CHAPTER IX.

THE REIGN OF SULTÁN BAHÁDUR.

It has been already mentioned that Bahádur Khán, son of Sultán Muzaffir II., had left the country, in consequence of the smallness of his personal estate, and his disagreement with his brother Sikandar. When Bahádur heard of his father's death, and his brother's murder, he mourned for four days, as is usual in such cases. Soon after having left Júnpúr, he set out for the capital, with all possible expedition; and arrived at the town of Mukrej, otherwise named Mahmúdnagar, where the nobles, who, through fear of Imádu-l-Mulk, had gone into retirement, now began to join him with troops from every quarter. On the 26th of Ramazán, of the same

year, he arrived at Ahmadábád, and entered the citadel there, which is commonly known by the name of Bhaddar. During the festival day of that month he went to the place of prayers, and caused the oration to be pronounced in his own name. Having soon after conferred titles on thirty-two persons, he ordered that they should be provided with suitable offices; and, on the
12th July, A.D. 1526. 2d of Shawál, set out for Mahmúdábád.

Imádu-l-Mulk, on hearing of the approach of the Sultán, became agitated; and sent an intimation to Latíf Khán, that, as Nasír Khán was now an infant, he, in the event of a war, would be able to conduct it. At length, however, through astonishment at the probable consequence of what he had done, he abandoned both Nasír Khán and Latíf Khán, and assumed to himself the royal authority. Sultán Bahádur in the mean time crossed the Mahindrí (Mahí river); and, regardless of his army, advanced rapidly with only a few followers. After making a pilgrimage to the grave of Sikandar at Halol, he appointed Táj Khán, with one hundred horsemen, to bring Imádu-l-Mulk captive. This commander plundered the house of Imádu-l-Mulk, who fled to the residence of the chief Díwán, and there concealed himself. During these proceedings, Sultán Bahádur entered Mahmúdábád,

with all the ensigns and pomp of royalty; and, after taking up his abode in the royal palace, ordered the seizure of Imádu-l-Mulk, which was effected after a little search. Imádu-l-Mulk was brought into the presence of the Sultán, who ordered him to be hung on a gibbet; and all those concerned in the base murder were punished according to their deserts. Latíf Khán, who arrived in the immediate neighbourhood of the capital during these events, now retired; and Sultán Bahádur having mounted the throne
11th August, A.D. 1526. on the 4th of the month Zú-l-kadah, A. Hij. 932, A.D. 1526, bestowed honorary dresses on the ministers and nobles. After giving instructions for a donation of one year's pay to be given to the soldiers, he conferred distinguished titles on one hundred and fifty persons.

At this time, being a year of scarcity, a charity-house was established by the king's order; whilst he himself, when riding out, never gave less than a gold mohur to any poor person.

As Latíf Khán[b], who had collected a body of Zamíndárs in the territories of Sultánpúr and

(b) The Tabakát Akbarí says that Latíf Khán fled to Pál, and was assisted by the Rájá named Rái Bhím. Briggs's Ferishta calls the Rájá Oody Sing. In Ferishta's history, these events are placed about the end of A. Hij. 932; and the Tabakát Akbarí says that they happened in the beginning of A. Hij. 933.

Nadarbár, occasioned commotions there, an army was sent against him, when, being wounded in action, he was taken prisoner and brought before the Sultán, at the station of Múrghidínah, where he died.

Sultán Bahádur, after causing Nasír Khán to be poisoned, on the 15th of the Rabí-ul-awal, of
Dec. 20, A.D. 1526. the year of the Hijra 933, A.D. 1526, went hunting in the direction of Khambáyat, whence he went to Sorath, in consequence of the quarrels among the children of Malik Ayáz Sultání. In returning, he came by way of Diú, where he remained a month, and entrusted that place to the care of Mujáhid Khán. When he arrived at Ahmadábád, Vikramajit, the son of Ráná Sanka, waited upon him. After remaining there three months, Bahádur went to Mahmúdábád, and, having punished the Rájá of Nadote, proceeded to the fort of Súrat. From this place he travelled in the course of one night and day to Mahmúdábád, where he took leave of the Ráná's son on departure to return.

The Sultán again visited Diú, and remained there several days, in the year of the Hijra 934. From thence going to Khambáyat, he sailed for Ghoga; and, after again visiting Diú, returned to Mahmúdábád, by way of Khambáyat. At this time, he gave orders that the city wall of Bhroch should be built[c]. After this he carried an army against Bágarh; when the Rájá of Dúngarpúr, coming to Mukrej, paid his respects. From thence he set out for Patan, and, by way of Ahmadábád, returned to Mahmúdábád with great celerity. The Sultán's perambulations, in these days, became proverbial in the mouths of men, "that one travelled with the celerity of Bahádur."

Were any one to attempt an account of all such expeditions, it would be almost impossible to detail the whole. I have, therefore, chosen to give a short and abridged explanation of them in these pages; but, should any one wish to know them more at length, let him turn to the pages of the Mirát Sikandarí.

In the year of the Hijra 935, A.D. 1528, he marched in the direction of Daulatábád, in order to assist his nephew, Mujáhid Khán, son of Ádil Khán Farúkí. During that expedition, it is said, nine hundred elephants of large stature accompanied him. After settling the important affairs of that quarter, he returned to his own capital, in the month of Shabán of the same year[d].

Shabán began the 10th April, A.D. 1529.

(c) The Tabakát Akbarí says that, having repaired the fort of Bhroch, he returned to Khambáyat, and that he did so after the conquest of Bágarh.

(d) The account of these events is confirmed by the Ahmadnagar history of Ferishta.

When he set out for the conquest of the Dekhan, in the month of Muharram, A. Hij. 936[e], A.D. 1529, many of the Dekhan kings, with Bohrji, the Rájá Baglánah, waited upon him at Dhar, and tendered their services. The united armies of Sultán Bahádur and his nephew were at this time ordered to march against Ahmadnagar, the fort of Chaiwal[f], and other places, which, with many cities in the Dekhan, were plundered. The oration was

Began Sept. 5, A.D. 1529.

(e) According to the Tabakát Akbarí, Bahádur heard from his nephew, the ruler of Khándesh, after he had returned to Khambáyat from Bhroch. He then marched to assist him, in the month of Muharram, of the year of the Hijra 935, (which month began the 15th of September, A.D. 1528; as the king of Nagar, Burhán Nizám Sháh, and that of Bídar, Amír Beríd, had attacked Imad Sháh of Bírar, and the ruler of Khándesh. While at Khambáyat, he heard that a Portuguese ship had stranded at Diú; and, while Bahádur waited for the army assembling at Baroda, Jam Fíroz of Sind, Narsingh, nephew of Man-Singh, of Gwalior, and Bírban Prithvi Ráj, nephew of Ráná Sanka, waited on him. The last is called Sreepelly by Colonel Briggs, but, in the original Ferishta, Sirvír.

(f) According to the Portuguese accounts, the siege of Chaiwal took place in A.D. 1527, on which occasion they were assisted by the king of Ahmadnagar, Burhán Nizám Sháh. This date is probably not correct. The kings of Ahmadnagar and Golkonda had confederated against Imad Sháh, Bahádur Sháh, and the king of Khándesh; and, as a coalition existed between the Portuguese and the Nagar State, such was in all probability the cause why Bahádur Sháh marched towards Daulatábád, A.D. 1528; but the expedition against Chaiwal could not have taken place until the end of A.D. 1529.

consequently read there in the name of the king of Gujarát. In the end of the month of Shabán, in that year, he resolved on returning, and, setting out for Mahmúdábád, accompanied by several persons, arrived there with great celerity.

In the year of the Hijra 937, A.D. 1530, he carried an army against Bágarh, in order to subdue that country; and thence going to Mandú, he completed its capture by approaches, as mentioned in the history before quoted. After having spent some days in besieging this fort, he entered it, on the 29th of Shabán, by that side where the buildings are most lofty: and on this occasion he himself led the way, accompanied by several other nobles. As Mahmúd Khiljí, who had defended Mandú, now fled, Sultán Bahádur took possession of his palace; and, on
August 26, A.D. 1531. the 12th of Muharram, A. Hij. 938, A.D. 1531, the former having returned with his sons, waited on the king of Gujarát, who gave them in charge to Alif Khán, Ikbál Khán, and Asif Khán. These officers were instructed to conduct them to Gujarát; but the king of Málwa and his sons were killed in a scuffle, which took place when the Rájá of Pál[g], and

(g) Pál is a district of Gujarát, on the Mahindrí, or Mahí, river; the Rájá in the Mirát Sikandarí is called Udai Singh. In Ferishta's "Native Annals of Málwa," the attack of the Bhíls and

the Kúlis about Dahad, had come for the purpose of liberating them. After this, the whole of the country about Mandú came into possession of the king of Gujarát, to which a governor and faujdár were appointed.

Sultán Bahádur passed the rainy season of that year in the upper fort of Mandú; and, having gone to Burhánpúr and Asír, on the 9th of Safar, of the year of the Hijra 939, A.D. 1532, he conferred the royal umbrella on Nizámu-l-Mulk, the prince of Ahmadnagar, and entitled him Nizám Sháh; since which time each of the rulers there is so entitled. Mahmúd Khán of Asír also received the title of Mahmúd Sháh; and the king of Gujarát, having undertaken a journey to Mandú, carried from thence an army against Silhaddí, the Rájá of Ujain. It is accordingly recorded that Silhaddí was made prisoner; after which the Sultán set out with all possible expedition, and arrived at Ujain, from which departing, he left the place in charge of Daryá Khán Mandwí. Having gone to Sarangpúr, he left that behind in charge of Mullú Khán, and afterwards took

and Kúlis on the Gujarát army is placed in the year of the Hijra 932, A.D. 1526, or the first year of Bahádur's reign, by which the battle between Latíf Khán and the Gujarát army and that which happened on this occasion have been confounded.

possession of Bhílsáh. From thence proceeding by stages to Raisein, then in possession of Lakshman Singh, brother of Silhaddí, he there encamped on the banks of the river, and ordered his officers to prepare batteries for capturing the fort. Rúmí Khán [h], unrivalled in his time for skill in preparing fireworks, destroyed and levelled, in the twinkling of an eye, one of the bastions by a gun, while twelve thousand Dekhaní foot-soldiers, who were in the Sultán's pay, sprung a mine beneath one of the bastions, and threw down a considerable part of the wall. The Silhaddí, who was then with the Sultán, observing these things, sent to say that he would embrace the Mohammedan faith; and, after causing the fort to be evacuated, would deliver up the place. He therefore sent for his brother, Lakshman Singh, who came and waited on the Sultán. While the two brothers, however, were seated in consultation on this matter, Lakshman Singh said to the Silhaddí, "Wherefore should you give up the fort? Bhópat [i], my son,

([h]) He is probably the Rúmí Khán who cast the Mulki Meidán, or large gun of Bíjapúr. The copy of the Táríkhi Ahmadí is here faulty; for, in the original of the Mirát Sikandarí, it would appear that such was levelled by a mine.

([i]) In the Táríkhi Sikandarí, from which the author of the Mirát Ahmadí has borrowed his account of these transactions, it is simply said, that Bhópat had gone to the Ráná, whose son, Vikramajit,

has gone to the Ráná, and he, with forty thousand cavalry, and infantry without number, is bringing us assistance. Till his arrival, it is necessary to procrastinate, and to employ caution and deceit." The Silhaddí, therefore, told the Sultán that Lakshman Singh would take his departure, and evacuate the fort on the succeeding day.

After some days had passed, however, without the promise being fulfilled, the Sultán was informed that the Ráná's son was approaching with assistance. Mohammed Sháh Asírí and Imádu-l-Mulk were nominated, to keep in check the Rána's son, but, the latter excusing himself to the Sultán, on account of the magnitude of the Rána's army, Ikhtiyár Khán was sent on the expedition. When the Sultán himself set out to join the army, he came up with it, as is said, in a night and a day, having travelled in that time seventy coss, accompanied by only thirty horsemen. The Ráná's spies, immediately on the Sultán's joining the army, acquainted their master of his arrival; and the latter, not thinking it advisable to front him, halted a stage in the rear. He at the same time sent one of his confidants into camp, who,

Vikramajit, was to bring assistance. Bhópat is called by Ferishta the son of Silhaddí.

under many pretended excuses, wished to ascertain whether the Sultán had himself joined the army or not. In the mean time, the Ráná, after ascertaining that Abigh Khán had arrived from Gujarát with thirty-six thousand cavalry, as an escort to the guns and elephants, sounded a retreat. The Sultán ordered that he should be closely pursued, and followed him to Chitore; but the Ráná, before the army could come up, had taken refuge in the fort. It was now resolved that the troops should capture the fort of Raisein, after which they were to lay siege to Chitore. Sultán Bahádur accordingly marched against the former place, where the besieged, seeing no prospect of assistance, yielded up the fort, as related in the history above quoted.

At this time, Sultán Álam Lódí, brother of Sultán Sikandar, had been driven from Kalpí, by the power of Jannat Makání Humáyún Pádsháh, and, accompanied by twelve thousand horse, sought an asylum with Sultán Bahádur. The latter presented him with the government of Raisein, Bhílsáh, and Chanderí, which had belonged to Silhaddí. He also ordered that Mohammed Sháh Asírí should seize on the town of Gagroní, which the Ráná had taken by conquest from Sultán Mohammed Khiljí.

About this time, Sultán Bahádur went to

Gondwánah for the purpose of hunting elephants, and obtained a great many. After capturing the fort of Kánúr, he gave it in charge to Alp Khán; and, having subsequently reduced Islámábád, Hushangábád, and other neighbouring districts dependant on Málwa, returned to Sarangpúr. From thence he went to Gagroní, which Mohammed Sháh Asírí had not yet reduced, and immediately received its submission on his arrival. He then appointed Imádu-l-Mulk to conquer the country about Mandásúr, whilst he himself marched back for his capital.

Soon after Sultán Bahádur's arrival at Mahmúdábád, intelligence was brought him from the port of Diú, that the Europeans had come there with many ships and other warlike means, in order to capture the place. He lost no time in hastening to Khambáyat: and the Europeans, hearing that the Sultán was advancing, took to flight[k]. After arriving at Diú, he ordered two large guns, with a hundred of smaller size, to be sent to Mahmúdábád for the capture of Chitore. From thence he went to Ahmadábád; and having subsequently arrived, in one day, at Mahmúdábád, sent orders to Mohammed

(k) See Briggs's Ferishta, IV. p. 123. This attempt on Diú is placed by the Portuguese Annals about February and March, A.D. 1531, being the end of A. Hij. 937.

Sháh Asírí to advance from Asír to the siege of Chitore. Khudáwand Khán[l] and Wazír Khán, who were with the army at Mandú, were ordered to join Mohammed Khán Asírí, whilst the Sultán himself posted from Mahmúdábád to Mandú in three days. At this time, Mohammed Khán Asírí and Khudáwand Khán received orders to march on Chitore; and when they with the army arrived at Mandásúr, the Ráná's agents came to say, that whatever the Sultán might be pleased to order he would perform it to the best of his ability, provided the intention of besieging Chitore was abandoned. This request not being complied with, the Sultán's army invested Chitore, and straitened the besieged. At length the mother of Vikramajit, the Ráná's son, sent to say, that she had been of old a servant of the Sultán, and that, if he consented to spare the place, and would march from thence, she would give him in return a golden waistband[m] and jewelled

(l) This is the same person as Rúmí Khán. He was a Turkish slave, whose original name was Saghra Áká. His subsequent titles were Khudáwand Khán and Rúmí Khán. According to the Haft Iklím, he founded the castle of Súrat A. Hij. 947, A.D. 1540; though Major Price in his Mohammedan History, vol. III. would place this foundation ten years earlier.

(m) This valuable belt was afterwards presented to Suleimán, the lawgiver, at the court of Constantinople; and the Chevalier Joseph

crown, which had been captured from Mahmúd Khiljí I. of Málwa, when the Ráná defeated him. Besides these jewels, which were incalculably valuable, she promised to pay five laks of rupees, one hundred horses, and ten elephants, as an acknowledgment of submission.

Malik Burhánu-l-Mulk and Mujáhid Khán were sent from thence with a large army to capture the fort of Rattanbhore; and Malik Shamshíru-l-Mulk was despatched with twelve thousand cavalry to reduce Ajmír. The Sultán at this time went to Mandú, by way of Mandásúr; and, soon after his arrival there, deputed Mohammed Sháh Asírí, with the most famous of the Gujarát nobles, to go against Nizámu-l-Mulk Dekhaní. Mohammed Sháh Asírí, after encountering the latter in the neighbourhood of the town of Bír, sent messengers to the Sultán,

Joseph von Hammer, in his Memoirs on the Diplomatic Relations of Dehlí and Constantinople, mentions it in these words of the Turkish historian:—" The Tátár armies of Humáyún, with which he had conquered the greatest part of Hindústán, having also taken possession of the countries of Bahádur Sháh, Sultán of Gujarát, this prince sent away his principal ministers, his harem, and his treasure to Medína; and at the same time despatched an ambassador to Constantinople with presents, who arrived there while the Sultán was absent at Adrianople. Besides other precious gifts, he brought a girdle valued at sixty krores of ducats, the krore being a hundred thousand; or, taking the ducat at fifty aspers, 30,000,000 aspers."

acquainting him of the circumstance; and twelve thousand brave horsemen were accordingly selected and sent to his assistance. The opposing armies, however, had come to action before the arrival of the others at Bír: and the Dekhan's troops, immediately on hearing of the Sultán's advance, took to flight[n]. A little time after, Burhán Nizám Sháh came to meet the Sultán, when he acknowledged his dependence; and the latter, having given him back his country, proceeded towards Mandú. At this time, Burhán Nizám Sháh, after accompanying the king of Gujarát several stages, obtained leave to return.

The Sultán again showed an anxious wish to take the fort of Chitore, but Mohammed Zamán Mírzá, grandson of Sultán Husain, king of Khorásán, happening at this time to fly from his relation, Jannat Áshiání Humáyún Pádsháh, of Dehlí, attached himself to Sultán Bahádur[o].

([n]) This expedition, which was the second against Burhán Nizám Sháh, is here wrongly placed. It is rightly placed by Ferishta, both in his Gujarát and Ahmadnagar histories, being after Shabán, A. Hij. 937, A.D. 1531.

([o]) We have been already told that Sultán Bahádur had laid siege to Chitore, and was induced to abandon it. According to Ferishta's Dehlí history, this happened A. Hij. 938, A.D. 1531; at which time Mohammed Zamán Mírzá, having conspired against Humáyún, fled to Bahádur Sháh. Humáyún on this very occasion advanced to Gwalior and returned; whilst the Ráná of Chitore

Humáyún was much vexed at this, and wrote to the king of Gujarát, either to send the fugitive back, or expel him from his country. The different letters on this subject which passed between them are to be found in the history before quoted; and, to terminate the matter, these produced a mutual enmity. About this time, Sultán Bahádur sent his army from Mandú to the siege of Chitore, and appointed Rúmí Khán as his deputy there; promising that, after capturing it, he would give it over to his care.

At the same period, intelligence was received that Humáyún Pádsháh had arrived at Gwalior, with the view of making war on Sultán Bahádur; who, while investing Chitore, and fighting with infidels, patiently waited the result. After being aware of Humáyún's intentions, he commanded Tátár Khán Lódí to make a demonstration against Dehlí, and to go by way of

tore paid a tribute of the waistband and crown. These events, which in his Gujarát history are placed A. Hij. 940, A.D. 1533-4, and have been confounded with the first siege of Chitore, are individually placed in the Dehlí accounts A. Hij. 938 and 941. But the dates of all these events appear very confused in Ferishta, and Abul-Fazl is certainly a better guide in this matter. Price, in his Mohammedan Annals, quoting this author says, Chitore fell to Bahádur the 3d of Ramazán, A. Hij. 941, March, A.D. 1535. If such be correct, Humáyún's first advance and return to Agra must have been A. Hij. 940, A.D. 1533-34.

Beyána, under an impression that, if Humáyún went into Gujarát, he himself would become master of Dehlí; or that the other, having nothing better left him, would order his troops to return. By the will of fate, and the mistakes of Tátár Khán Lódí, these measures were not accomplished, and the Gujarát army was accordingly defeated by Hindal Mírzá, the brother of Humáyún. Notwithstanding this, the siege of Chitore continued; and the besieged at length, being straitened, surrendered the fort.

Though Sultán Bahádur had promised to give Rúmí Khán the command of Chitore, he did not do so on various accounts. Rúmí Khán, offended at this, wrote privately to Humáyún, and at the same time threw difficulties in the way of the king of Gujarát, whenever any thing was to be done, as is to be found detailed in the above history. Sultán Bahádur was at length forced to take shelter in the fort of Mandú, but, on the capture of this place by Humáyún, escaped to Chámpánír, and left Mandú to the care and protection of Ikhtiyár Khán and Rájá Narsingh Deo. From thence going to the country of Sorath, he took up his residence in the island of Diú[p]. Soon after this, Chámpánír fell

(p) In Col. Miles's account of Chámpánír (Bombay Transactions, 1. 1431) Abul-Fazl is quoted; from whose account it appears into the power of Humáyún, who went to Ahmadábád; but, as he was obliged to return to the capital of Agra, in consequence of the insurrection of Shír Khán Afghán, otherwise entitled Shír Sháh, he left his brother, Mírzá Askarí, at Ahmadábád, Kásim Beg in the Sirkar of Bhroch, Yádgár Násir Mírzá in the Sirkar of Patan, and Baba Beg Jallairí in the fort of Chámpánír. At this time, Sultán Bahádur's commanders, such as Malik Amín Darwísh, who had been appointed to command Rentumbhore, Malik Burhánu-l-Mulk, the commandant of Chitore, and Shamshíru-l-Mulk, the commandant of Ajmír, having effected a junction, advanced with forty thousand cavalry to the neighbourhood of Patan, whence they sent to tell the Sultán that, if it was his pleasure, their troops would attack those of Yádgár Násir Mírzá. The Sultán replied that he was about to join them, and that they must not engage the Mírzá until he came. Soon after Sultán Bahádur joined the troops, Yádgár Násir Mírzá hearing that he had arrived, kept aloof, and hastened to Ahmadábád. The former, on learning that soldiers from all quarters were flocking to join him, advanced against Ahmadábád; soon after which Mírzá

pears that Bahádur was defeated at Mandásúr, A. Hij. 941, A.D. 1534-5, and that the fort was not taken until Safar, A. Hij. 942, or August A.D. 1535.

Askarí and the others gave him battle near Mahmúdábád. The Dehlí commanders, however, perceiving that it would be impossible to keep their footing in a strange country, went soon after to join Humáyún. Mírzá Askarí and the others were in possession of Gujarát nine months and some days.

Sultán Bahádur, at this period, went to Chámpánír, where he remained for some time; but, being annoyed by the intrigues of the Europeans, and vexed with them for building a fort in the island of Diú, was continually contriving how he might expel them. The account of building this fortification may be found in the Mirát Sikandarí.

When the Sultán, accompanied by a few other persons, went to have an interview with the treacherous European infidels, he was murdered, it is said, by them, and thrown into the sea[q].

([q]) The death of Bahádur Sháh of Gujarát, who was killed in an affray with the Portuguese at Diú, has been represented by some Mohammedan authors in a most unfavourable light for the latter. Colonel Briggs, in his translation of Ferishta, has extracted a passage of the history called the Táríkhi Sikandarí, from which, and the Portuguese accounts, it would appear that the parties were suspicious of each other, and were plotting accordingly. Bahádur Sháh intended to imprison Nuno de Cunha, Governor General of Portuguese India, and Emanuel de Souza, Governor of Diú, by which he hoped to drive these foreigners from

These events happened on the 3d of Ramazán, A. Hij. 943; and from this time the port of Diú has been possessed by the Europeans, Ikhtiyár

from Diú, and obtain possession of the place; while the latter were desirous of seizing Bahádur and thwarting his designs. Some misunderstanding and quarrel having taken place between their followers, at a meeting on board the Portuguese ship, Bahádur was put to death in the squabble. The author of the Mirát Sikandarí wrote sixty-two years after this transaction, and probably derived his information from those cotemporary with the actors in it. This account is supported by the author of the Tazkaratu-l-Mulúk, who wrote about the same time, and arrived in India little more than twenty years after the event of Bahádur's death. The latter says, "at this time it was reported that the Governor of Gova had arrived at the port of Diú, with the design of carrying on hostilities in this part of the country. Sultán Bahádur, therefore, accompanied by a large force, went to Diú, with a view of thwarting their designs; and, as all the places on the sea coast were soon after given in charge to the Gujarát commanders, and their Sipáhís, all ingress to the Europeans was thus prevented. Skirmishes between the Mohammedans and the latter daily took place on the sea coast, and several were killed on each side; but a peace was at length agreed upon between them, as both were tired of this warfare. It was settled at this time that the parties should meet on shipboard, from whence the Europeans in amity with the Mohammedans were to come on shore to an entertainment. Several of the nobles about Sultán Bahádur were averse to his going on shipboard, lest something unfortunate might happen, and thus frustrate his intentions; but the Sultán, heedless of their wishes, determined to go there: thinking that the Europeans would be thus induced to attend an entertainment, where he might put the whole to death, and find opportunity for afterwards seizing on their ships and other property. The Sultán, accompanied by some friends, imprudently went on shipboard, where

Khán, the king's minister, has written the date thereof in these words :—*Sultánu-l-barr Shahídu-l-bahr*—"The king of the land was a martyr at sea."

The length of his reign was eleven years; and his death happened when he was only thirty-one years of age.

After the murder of Bahádur, his minister and nobles sent to his nephew, Mohammed Sháh Farúkí, of Khándesh, then at Ujain, commanding seven thousand horse; and, after acquainting him with the circumstances, requested he would come to Gujarát to be invested with power, according to the will of his late uncle.

Mohammed Zamán Mírzá, pleased at the confusion which at this time prevailed in Gujarát, took up a position at the town of Awan, three koss from Diú. The nobles, aware of his intentions, sent Imádu-l-Mulk with a strong force against him; when, after a battle fought in that neighbourhood, the Mírzá was defeated, and took his departure.

Sultán Mohammed Sháh Farúkí, on receiving the intelligence of Sultán Bahádur's death, did not communicate the event to any one; but was

where his enemies slew him at this meeting, and all the Mohammedans who were with him. After having subsequently plundered many parts, the Europeans returned to Gova.

so much grieved at being thus separated from him, that his death also happened seventeen days afterwards. When the Gujarát nobles were made acquainted with this event, they saw that there was no heir to the throne, except Mohammed Khán, son of Latíf Khán, and nephew to Bahádur. As he had been imprisoned, at Bahádur's request, by the late Mohammed Khán Farúkí; the nobles, therefore, wrote to Shamsu-d-dín, in whose care he was, that he might send him to Gujarát. Shamsu-d-dín accordingly sent him to be installed in the manner of his ancestors.

After the defeat of Sultán Bahádur, much disorder and sedition found their way into the affairs of Gujarát; and, from that time, the tribute from the kings of the Dekhan, and the ports possessed by the Europeans, was no longer received.

CHAPTER X.

THE REIGN OF SULTÁN MAHMÚD II., SON OF LATÍF KHÁN.

A. Hij. 943, A.D. 1536. Mahmúd Khán, in A. Hij. 943, A.D. 1536, commenced his reign at the age of eleven. On this occasion, Imádu-l-Mulk obtained the office of prime-minister; and Daryá Khán received the title of Majlis Girámí. These two agreed to carry on the affairs of the government, and watched the Sultán so narrowly, that he appeared as if placed between two planks of wood. No one, excepting these two noblemen, ever visited the Sultán; and, though much annoyed at this, he very wisely and judiciously never gave the least indication of his vexation. He appeared so much taken up with amusements and hunting, that you would have said he had no thought for his kingdom or his army. He continued to say, both privately and openly, that a king, having such ministers as Imádu-l-Mulk and Daryá Khán, need not give himself any trouble about his government; and often he would ask, What kind of a place is Mekka? and what like is Medínah? The ministers, pleased to hear him talking in this manner, conducted the affairs of government without any trouble. But the Sultán very wisely, and from necessity, played the simpleton; and whatever of good or bad he might hear, either publicly or privately, he repeated to them without alteration. They were, therefore, much astonished at the Sultán's conduct.

At length, Daryá Khán wished to remove Imádu-l-Mulk from any interference with the government. To further this design, he carried the Sultán on a pleasure trip to a tank near the Mahindrí River, and distant from the city thirty koss; where, having collected together a large force from the neighbouring districts, he commanded Imádu-l-Mulk, in the name of the government, to quit the city of Ahmadábád, and retire to his personal estate. The latter, having no alternative but compliance, went to his estate in Jhaláwár. On this occasion, Daryá Khán, accompanied by the Sultán, pursued Imádu-l-Mulk, and, after following him to the confines of Burhánpúr, sent a message to Mubárak Sháh Farúkí, requesting he would seize the fugitive, and send him to him. Mubárak Sháh, who would not comply with this request, was now at war with Daryá Khán; and, in an engagement fought near Wankírí, the former being defeated, fled to Assír, while his famous elephants, and other ensigns of royalty, fell into the power of Mohammed Sháh II. of Gujarát. Imádu-l-Mulk, continuing his flight from thence, went to Kádir Sháh of Mandú, then Governor of Málwa; and the Sultán, after remaining several days at Burhánpúr, entered into a treaty, stipulating that the oration at the mosque, and the currency of Burhánpúr and Asír, should be in his name.

Soon after this, Daryá Khán, accompanied

by the Sultán, returned to Ahmadábád; and, being now at leisure, subjected the whole of Gujarát to his control. He pretended to act in the name of Mohammed Sháh, whom he retained as a pageant. Being much addicted to luxury, he made an agreement that Álam Khán Lódí, one of his confidants, should provide for the custody of the Sultán, whom he gave over to his charge.

The people of Gujarát, they say, whether rich or poor, were pleased and gratified by the propriety of Daryá Khán's kindness, presents, gifts, and pensions. It was his practice to keep by him blank grants of land, sealed with the royal signet, and ready for presentation, in order that the deserving might not be kept waiting.

In this manner, Daryá Khán, for the space of five years, enjoyed himself; and, though the Sultán was informed of his excessive luxury, he took no notice of it. The former continually endeavoured to discover the other's secret thoughts, but was never able to do so, and was wont to say, "I am astonished at the conduct of the Sultán, who is either very knowing or a fool who has no equal."

Álam Khán Lódí subsequently obtained Daryá Khán's permission to go to his own estate, as he was displeased with his benefactor for the reasons found written in the Mirát Sikandarí. It was reported that Imádu-l-Mulk, in Málwa, had at this time become more and more intimate with Kádir Sháh. Daryá Khán, who was much vexed at hearing this, sent an order in the name of the king of Gujarát, that Kádir Sháh should either seize and send Imádu-l-Mulk to Gujarát, or expel him from his country. The Governor of Mâlwa wrote in answer that he did not chose to comply. Daryá Khan was enraged at this reply; and, having ordered the king's tents to be brought out, encamped at the palace of Ghattámandal, near the Kankriya tank, with the intention of marching an army against Kádir Sháh. He also issued a firman for the assembly of troops from all quarters of the kingdom; during which time he daily passed two or three hours with the Sultán, and was wont, after returning to his own house, to spend his time in pleasure and amusement.

The Sultán, while yet young, had acquired a habit of bearing whatever might come; and, though consequently grieved, had no power of doing otherwise. Daryá Khán one day invited him, along with Sayyid Mubárak Bokhárí, to an entertainment, where the dancing and singing had induced him to remain all night a spectator. About the latter part of the night, the minister, rising up, retired with one of the dancing girls, and left the Sultán quite alone; at this very improper treatment, the latter manifested his indignation; but, restraining his passion, whispered to the Sayyid, "Do you behold the impudence of this slave, who leaves me alone, and, in getting up, forgets the usual respect that should be paid me?" The Sayyid told him that it was now necessary to bear and wait patiently, to see what might turn up.

Álam Khán Lódí, then living on his estate at Dhandukáh, and who had a grudge against Daryá Khán, hearing what had happened, sent privately to the Sultán, saying, "that if he chose to favour him, and would give the orders for the removal of Daryá Khán, such would be accomplished." This measure being finally resolved on and agreed to between the parties, through the mediation of a bird-catcher named Charúnjí, the Sultán one night secretly took flight, and went over to Álam Khán Lódí. He was accompanied, on this occasion, by twenty-two horsemen, who had escorted some draught carriages sent by the latter. One day had elapsed before Daryá Khán became acquainted with the Sultán's flight, and was now at a loss how to proceed. As he was in possession of the treasure, he elevated to the throne a grandson of Sultán Ahmad II.; and, having entitled him Sultán Muzaffir, caused the currency to be struck, and the oration at the mosque to be pronounced in his name. After having, moreover, collected fifty thousand cavalry, he came out to oppose Álam Khán Lódí and the Sultán, who, in a severe battle fought soon after, sustained a defeat.

Daryá Khán, thus victorious, left the Sultán to himself, and went to Dholka. The latter, notwithstanding their defeat, collected another army, by people flocking to their standard from every quarter, and from among the numerous deserters of Daryá Khán's army. The other, not thinking it advisable he should remain at Dholka, marched to Ahmadábád. On arriving there, the people refused him admittance; but, entering the city by force, he endeavoured to conciliate the soldiers and the people. Notwithstanding this, his men deserted and went over to the opposite party. Daryá Khán, who was now suspicious that the townspeople would seize and deliver him up to his sovereign, sent his family and effects to the fort of Chámpánír; whilst he himself went to Mubárak Sháh at Burhánpúr. These events happened in the year of the Hijra 950, A.D. 1543.

Mohammed Sháh II., after entering Ahmadábád, went to Chámpánír; and, having captured that fort, obtained possession of Daryá Khán's women and treasures. The Sultán, now invested with absolute dominion, conferred the office of prime-minister on Burhánu-l-Mulk Babí, and made Álam Khán Lódí commander-in-chief. His affairs had thus continued prosperous for six months; when, at the intercession of Álam Khán Lódí, Imádu-l-Mulk was called to court, and Charúnjí, through his representation, obtained the title of Muháfiz Khán. The latter was made a companion of by the Sultán; and, though naturally a mean wretch, became his adviser, frequently declaring that he was a friend and well-wisher of his sovereign.

Imádu-l-Mulk, who had in the mean time arrived from Mandú, paid his respects to the Sultán; and, after obtaining the sirkar of Bhroch, with the port of Súrat as his jágír, received permission to go there and take possession. At this time, Muháfiz Khán, when the Sultán was one day heated with wine, advised him to dismiss all the old nobles, and promote others. But, to accomplish this object, it was necessary first to remove Alá-ud-dín Lódí, brother of Sikandar Lódí, of Dehli, and who, in the time of Bahádur Sháh, entered the service of Gujarát; and, secondly, Shujáat Khán, who had accompanied him in the war carried on against Daryá Khán. The Sultán, without consulting any of his ministers or nobles in this matter, ordered that these two noblemen should be put to death on the gallows ; and they were accordingly executed.

At this time, Sultán Mohammed retired to his private apartment, and ordered that no one should for three days be admitted to see him. On the third day, Álam Khán Lódí told Imádu-l-Mulk, that, as Sultán Alá-ud-dín had now been dead for three days, it would be necessary to tell the Sultán that he must be buried. Imádu-l-Mulk consequently went to the *darbár,* where Muháfiz Khán, coming from the presence of the Sultán, asked what he wanted, after having received permission to proceed to his jágír. The former replied, he must tell the Sultán that, if it was his pleasure, he would bury Sultán Alá-ud-dín. The wretch Muháfiz Khán, laughing contemptuously, said to him in a familiar manner, " Oh, Malik, these two ungrateful servants have suffered death, and a crowd of others will be made to follow them !" Imádu-l-Mulk, on hearing this speech, was angry ; and, going to Álam Khán Lódí, told him what he had heard. At the same time, he advised him that Muháfiz Khán should be put to death, if he himself had a wish to live many days; and that the Sultán should be closely watched. Imádu-l-Mulk immediately after went to his jágír; but Álam Khán, Wajíhu-l-Mulk, and others, who were assembling troops for the purpose of having Muháfiz Khán put to death, resolved that they would not *salám* to the Sultán till such had been accomplished.

After burying Alá-ud-dín Lódí, the conspirators assembled in a mosque near the royal court, where, seating themselves, they besieged the Sultán for three days. At the end of this time, the latter, being no longer able to endure his confinement, sent to ask them why they were assembled. They unanimously answered, "they were the Sultán's servants, but that his confidant, Muháfiz Khán, who was not a proper person to serve him, must be delivered over to them." The Sultán would not consent to this, but soon after called these noblemen to him, that they might pay their respects. As one among them was in some way connected with Muháfiz Khán, the same sent to tell him that it would not be proper that he should be present at the meeting. The fool, either from pride or reliance on the Sultán's favour, did not attend to this warning; and, having accordingly come, stood behind the king's throne. When Álam

Khán Lódí saw him standing there, being no longer able to contain himself, he made a signal to his followers: on observing which, Muháfiz Khán, through fear of his life, took shelter below the throne. The mutineers, after dragging him by the hair of the head from below the throne, cut him in pieces; and, although the Sultán urged them to forbear, yet no one attended to his request. The latter, being quite petrified at this transaction, drew his dagger, with an intention of killing himself; and, although the conspirators almost immediately wrested the dagger from his hand, a small part of the point had however penetrated his belly. After dressing his wound, they gave him into custody, to be confined as before: and Álam Khán Lódí, with Wajíhu-l-Mulk, Mujáhid Khán, and Mujáhidu-l-Mulk, who were the principal nobles, were appointed to have charge of him. They, having conducted him to Ahmadábád, continued to watch him narrowly as before; but, as an intrigue had been now set on foot among themselves, their vexation was manifested at being thus obliged to guard him. After consulting what ought to be done, they proposed to blind him with a hot iron, and raise a child to the throne; but some said that there was n necessity for even a child; and that, by dividing the country among themselves, each might govern his own domain. It was, therefore, agreed on that the country should be divided, and that each should have a determinate portion in certain districts. This design was never accomplished; as one of them, Tátár Khán, privately told the Sultán what he had heard; and the Sultán, going with a party of horse at night, ordered that the houses of Álam Khán Lódí and Wajíhu-l-Mulk should be plundered. Those who were the leaders of the nobles consequently took to flight; and a detailed account of the same may be found in the Mirát Sikandarí. The Sultán, having again become master of his kingdom, gave the office of prime-minister to Asaf Khán, who had before held the same office under Sultán Bahádur; and who, with Khudáwand Khán and several others, were promoted to high offices.

As Álam Khán Lódí, after his flight, wrote to Daryá Khán, then living in poverty among the cities of the Dekhan, and requested he would join him, the latter, accordingly, came, and met Imádu-l-Mulk at Bhroch: but with this event the Sultán became anxious and uneasy. In the mean time a communication came from Imádu-l-Mulk, representing that as Álam Khán and Daryá Khán were old servants of his government, it would be wrong to allow them to go to Shír Sháh, the king of Dehlí, and that he should give them jágírs on the frontiers; where they might do him great service. To this proposition he agreed; but, as Álam Khán's brother, with his family, had fled, the fulfilment of the promise was delayed. The Sultán, being ever on the watch, lest Daryá Khan, Álam Khán, and Imádu-l-Mulk, should join to raise a disturbance in the country, ordered the latter to come to him with all possible expedition, in order that he might consult him on these matters. Sayyid Arab Sháh was accordingly despatched to Imádu-l-Mulk, who, having come to Chámpánír, with ten or twelve thousand cavalry, experienced the royal favour.

Soon after, it happened that some one at night set up the cry that it was the Sultán's order to plunder Imádu-l-Mulk. The people rushing from all quarters, in consequence of this false assertion, plundered Imádu-l-Mulk and his followers; on which the former, being much hurt at heart, and greatly injured, sought an asylum with Sayyid Mubárak. The Sultán, when made acquainted with this transaction, was much vexed; and, after causing those who had occasioned this commotion to be seized, ordered them to be executed. He also endea-

voured by every means to conciliate Imádu-l-Mulk; but, as he mentioned his intention of visiting the holy cities of Mekka and Medínah, the Sultán complied with his wishes, and forwarded him to the port of Súrat; where he was
A. Hij. 952, A.D. 1545. killed soon after, on the seventeenth of Ramazán, of the year Hijra 952, A.D. 1545.

Succeeding these events, the Sultán appointed Sayyid Mubárak to command a force against Daryá Khán and Álam Khán; and he, after gaining a battle, drove them from Gujarát, when they both went to Shír Sháh of Dehlí.

At this time, the Sultán abandoned the pleasures of the harem; and the government having thus received an accession of power, both nobles and soldiers fell so completely under its management, that they had not the power of disobeying. There was now some desire manifested of seizing on Málwa; but, when the Sultán consulted his minister, Asaf Khán, in this matter, he was told that he might obtain a country equal to Málwa by merely attaching a fourth of the Gujarát province, or that part called the apportioned lands, then possessed by Rájpúts, Grássias, and Kúlis. "If," said the minister, "that fourth was only brought under government management, it is sufficient, as a jágír, to maintain twenty-five thousand horse;"

and the order was accordingly given for its resumption. The Grássias of Ídur, Sirohí, Dúngarpúr, Bánswárah, Lonawárah, Rájpípalah, the banks of the Mahindrí river, and Halwad, began on this account to disturb the country. The parties of soldiers stationed at Sirohí, Ídur, and other places, were therefore ordered to extirpate the very name of Rájpút and Kúli from such places; excepting, however, those who were the armed police of the country, or such as were engaged in trade, and who were to be distinguished by a specific mark on the right arm. Should any of this class be found without this mark, they were to be executed.

In consequence of such orders, the Mohammedan faith obtained such a superiority in those parts, about the latter part of this reign, that no Hindú was allowed to ride on horseback through the city; and those on foot were not allowed to wear clothing, unless distinguished by a red patch of cloth sewed on the shoulder. They were, moreover, prevented from exhibiting any public marks of infidelity, such as the idolatries of the Húlí and Dewálí festivals. It is therefore related that after the villain Burhán murdered the Sultán, the Grássias and Kúlis set up an image of the murderer, which they worshipped, and addressed it, saying, "This is our protector, who has saved us from perdition."

The author of the Mirát Sikandarí, who has mentioned the Sultán's contemporaries and friends, says that he was a great friend to Fakírs, and that, having a great regard for the unfortunate among this class, he built many places for their reception, where servants were appointed to supply them with whatever they required. He was also wont to give the devout, frequenting mosques and colleges, good clothing during the winter season, and make them presents of coverlets. As many of the dissipated among them were, however, in the habit of selling the latter, he ordered that such should be made large enough for covering several persons, as they would not be then unanimous in their resolution to sell them.

The Sultán, having rid himself of the domi-
A. Hij. 953, A.D. 1546. neering nobles, set out, in A. Hij. 953, A.D. 1546, on a trip of pleasure to Mahmúdábád[r]; where he resolved on erecting some magnificent works, called the deer park. The latter, which was two farsangs long, and in breadth nearly as far as a horse could run, contained at each corner a palace, the walls and

(r) This city was founded by Mahmúd I, surnamed Bígarrah, in A. Hij. 880, A.D. 1475.

roof of which were gilded. On the right hand side of the doors, leading to each of these palaces, he caused a fine bazár to be made; where in every shop a Peri-faced damsel was stationed, to dispense to customers every thing which contributed to pleasure. The Sultán often, when engaged on a hunting party, was wont to entertain and amuse himself there with these fair damsels; and, once every year, from the 1st to the 12th of Rabí-ul-awal, the nativity of the Prophet Mohammed was celebrated, when all the Ulamás, Shaikhs, and learned men, attended the Court, and rehearsed the traditions. On the 12th day, the Sultán personated the Sharíf of Mekka in that assembly, after having ordered the whole to be fed at a banquet. This practice had been continued downwards from the time of Muzaffir II.

When Sultán Mahmúd II. had exerted himself at the celebration of this festival, held in the year of the Hijra 961, A.D. 1533-4, he retired to rest, after having taken farewell of the people then assembled. Having slept a little, he awoke, and called for some sherbet and water; when Burhán, whose office was to prepare these things, mixing poison with the draught, gave it to the Sultán. The latter soon after felt unwell, and, having vomited, asked

Burhán what kind of sherbet he had given him. The latter replied that, as the Sultán's illness had been solely brought on by his exertions, it was necessary for him to take rest, that he might drive it away. Another hour of the night passed, and the Sultán, again going to sleep, was murdered by Burhán with a dagger. This event happened on Friday, during the nativity of the Prophet, A. Hij. 962, A.D. 1554. As nearly eighteen years had passed from the time he was first enthroned, and as he was in his eleventh year, he must have attained his twenty-eighth year at the period of his death.

The wretch Burhán, with his wicked accomplices in this infamous transaction, resolved to finish the business, by concealing, in the antechamber of the royal apartments, a party of armed men, to whom instructions were given to kill every one who should approach. After this arrangement was made, a person was sent to Asaf Khán, the prime-minister, with a message to say "that the Sultán was calling him, and that he was on no account to make the least delay." The minister accordingly went; when Burhán, rising up, received him with much respect, telling him that it was the Sultán's order that he should wait in the ante-chamber, where the armed men had been concealed. The wretch soon after made the minister advance before him; and, whilst he himself drew back, the latter was slain on entering the ante-chamber: as was also Khudáwand Khán, who was sent for in the same manner. Itimád Khán had been also sent for; but he, wisely supposing that there was some pretence for doing so, went not. About the same time, another of the ministers, Afzal Khán, was sent for; on whom Burhán, seeing him approaching, began to smile, and flattered him, saying, "That if the Khán gave him his assistance, he would grant him whatsoever he might desire." To this, Afzal Khán replied, "Wretch! what are your thoughts? and what is this you talk of?" Burhán at length, despairing of gaining over Afzal Khán, caused him also to be put to death.

The wretch, having thus glutted his vile heart with these and many other murders, laid his hands on the royal treasure and effects; and, having dressed himself in fine attire, binding on his neck a collar of great value, studded with jewels, which had been worn by the Sultán, seated himself like a dog on the royal jewelled chair, making manifest the saying, "that the dog sits in the cook's place."

Having thus commenced to govern, he gave away the king's best horses as presents to his accomplices, along with their saddles, their gold and silver head-ornaments; and ordered that all the prisoners in jail should be set free. Those who joined him took the money and the horses, but, soon after seceding from his party, left him with only a few.

In the mean time, these events became generally known. The confidants of the late Sultán, such as Imádu-l-Mulk[s], the leader of the Turks, and Alagh Khán, chief of the Abyssinians, now went with all possible expedition to the palace, and, having locked up the treasure, gave it in charge to trustworthy persons. They next proceeded to expel Burhán; who, with those he had collected, came out; and as one of the nobles, named Shírwán Khán, had advanced in front, Burhán said to him, "Come on, Shírwán Khán; you have arrived in time!" To this the Khán replied, "I have indeed!" and, spurring on his horse, so cut him across the shoulder with his sword that he fell at his feet. All who were with him were also put to death.

Sayyid Mubárak now called together all the great nobles, such as Itimád Khán and others,

(s) This is the Imádu-l-Mulk mentioned in the Mirátu-l-Mamálik, who must not be confounded with him who died at Súrat. His original name was Malik Arslán.

that they might deliberate how government should be carried on. The late Sultán having left no heir behind, Rizá-ul-Mulk was despatched to Ahmadábád, to bring one of his relations, named Ahmad Khán. The messenger, who found him at a merchant's shop, purchasing grain, brought him accordingly to Mahmúdábád.

CHAPTER XI.

THE REIGN OF AHMAD KHÁN II. SON OF LATÍF KHÁN, WHO WAS GRANDSON OF SHUKÁR KHÁN, THE SON OF SULTÁN AHMAD I.

A. Hij. 961, 28th February, A.D. 1554.

On the 15th of Rabí-ul-awal, A. Hij. 961, A.D. 1554, Sayyid Mubárak, assisted by the grandees and great nobles of state, taking Ahmad Khán by the hand, placed him on the throne, and entitled him Ahmad Sultán. From this date, the Sultán confided much in Sayyid Mubárak, and Itimád Khán was made prime-minister.

As Ahmad Sultán was yet a minor, the nobles agreed to divide the treasure and country among each other, until he attained maturity; and every one in his own domain was to guard against disturbances of the public peace, and protect the frontiers. When Mubárak Sháh, of Khándesh, became aware of this state of affairs in Gujarát, he undertook an expedition to that quarter, and encamped with his army on the Nerbuddah, opposite Bhroch. The Gujarát nobles, marching thither, encamped opposite to him. After an interchange of messages between the parties, a peace was at length concluded, through the mediation of Sayyid Mubárak; when the nobles returned towards Ahmadábád; but, having soon after split into two factions, one of them joined Itimád Khán, and the other followed Násiru-l-Mulk. Sayyid Mubárak, who was a brave and honourable man, continued to support Itimád Khán. The two opposite factions continued watching each other, until they arrived in the neighbourhood of Baroda, where a battle was fought between Sayyid Mubárak and Násiru-l-Mulk, in which the former suffered a defeat. As this had happened in consequence of Itimád Khán having withheld his assistance, Sayyid Mubárak took his departure for his jágír of Kapparwanj; and the former, without fighting, soon after joined him at that place.

Násiru-l-Mulk carried Sultán Ahmad along with him; and, having entered Ahmadábád with uncontrolled power, administered the affairs of government in this manner for two months. At the end of that time, he carried his troops against Kapparwanj, for the purpose of expelling Sayyid Mubárak and Itimád Khán, who came out to oppose him. As Alagh Khán Habshí and Imádu-l-Mulk Rúmí, who had charge of the Sultán, came to the resolution, at this time, of going over with him to Sayyid Mubárak; and were afraid that, if Násiru-l-Mulk succeeded against the Sayyid and Itimád Khán, he would proceed against them in turn; they accordingly carried the Sultán over to the enemy, one morning at daybreak: in consequence of which Násiru-l-Mulk took to flight.

Sayyid Mubárak and Itimád Khán carried the Sultán with them to Ahmadábád: from whence they went in pursuit of Násiru-l-Mulk, who had gone into the mountainous country about Pál. Itimád Khán, on this occasion, appointed Ikhtiyáru-l-Mulk his deputy in Ahmadábád; but as the latter, two days after the departure of the Sultán with Itimád Khán, gave his support to a person named Sháhú, the Sultán's paternal uncle, discord was renewed afresh.

Sayyid Mubárak and the others, on being made acquainted with this proceeding, marched from Bhroch for Ahmadábád; but had only advanced as far as Mahmúdábád, when the supporters of Sháhú marched out to meet them. A battle having consequently taken place between the parties, at the town of Upráh, four koss distant from Ahmadábád, Sháhú and the rebellious nobles who supported him were put to flight. Sayyid Mubárak now carried the Sultán along with him, and entered Ahmadábád in triumph. Soon after, the nobles having divided the country in the manner agreed on[t], each took possession of his portion; whilst the Sultán and Itimád Khán remained at Ahmadábád, and were absolute there.

But, when was discord ever known to cease? About this time, Daryá Khán dying, his companion in exile, Álam Khán Lódí, who was with Shír Sháh of Dehlí, wrote to say that he could not remain there; and soon after, coming to Ahmadábád, endeavoured to bring about a union between himself and Sayyid Mubárak. Itimád Khán and Imádu-l-Mulk, who were now displeased with Sayyid Mubárak, had at length, through the intrigues and evil advice of Álam

(t) The division of the country here noticed is detailed in a note at the end of this chapter, supported by the authority of a contemporary historian. It is not the same division which took place during the reign of Muzaffir III., as mentioned by Ferishta, and subsequently in this work.

Khán Lódí, come prepared for war against him; and these nobles, having carried the Sultán along with them, went forth for battle. But, when it was known that Álam Khán Lódí had caused all this, a meeting took place between them, when the Sultán was again sent back to Sayyid Mubárak. Álam Khán Lódí now fled to the mountainous country about Pál; and the two commanders, after following him for some distance, returned to Chámpánír.

Mubárak Sháh, of Khándesh, on learning this state of affairs, again entered Gujarát with an army, and returned without effecting any thing. Though the Sultán, at this time, entertained several private servants, Itimád Khán and Imádu-l-Mulk retained the whole power of the government; and, as each strove for the superiority, the confidential servants of either alternately kept watch on the Sultán. The kings and nobles of Gujarát, who were now doomed to destruction by the will of God, ended the business by going to war with one another; and, though a treaty of agreement had been renewed, and sworn to falsely, they bartered their faith for the mean idea of gain. Sayyid Mubárak, who was peaceably inclined, continually endeavoured to mediate between them, and smother the flame of discord.

Some time had passed in this manner, when the enmity existing between Imádu-l-Mulk, Rúmí, and Itimád Khán, became apparent by the Sultán uniting himself with the former, in order that he might free himself from the control of the other. Itimád Khán, being vexed at this, went to Mubárak Sháh of Khándesh; and, bringing the latter along with him, advanced on Gujarát, when Sayyid Mubárak's good advice induced the Khán to return to his former situation of minister. The Sultán, having now no expectation of obtaining the direction of government affairs, through means of Imádu-l-Mulk, and perceiving that he must again fall into the power of Itimád Khán, came privately, with several friends, to Sayyid Mubárak, at Sayyidpúr, near Mahmúdábád, a place rendered flourishing by the Sayyid. The Sayyid, not being pleased at his coming in this manner, reproved his friends, and told them that they had acted improperly in bringing him in this way.

About this time, Hájí Khán, one of the best commanders of Islám Sháh, king of Dehlí, having left that capital, on account of its conquest by the troops of Humáyún Pádsháh, set out for Gujarát, with fifty thousand horse and one hundred elephants. The Khán, on his way hither, having engaged the Ráná, defeated him; when, being thus victorious, he turned towards Gujarát. As Itimád Khán and Imádu-l-Mulk supposed that Hájí Khán had come at the request of the Sultán and Sayyid Mubárak, they resolved on putting to death the latter, before the Hájí had yet joined Sayyid Mubárak and the Sultán. The two commanders accordingly marched out with thirty thousand cavalry, accompanied by guns; and, having encamped in the neighbourhood of Mahmúdábád, fought a battle there, after a frequent exchange of messages. On this occasion, Sayyid Mubárak was killed, and Sayyidpúr plundered. His family was, however, respected; as it is customary with the people of Gujarát, on such occasions, not to injure the honour of their opponent's family, however much they be their enemies or wish them evil.

The leaders, with their troops, having now separated, removed from one another a distance of ten or twelve koss; but parties from each camp continued to frequent the city. After some days, a peace was concluded, through the interference of mediators. In short, Sayyid Mírán, the son of Sayyid Mubárak, went to Kapparwanj, with his family and people, whilst the two commanders, taking the Sultán along with them, went to Ahmadábád, where they entered into a private treaty with each other.

Sayyid Mírán came to Ahmadábád, a short time after, having been requested to do so by Imádu-l-Mulk and Itimád Khán. As some fresh cause of disagreement between the two leaders happened at this time, the Sultán was again privately intriguing with Imádu-l-Mulk, who sent for his son, Jangíz Khán, from Bhroch. Itimád Khán also sent for Tátár Khán Ghází from Júnagarh; and, after having left Ahmadábád and collected an army in the neighbourhood, sent a message to Imádu-l-Mulk that he must leave the city, and go to his own personal estate. Imádu-l-Mulk, perceiving that he could not remain there, left it along with Alagh Khán Habshí, and went to Bhroch, on which occasion the latter obtained Baroda from him.

Itimád Khán now appointed his confidential friends to watch over the Sultán: and, being free from all responsibility and uneasiness with regard to governing, gave half the parganah of Karrí, in jágír, to Hájí Khán, whom he entertained in service. He also permitted Músá Khán and others to go to their own estates.

Intelligence was at this time received that Imádu-l-Mulk's brother-in-law, named Ikhtiyár Khán[u], who was then at Súrat, had put him to

(u) The person here noticed is called Khudáwand Khán by a contemporary, the author of the Tazkaratu-l-Mulúk, and had married

death; and that, some months after, the son of the former, Jangíz Khán, had revenged his father's murder by slaying his murderer. During these proceedings, Itimád Khán carried an army against Bhroch; but, immediately after, returned to Ahmadábád, on account of disturbances happening at this time in the Zillahs of Patan and Rádhanpúr. Itimád Khán was now employed in guarding against the Sultán's intrigues, as men from all quarters had collected in Gujarát, with whom the Sultán had a community of feeling. The minister, impressed with an idea that some calamity might happen, for which he might not be prepared, passed his time in much anxiety. As Sultán Ahmad was of an evil and subtile disposition, he would often, when drunk with wine, take a sword, and, cutting a plantain tree, would say, "I have cut off the head of Itimád Khán, and divided Imádu-l-Mulk's body into pieces." In this manner he spoke of several of the nobles; on which account, Wajíhu-l-Mulk, who was Itimád Khán's assistant, was continually advising them to put the Sultán to death, before he could effect any thing treacherous.

ried a daughter of Imádu-l-Mulk Malik Arslán. This same Khudáwand Khán was in possession of Súrat at this time, as appears from the mention of him by the Mirátu-l-Mamálik. (*Bombay Literary Transactions*, vol. ii., p. 1.)

Sultán Ahmad was at this time so powerful, as to be capable of riding three koss either for the sake of amusement or the chase; and, as he often came to Itimád Khán's house at unseasonable times, the Khán received him with fear and trembling. Although Wajíhu-l-Mulk continued to urge Itimád Khán to put the Sultán to death, he continued to delay the measure. One day, however, Wajíhu-l-Mulk sent a message to the Sultán, saying, that if a promise of succeeding as prime-minister was given him, he would put Itimád Khán to death. The Sultán, unconscious of any thing being intended, encouraged him by a promise of succeeding the minister; but, when Wajíhu-l-Mulk told this to Itimád Khan, he would not, he said, give credence to such a thing, without having heard it with his own ears. Wajíhu-l-Mulk, therefore, having carried the Khán at night time to a house near Bhaddar, concealed him in an antechamber; whence he sent this message to the Sultán, "that, as he could not venture to publicly meet the Sultán for fear of Itimád Khán's spies, he begged the latter would take the trouble of meeting him, in order that an agreement might be drawn up. Wajíhu-l-Mulk then prepared a royal seat for the Sultán at the door of the antechamber where he had concealed Itimád Khán. The Sultán

accordingly came and took his seat, when Wají-hu-l-Mulk recapitulated to him what he had before said, requesting that an agreement between them might be drawn up. The former, without hesitation, repeated all that had already passed between them; when Itimád Khán, who had overheard the whole conversation, presenting himself from the antechamber, asked the Sultán what he had ever done that he should conspire against his life. The Sultán, who became petrified with astonishment, was immediately killed by Itimád Khán's servants, who, according to order, inflicted on him several blows of a stick. Having afterwards taken up his dead body, they threw it on the sands of the Sabarmatí river, which is close by the houses of Bhaddar. These events happened on Monday,
April 12, A.D. 1561. the 5th of Shabán, A. Hij. 968, A.D. 1560-1 [x].

([x]) Rafí-ud-dín Shírází, author of the Tazkaratu-l-Mulúk, was in Ahmadábád at this time, and mentions the death of Ahmad Khán II. of Gujarát in these words; سلطان احمد کجراتي بعد از قتل سلطان محمود برتخت سلطنت قرار کرفت امّا از سلطنت همين نامي بود و منزلي از براي او تعين کرده بودند و چند خدمتکاران مقرر ساخته ديکر کسي‌را سلطان نميديد و اعتماد خان با جهجهار خان والغ خان حبشي ساخته در شهر مي‌بود و باقي امرا در ولايت خود دم استقلال مي‌زدند موسي خان و حاجي خان و ملک ارسلان عماد الملک در بهروچ و امين خان در بيچانکر

Those who found the body thought some of his intimate associates must have murdered the Sultán; and, on removing it from thence, it was buried in the vault of Sultán Ahmad I.

باستقلال تمام زندكاني ميكردند و سكه و خطبهٔ سلطان احمد روان مي‌داشتند و سلطان احمد در مدت هفت سال دو مرتبه از اعتماد خان كريخته پناه بامرا برد شايد كه بامداد ايشان استقلال پيدا كند چون قابليت اين كار نداشت كاري از پيش نبرد باز از ايشان كريخته پيش اعتماد خان آمد و بتاريخ سنه نهصد و شصت و هفت صبحي سلطان احمدرا بي‌سر در ميان رودي كه بر كنار شهر جاريست يافتند اتفاقا همان روز مسود اوراق بحوالي شهر احمد آباد رسيده خبر شنيد كه بوقت شب سلطانرا سر بريدند از اين سبب خوف وهراس بر طبعيت مستولي شد كه فتنه بر خاسته و آشوبي بهمرسيده انقلاب بسيار خواهد شد خودرا بشهر رسانيد چنانچه در شهر هيچ فتنه و آشوبي نبود ديكريرا بر جاي او نصب كرده بودند "After the murder of Sultán Mahmúd II. of Gujarát, Sultán Ahmad II. was seated on the throne; but the latter only possessed the name, without the power, of governing, as several of his servants had appointed a residence for him, where their associates were stationed, and permitted no other person to see him. The Sultán and Itimád Khán, with Jahjahár Khán and Alagh Khán, Abyssinians, occupied the capital, while the other nobles declared themselves independent on their own estates. Músá Khán, Hájí Khán, and Malik Arslán Imádu-l-Mulk in Bhroch, and Amír Khán in Bíjnagar [not Bíjnagar in the Dekhan, but the city of this name in Gujarát], enjoyed absolute authority, but read the *khutba* and coined money in the name of their sovereign. Sultán Ahmad, in the course of seven years, had twice escaped from Itimád Khán, and taken refuge with the other nobles, in order that, through their assistance, he might establish

Previously to the Sultán's murder, Beirám Khán had been murdered at the city of Patan, on his way to Mekka; as Arsh Ashiáni Akbar Pádsháh, on that very year, for the several reasons detailed in the Akbar-Námah, had given him permission to go to the Holy City, on a pilgrimage. Beirám Khán, on arriving at Patan, encamped there on the plain, intending to rest himself for some days. As Músá Khán Faoládí was at this time in uncontrolled power in that quarter, a crowd of Afgháns, who increased the disorders of the country, had collected about him. Among others, was a person named Mubárak Khán Lohání; who, as his father had been inadvertently killed, in the battle of Máchíwáráh, by Beirám Khán, was now determined to take revenge. The Afgháns accordingly excited a tumult, both on account of this occurrence, and

establish his own authority. Having failed in doing so, however, he left them, and returned to Itimád Khán, when, one morning, in A. Hij. 967, A.D. 1559, the people found Sultán Ahmad without a head, in a small water-course which flows near the city. The writer of these pages chanced at this time to arrive in the environs of Ahmadábád; when, having heard that they had beheaded the Sultán during the night, and being afraid that seditious risings and disturbances would follow, he went into the city, where neither sedition nor tumult existed, in consequence of a successor having been appointed."

because a Kashmírian woman, the wife of Selím Khán, by whom she had a daughter, after betrothing her to the son of Beirám Khán, was now accompanying him on his pilgrimage to Mekka. One day, Beirám Khán had gone to a pleasure seat, situated in the midst of a large lake, near the city; and had returned in the boat which had conveyed him there, when the above-mentioned Afghán, accompanied by thirty or forty others, arrived on the borders of the lake, just as Beirám Khán had mounted his horse. On this occasion, the dishonourable Afghán, though the Khán had requested the whole to come to him, so struck him on the back with a dagger that it passed out at his breast. The others, then drawing their swords, completed his business, and put him to death. His followers and attendants, distracted and astonished, took to flight; and left the Khán's bleeding body in the dust, where it was allowed to lie, until some Fakírs and inhabitants carried it away, and buried it near the mausoleum of Shaikh Hissám. This event happened on Friday, the 14th of Jumádá-ul-awal, A. Hij. 968,
22nd January. A.D. 1561. A.D. 1560-1.

Beirám Khán's body was afterwards carried to the holy Mashhad, and buried there, through the exertion of Hussain Kúli Khán.

After Beirám Khán's death, the robbers of Patan plundered his followers, and left them nothing. Khoájah Malik, and several others, who brought away Abdú-l-Karím, (son and rightful heir of the Khán,) with his mother, saved them from that calamity, and sent them to Ahmadábád; whence, after four months, they went to the capital, (Dehlí) by desire of the Emperor Akbar.

CHAPTER XII.

THE REIGN OF SULTÁN MUZAFFIR III, COMMONLY CALLED NATHÚ, WHO WAS THE LAST OF THE RACE OF GUJARÁT KINGS.

A. Hij. 968, A.D. 1561. After the murder of Sultán Ahmad in A. Hij. 968, A.D. 1561, Itimád Khán seated Muzaffir on the throne. According to the faith of most historians, Itimád Khán, who had all the power of government in his hands, seeing that there were none of the late Sultán's relations fit for the government, produced a young boy, named Nathú; and having in open assembly taken an oath that such was the son of Sultán Mahmúd II, he explained that his mother, when pregnant, had been delivered over to him, for the purpose of procuring an abortion; but that this child had been brought forth: as, five months of her pregnancy having passed, no abortion could take place. He said, moreover, that he had brought him up in secret, and that there was no heir to the government excepting him. Every one, assenting to this, and supporting his claim to the throne, entitled him Muzaffir Sháh.

After a lapse of some months, Itimád Khán carried an army against Músá Khán and Shír Khán Faoládí, at Patan, for the purpose of being revenged on Fat'h Khán Balúch. The nobles, now aware of the circumstances attending the Sultán's murder, were annoyed with Itimád Khán; and only remained attached to him through fear of their own lives. When the minister arrived at Patan, having given Músá Khán and Shír Khán battle, he sustained a defeat: and the nobles, without fighting, came back to Ahmadábád. Itimád Khán resolved again to raise troops, and exerted himself to the utmost, notwithstanding none of the nobles were on his side, and all of them had gone to their own estates. He, at length, proceeded against Músá Khán and Shír Khán, with the army he had; and after sustaining a second

defeat, came to Ahmadábád. These events hap-
A. Hij. 969, A.D. 1561-2. pened in A. Hij. 969, A.D. 1561-2.

Finally, enmity among the nobles, and a contest for superiority, happening at this time, Itimád Khán left the capital; and Jangíz Khán took possession of it, when he also was killed by the Abyssinians. An account of these things, and of the anarchy which was thus produced in the kingdom, may be found in the Mirát Sikandarí.

The victories gained in Gujarát by the army of Arsh-Áshiání Akbar Pádsháh, with the termination of Sultán Muzaffir's reign, and the government of Azím Mírzá Azíz Koká, for a
A. Hij. 1000, A.D. 1591. second time, in A. Hij. 1000, A.D. 1591, will be yet detailed. But now, please God, we may proceed to give a short account of the conquest of the country by Akbar, and of such things as happened under the rule of the Názims, who from that time were appointed to Gujarát. We, therefore, deem it necessary to write down whatever may have happened under the government of those permanently appointed to the office of Názim, or those acting as deputies for a time. And, as the Mirát Ahmadí principally consists of revenue regulations and assessments, with the greater part of the orders, issued and observed in settling the province in

the name of the collectors-general, the several Díwáns, under each individual reign, are therefore mentioned, along with the Názims, or provincial governors. From a deficiency of information regarding the Faujdárs and Ámildárs, any lengthened account of them has been omitted. Several of these are, however, occasionally mentioned: and, as the offices of revenue minister and governor were akin to each other, the account has been abridged accordingly.

SECTION III.

THE CONQUEST OF GUJARÁT BY THE EMPEROR AKBAR, WHEN IT WAS UNITED AS A PROVINCE TO THE MOGHUL EMPIRE OF DEHLÍ.

CHAPTER I.

A GENERAL ACCOUNT OF THE CELEBRATED DESCENDANTS OF SAHÍBI KIRÁN AMÍR TAIMÚR KÚRKÁN, WHO HAVE REIGNED IN HINDÚSTÁN.

It is truly wonderful to think on what a celebrated line of ancestry the members of this family can show ; whose forefathers, from Adam downwards, have been kings and emperors of great fortune and dignity. Such have been the habits of justice and equity, of beneficence and liberality, with which they have been endowed by the great Giver of all things, that, if inquirers into history will diligently search, they will find that the kings, princes, and potentates of the seven climates have derived their power from them. From them, also, contrary to the customs of other kings, every one travelling hither from Irán, Túrán, Rúmelia, Assyria, Arabia, and Abyssinia, obtains his desires. But, notwithstanding the amazing extent of their possessions, their power and opulence, it can never be said that they have either been so proud or arrogant as to treat with contempt the meanest of their servants; whilst they have also supported the usages of our exalted religion. It is related, that Sahíbi Kirán II., or Sháh Jahán Pádsháh, on the commencement of his reign, after seating himself on the Peacock throne, which cost one krore of rupees, equal to several years' revenue of Egypt, gave thanks to God, after having twice knelt, saying, "though Pharoah in Egypt, when on his ivory throne, claimed equality with the great God of truth, and said, 'I am thy God the highest,' yet, master as I am of such a country, I dare not address to him such language." How proper and becoming is such a faith!—and, by thus continuing to glorify God, we trust that he will continue to support this noble family on the throne. Wherefore, it has come to pass that, amidst the disturbances and revolutions which have happened throughout the world, both in Irán and Túrán, the princes of this family are still lords of Hindústán: for which we ought to be thankful.

As must be generally known, Amír Taimúr Sahíbi Kirán captured the capital of Hindústán,
A. Hij. 801, January, A.D. 1399. in the beginning of A. Hij. 801, A.D. 1398-9; and, after subduing the whole of the country in the course of a year, marched for his capital of Samarkand, at the end of that very year. Sultán Mahmúd Toghluk, who was then king of Dehlí, being defeated by Taimúr, fled to Gujarát, where Muzaffir Khán had assumed the style and title of a king; and, as Mahmúd Toghluk met with no encouragement in Gujarát, he went from thence to Málwa, as has been already detailed.

His Highness Firdaus-Makání Zahíru-d-dín Mohammed Bábar, who was the son of Omar Shaikh Mírzá, the son of Abú Saíd Mírzá, by Mírán Sháh, the son of Taimúr, having left Kábúl for the conquest of Hindústán, in the year of the Hijra 932, A.D. 1525-6, captured Dehlí

and Agra, with several other cities in the East. This happened about the latter part of the reign of Sultán Muzaffir II. of Gujarát, who was succeeded by Sultáns Sikandar and Bahádur; and, in the fifth year of the latter's reign, Bábar having departed this life, at Agra, on the 6th
A. Hij. 937, 25th Dec. A.D. 1530. of Jumádá-ul-awal, A. Hij. 937, A.D. 1530, was carried to Kábúl and buried there. Bábar therefore reigned about six years.

His son, Nasíru-d-dín Humáyún Pádsháh, named Jannat-Áshiání, succeeded him; and commenced his reign at Agra on the 9th of Jumádá-ul-awal, A. Hij. 937. The date of this event is contained in the words "Kheir-ul Mulúk;" and at this time Sultán Bahádur was reigning in Gujarát. As Humáyún was vexed with the latter, on account of the affair of Mohammed Zamán Mírzá; he brought an army against him in A. Hij. 941, A.D. 1534-5, while the latter was besieging Chitore; and, after defeating him, captured the fort of Chámpánír. These transactions are partly detailed in the Mirát Sikandarí, and more at length in the Akbar-Námah.

After a lapse of some years, Humáyún went to Irán; and, on his return from thence, in the middle of the month of Zú-l-hijjah,

Zú-l-hijjah then began 17th Sept. A.D. 1555. A. Hij. 962, A.D. 1555, took the country a second time from those who had rebelled against him, and made it wholly his own. In the mean time, Sultán Bahádur of Gujarát had been removed, Sultán Mahmúd II. killed, and Sultán Ahmad II. placed on the throne: when, on the 13th of Rabí-ul-awal, A. Hij. 963, Humáyún himself died, at Dehlí, and was buried there in the mausoleum, now called Humáyún's. His reign, from the time he was first enthroned in Hindústán, lasted twenty-five years, two months, and two days.

13th Rabí-ul-awal, 26th Jan. A.D. 1556.

After the decease of Humáyún, his son Arsh-Áshiání Jalálu-d-dín Mohammed Akbar commenced his reign, at the *ídgáh,* in the city of Kalanúr, about midday of Friday, the 2d of Rabí-us-sání; at which time Sultán Ahmad II. was reigning in Gujarát. On the 14th of the month of Rajab of A. Hij. 980, when thirteen complete years had elapsed from the beginning of the reign of Muzaffir III. the whole of the country of Gujarát came into possession of Akbar, as detailed hereafter, among the affairs of Hindústán. Akbar died on Wednesday, the 12th of Jumádá-s-sání, A. Hij. 1014; and was buried in the mausoleum, which exists at Sikandrah. His reign

14th February, A.D. 1556.

14th Rajab. 18th November, A.D. 1572.

15th October, A.D. 1605.

lasted fifty-one lunar years, two months, and nine days; during which time nine persons were appointed to the government of Gujarát.

His son, Jannat-Makání Núru-d-dín Mohammed Jahángír, succeeded him; and commenced his reign at Akbarábád, or Agra, on Friday the
17th Oct. O.S. 14th of Jumádá-s-sání of the above year. He died on the afternoon of Sunday the
28th Safar, 29th Oct. O.S. A.D. 1627. 28th of Safar, A. Hij. 1037, at the station of Jannak Hattí, when returning from Kashmír to Lahore, which was the seat of government. He was buried in the mausoleum near Lahore, after having reigned twenty-one years and a month. During this period eight persons were honoured with the government of Gujarát.

Sháh-Jahán Pádsháh, otherwise named Firdaus-Áshiání, and Sahíbi Kirán II., succeeded
13th Jumádá-s-sání, A. Hij. 1037, 11th Dec. O.S. A.D. 1627. his father Jahángír, on Friday the 12th of Jumádá-s-sání, A. Hij. 1037.
22nd Jan. O.S. A.D. 1666. He died on Monday the 26th of Rajab, A. Hij. 1076, A.D. 1665-6, and was buried in the mausoleum which exists at Akbarábád (Agra), after having reigned thirty-two years. For the last seven years of his life, he was kept under restraint, in the fort of Agra; during which time there were twelve persons who held the government of Gujarát.

On the death of Sháh-Jahán, his son, Mohei-ud-dín Mohammed Aurangzíb, otherwise named Khuld-Makání, succeeded to the government. He first commenced to date his reign at the
A. Hij. 1068. 1st Zú-l-kadah, 30th July, O.S. A.D. 1558. garden of Aiz Khán, on Friday the 1st of Zú-l-kadah, A. Hij. 1068[y]; and a second time, when the coins of the empire and the oration at the mosque were proclaimed
24th Ramazán, A. Hij. 1069, 24th June, O.S. A.D. 1659. under his title, corresponding to Sunday the 24th of Ramazán, A. Hij. 1069. This prince died at Ahmadnagar, a province of
27th Zú-l-kadah, A. Hij. 1118, 19th Feb. O.S, A.D. 1707. the Dekhan, on Sunday the 27th of Zú-l-kadah, A. Hij. 1118; and his body was sent from thence to Khuldábád, known by the name of Roza, where it was buried side by side of Burhánu-d-dín Auliá, in the mausoleum called after him. The length of his reign was fifty years, two months, and four days; during which time ten persons were sent as governors to Gujarát.

On the death of Aurangzíb, his son, Sháh Álam Bahádur, otherwise called Khuld-Manzal,

(y) This is not quite accurate, regarding the mode of reckoning Aurangzíb's personal era, as it also appears to be counted from A. Hij. 1067. The inscription placed by his order on the Mulki-Meidán, or great gun of Bíjapúr, is the 30th year of his reign, or A. Hij. 1097, A.D. 1686; and, as Bíjapúr was taken in Zú-l-kadah, the 11th Mohammedan month, he had just completed his 30th year from A. Hij. 1067.

succeeded under the title of Mohammed Moazzam; and, after his victory over Mohammed Azím, commenced his reign on the 19th of Rabí-ul-
9th June, O.S. A.D. 1707. awal, A. Hij. 1119, A.D. 1707, at the garden of Dhora, near Agra. He departed this
16th Feb. O.S. A.D. 1712. life on the 19th of Muharram, A. Hij. 1124; and was buried near the sepulchre of Khoájah Nasíru-d-dín, the lamp of Dehlí, which exists at Sháhjahánábád. The length of his reign was four years and nine months; during which time only one person came as governor to Gujarát.

Moizzu-d-dín Mohammed Jahándár Sháh, who now mounted the throne, commenced his reign
February. A.D. 1712. during the month of Muharram, A. Hij. 1124, in the neighbourhood of Lahore; and, dying one year, ten months, and twenty days afterwards, was buried in the mausoleum of Humáyún Pádsháh. During his reign, only one person obtained the government of Gujarát.

Abú-l-Muzaffir Moínu-d-dín Mohammed Farrukhsír, the son of Mohammed Azímu-d-dín, and grandson of Khuld-Manzal Bahádúr Pádsháh, after being victorious over his uncle, Jahándár Sháh, mounted the throne, in the neighbourhood of Agra, on the 13th of Zú-l-hijjah, A. Hij. 1124; at which time he ordered that the oration at the mosque should be pronounced, and coins struck in his name.

After having been put under restraint, he was
A. Hij. 1131. Rabí-ul-awal, 26th January, A.D. 1719. subsequently murdered on the 18th of Rabí-ul-awal, A. Hij. 1131[z]; and was buried in the mausoleum of Humáyún. The length of his reign, including that of Jahándár Sháh, was six years and twenty-five days; during which time there was no one honoured with the government of Gujarát.

9th May, O.S. A.D. 1719. On the 18th of Rabí-ul-awal, of the same year, Jannat-Arámgah Mohammed Rafí-ud-durját Pádsháh, son of Rafí-us-shán, and grandson of Khuld-Manzal Bahádur Pádsháh, mounted the throne, at Sháhjahánábád; and
9th May, O.S. A.D. 1719. died of a severe fever, on the 3d of Rajab following. He bequeathed the throne to his elder brother, after having reigned four months and fifteen days; and was buried in the mausoleum of Humáyún. During his reign, there was no change in the government of Gujarát.

His brother, Rafí-ud-dauláh, entitled Sháh Jahán II., another grandson of Bahádur Sháh, succeeded, according to the above will; and
26th May. commenced his reign on Sunday the 20th of Rajab of the same year. With a view

([z]) It would appear from Scott's Dekhan and Fraser's History of Nádir Sháh, that his death took place in February or Rabí-us-sání.

of quashing the rebellion of Mohammed Nekasír, having gone to Agra, he died in the month of September. Zú-l-kadah following. His reign lasted four months; during which time there was no change in the provincial government.

Násiru-d-dín Mohammed Sháh, a grandson of Bahádur Sháh, by his son, Jahán Sháh, next mounted the throne, and is otherwise styled Firdaus-Arámgah. When Sháh Jahán II. died, the minister Sayyid Abdallah Khán, with Hussein Alí Khán, chief of the nobles, and his brother Najjámu-d-dín Alí Khán, then governor of the province of Dehlí, wrote to Mohammed Roshan-Akhtar, requesting him to send, with all possible expedition, one of the princes who might fill the throne of his ancestors. The son of Jahán Sháh, having been accordingly selected, mounted the throne on the 15th of Zú-l-kadah, in that year, and assumed the title of Mohammed Sháh. He died in the month of Rabí-us-sání of the year Hijra 1161; and was buried in the sepulchre of Nizámu-d-dín Auliá, at Dehlí. The length of his reign, including the time from the first of Rafí-ud-durját, was thirty years and twenty-six days: during which period there were six persons who held the government of Gujarát.

His son, Mujáhidu-d-dín Ahmad Sháh, commenced his reign at the station of Gondrah, on

Sunday, the 1st of Jumádá-l-awal of the above year; after having returned from his victory over Ahmad Abdallí. In consequence of dissensions among the ministers, he was placed in

A. Hij. 1167. May, A.D. 1754. confinement, during the month of Shabán, A. Hij. 1167, A.D. 1754 [a], after a reign of six years, three months, and nine days, during which time Rájá Bakht Singh governed Gujarát.

On the very day that Ahmad Sháh was deposed, Arsh-Manzal Mohammed Álamgír II. was elevated to the throne, at Sháhjahánábád. He was subsequently murdered at the instigation of his minister, on Thursday, the 8th of Rabí-us-sání, of A. Hij. 1173, after having reigned five years, seven months, and twenty-seven days; during which time there was no governor sent to Gujarát, in consequence of Ballají Ráo Marat'ha having taken possession of it.

Succeeding this, Sháh Jahán Pádsháh III. was invested with the authority, on the very day of the murder; and with him ends our account of the descendants of Taimúr.

(a) Mr. Mills's history is out a year in this date, by giving A.D. 1753.

CHAPTER II.

THE COMMENCEMENT OF INSURRECTION IN GUJARÁT, THE ARRIVAL OF THE MÍRZÁS IN THE COUNTRY, THE TERMINATION OF THE POWER OF ITS KINGS, AND ITS INCORPORATION WITH THE KINGDOM OF HINDÚSTÁN, UNDER JALÁLU-D-DÍN MOHAMMED AKBAR.

The learned and observing well know that a cause for the decline of every empire, which has existed since the beginning of the world, may be found in the animosities of its nobles, assisted by rebellious subjects, whose mutiny and endeavours, thank God! generally revert on themselves, so that some more fortunate rival steps in and profits thereby.

Such was the end of the kings and nobles of Gujarát, as will be here explained. Fate having decreed the destruction of the government, its servants, by disregarding all sacred ties in the midst of rebellions, went to war among each other; so, under the semblance of friendship, they openly committed acts of hostility, until, at length, those parties being set aside, the powers and seals of this kingdom were transferred to the hands of the illustrious descendant of Taimúr Jalálu-d-dín Mohammed Akbar.

To be brief, Mohammed Hussein Mírzá,

Masúd Hussein Mírzá, and Aligh Hussein Mírzá, sons of Mohammed Sultán Mírzá, a descendant of Taimúr, after raising disturbances in the country of Hindústán (whilst their father, on account of old age, remained at his jágír of Sambal, in the Panjáb), were obliged to leave that quarter, in consequence of the advance of the imperial troops. They subsequently plundered several places; and, having put to death some Jágírdárs, invested the city of Dehlí. These proceedings gave rise to insurrections in the country, and many people were consequently oppressed. Akbar, on hearing what had taken place, advanced for the relief of Dehlí; and the Mírzás, after desisting from their attempts against that city, hastened into Málwa, which they subdued as far as Hindíah, taking the country from the Imperial Governor, Mohammed Kúli Bírlás. The Emperor now sent his victorious troops from Dehlí to exterminate the Mírzás; at which time the rebellious nobles of Gujarát, subsequently to the murder of Mahmúd II., had conferred the throne of that country on a child, said to be a grandson of Sultán Ahmad I., and who had no just claim to the government. The nobles, who gave him the title of Ahmad II., had retained all the power in their own hands; but, as he at this time arrived at man's estate, they completed his business, and elevated to power another child, who was said to be a son of Mahmúd II. The latter was entitled Muzaffir III.; and, though many knew the story of his birth to be a lie, they only talked of it, without doing any thing, as the nobles were then in absolute power. At this time, the latter divided the country among themselves, when Ahmadábád, with the port of Khambáyat, and much more of the country, was possessed by Itimád Khán; the sirkar of Patan by Músá Khán and Shír Khán Faoládí; the districts of Súrat, Bhroch, Chámpánír, and Baroda, by Jangíz Khán; Dhandúka and Dholka, with other parts, by Sayyid Hámid[b], the grandson of Sayyid Mubárak; and Júnagarh, with the country of Sorath, by Amír Khán Ghorí.

After these powerful but unworthy rulers had governed for some time, and had introduced every species of oppression and injustice, they began to quarrel and attack one another. As the Mírzás saw no prospect of being able to hold out against the imperial army in Málwa, they came into Gujarát during these disturbances, and sought an asylum with Jangíz Khán, at Bhroch. The latter was then carrying on war with Itimád Khán, in the neighbourhood of

(b) Briggs's Ferishta says, Sayyid Mírán, his son.

Ahmadábád ; and, being afraid that the Mírzás would plunder him, he conferred on them the district of Bhroch in jágír.

After this, Shujár Khán [c], having imprisoned Jangíz Khán at Ahmadábád, put him to death: on which the disturbances in Gujarát increased. The Mírzás, who deemed this a fit opportunity, captured the forts of Chámpánír and Súrat; and, having also taken possession of the fort of Bhroch, thus acquired power. Itimád Khán had at this time taken on himself the responsibility of governing, when Sultán Muzaffir III., at the instigation of Shír Khán Faoládí, flying from Ahmadábád, joined the latter at Patan. After effecting this junction, Sultán Muzaffir advanced against Ahmadábád, with an army; and Itimád Khán, now besieged, formed a union with the Mírzás: but, sending a message at the same time to Akbar, representing the state of affairs, entreated him to enter Gujarát, and take possession of the country.

Akbar, who now resolved on quelling these disturbances, commenced his preparations, for an expedition against Gujarát, on Tuesday the
A. Hij. 980. A.D. 1572. 20th of Safar, A. Hij. 980, A.D. 1572;

He is called Hajáz Khán in Briggs's copy of Ferishta, a mistake easily committed from the similarity of the letters in Persian.

and appointed Khán Kilán, Sayyid Mohammed Barhá, Kúlí Khán, Sádik Khán, and Sháh Fakh-ru-d-dín, with several other great chiefs, to command the army, sent in advance. The Emperor himself left Ajmír for Gujarát, on Monday the 22d of Rabí-us-sání; and, on the arrival of the troops at the station of Nagore, Khán Kilán, with the other commanders, went as ambassadors to Sirohí. The mad Rájá of this place, named Mán Singh, being intent on treachery, sent a friendly message to Khán Kilán. The deputation of Rájpúts who brought it had been received, and were about to take leave, when Khán Kilán, as was the custom in Hindústán, called each of them up, in order to receive the betel nut. At this time, a Rájpút, advancing to Khán Kilán, struck him so forcibly with a dagger, on the back of the shoulder, and at its lower part, that three fingers' length of the instrument appeared from below the shoulder-blade. One of Khán Kilán's attendants, named Bahádur Khán, seized the Rájpút, and threw him on the ground; when Sádik Khán and Mohammed Kalíj Khán finished his business with a sword, and put all who were with him to death.

The Emperor's army soon after joined the advance; and, as it was known how improperly the people of Sirohi had behaved, several brave men were ordered to go there, and extirpate the people. In consequence of this order, many of the Sirohí people were brought to ruin; and some took shelter in the defiles of the mountains; whilst several of those, called in Gujarát "Machators [d]," were put to death, at the Hindú temples.

The army had, at length, encamped in the neighbourhood of Patan; when Sháh Fakhru-d-dín was ordered to go and offer words of assurance to Itimád Khán; who, having written a friendly letter, requested that he might be permitted to come into the imperial camp. On the arrival of the troops near Dísa, it was reported that Shír Khán Faoládí, who invested Ahmadábád, had abandoned the siege of that place, on learning that the imperial army approached; and that, after hastening into the country of Sorath, he had sent his sons, Mohammed Khán and Baddar Khán, in order that they might station his family and domestics in a place of security. In the mean time, his sons, having sent his family and domestics in advance, turned towards Ídur; and Ibrahím Husain

(d) These would appear to have formed a caste of soldiers among the Rájpúts, much addicted to opium-eating, and ready for any desperate enterprize.

Mírzá, who had accompanied Itimád Khán's troops, returned to that part of the country which owed him allegiance: as the latter wished to submit. After this, the Emperor ordered Mán Singh to proceed, with a body of troops, and seize the family of Shír Khán Faoládí; but, although the Rájá came up with his baggage, and plundered it, the Khán's sons, who had previously received information of this movement, threw themselves into the defiles of the mountains, and escaped.

On Sunday the 1st of Rajab, in the above year, while the army was encamped at Patan, Hakím Ainu-l-Mulk and Mír Abú Túráb were sent to conduct Itimád Khán to camp. After their arrival at the town of Chotánáh, several representations were sent to the Emperor, informing him that Muzaffir Sháh Gujarátí III, who had separated from Shír Khán Faoládí, was then wandering about that neighbourhood. Wherefore, Mír Khán, Master of the Horse, with Faríd of the guard, Mír Abú Kásim Túmkín, and Karam Ali, were despatched to make him a prisoner. When they had advanced a short way, they seized his royal umbrella and canopy; and, after some search, found him hid in a field of grain. Having immediately seized him, they brought him to the

Emperor, who very benevolently granted his life, and gave him in charge to Karam Ali. But, on this subject, the author of the Mirát Sikandarí says, that Muzaffir came and submitted, previous to any of the Gujarát nobles doing so.

At this time, Sayyid Mohammed Bokhárí and Alagh Khán Habshí came with their people, in proof of their allegiance. Succeeding this, Sháh Fakhru-d-dín, Ainu-l-Mulk, and Mír Abú Túráb, came to represent that Itimád Khán, having sent in his submission, was on his way to pay his respects; and that he had previously sent them, with Wajíhu-l-Mulk and Mujáhid Khán, to appease the Emperor.

After this, Sháh Fakhru-d-dín hastened to Itimád Khán, accompanied by a crowd of attendants; and Hakím Ainu-l-Mulk followed him. The Gujarát nobles, having deliberated for some time, now came to the resolution of having coins struck, and the oration at the mosque pronounced in the name of Akbar.

Itimád Khán, on his arrival near Karri, a town distant from Ahmadábád twenty koss, sent forward Sháh Fakhru-d-dín, to declare his attachment to Akbar's government; and, on the following day, when the Emperor marched from Chotánáh, Khoájah Khán and Mír Abú

Túráb, were ordered to go and bring Itimád Khán to pay his respects. Itimád Khán came accordingly; on which occasion, the Emperor was mounted on a large elephant, escorted by foot soldiers. Subsequently, Ikhtiyáru-l-Mulk, Maliku-s-Shark, Shujár Khán Habshí, Wajíhu-l-Mulk, and Mujáhid Khán, came to pay their respects, and were each distinguished by marks of imperial favour, according to their rank. Itimád Khán and several others were directed to ride near the Emperor; and, when the imperial standards arrived at Karri, Sádik Khán, and several of those who had accepted service, were sent to Mahmúdábád, with a view of inducing Seifu-l-Mulk Habshí and others to come in and pay their respects.

As Akbar was solicitous to settle and protect the country, he at this time assembled all the Gujarát nobles; telling them, "that, as he had spared the country, through the intercession of Itimád Khán, he would grant whatever they should ask through him; but that they must give respectable security to preserve the peace of the country." Mír Abú Túráb became Itimád Khán's security; and the latter became security for all the others, excepting the class of Abyssinians. As the latter were the slaves of Sultán Mahmúd, the Emperor ordered that they should be numbered among those belonging to himself, and that there would be consequently no occasion for bail. Soon after, however, he ordered that they should be distributed among the great officers of state, to perform the different duties connected with the government.

The army encamped the next day at Hájípúr, when a set of vagabonds raised a cry that there was an order for plundering the Gujarát camp. A crowd of men given to robbery consequently entered the Gujarát line, and plundered it, on which occasion a great tumult was produced. When this dishonourable affair was represented to the Emperor, he ordered that the quartermasters and their deputies should see the robbers punished, and not permit one to be left alive. Wherefore, all the things plundered from the Gujarátís were recovered, and given to the rightful owners.

The Emperor at this time, mounting a throne, gave a general audience to the people; and ordered all concerned in the plunder to be trampled under the feet of furious elephants. Confidence and tranquillity being thus restored, the imperial colours were pitched soon after, within sight of Ahmadábád, on the 14th of
18th November, A.D. 1572. Rajab, in A. Hij. 980, A.D. 1572; when a crowd of people, both high and low, came separately to pay their respects.

Thus was Gujarát conquered without a battle;

and which is in every respect allowed to be the finest country of Hindústán. Such was once its populous state, that it contained three hundred and eighty púrahs; and a púrah is itself a considerable quarter, containing good buildings and bazárs, filled with every thing valuable and rare, so that each is almost a city.

Some days after, Amín Khán Ghorí sent a letter, with a suitable tribute; and, though Ibrahím Husain Mírzá also sent a tribute, the latter was not accepted, as the Emperor did not think it was given with a sincere intention. The government of Ahmadábád, with the settlement of the country, was now entrusted to the great Khán Mírzá Azíz Koká; who received, in jágír, the parganahs situated on this side of the river Mahindrí. The other parganahs, such as Baroda, Chámpánír, Súrat, and others, then in possession of the Mírzás, were given to the Gujarát nobles, who had lately renewed their allegiance, and now undertook the task of driving out the Mírzás.

Some days afterwards, the Emperor, desirous of having some amusement on the sea, marched for Khambáyat, on the 2d of Shabán. The nobles of Gujarát remained behind some days at Ahmadábád, and asked permission to do so, that they might prepare for the journey. Hakím Ainu-l-Mulk, who had formed a friendship with them, was left behind to watch, and bring them along with him. The Emperor, while on the road, received intelligence that Ikhtiyáru-l-Mulk had fled to Lúnawáráh, and that Itimád Khán and other Gujarátís were irresolute, and disposed to be ungrateful for the benefits they had received. Shábáz Khán was accordingly ordered to proceed, with all possible expedition, to Ahmadábád, so as not to give them an opportunity of being treacherous, and was instructed to collect them, and bring them along with him.

When the Emperor arrived at Khambáyat, he was met and welcomed by the merchants and inhabitants of the place; and soon after, going on board a boat, he amused himself with sailing on the sea. After Shábáz Khán had returned with Itimád Khán and the other Gujarát nobles, Akbar, with a view of preserving the peace of the country, and preventing quarrels in the government, stationed one of his own confidential people with each of the Gujarát nobles.

Being now at leisure, the Emperor proposed to drive out the aggressive Mírzás; and appointed Husain Khán, the paymaster of the army, to be governor of Khambáyat. On leaving this place, the imperial banners went to Baroda; from whence Mírzá Azíz Koká took his departure for his government of Ahmadábád, whilst Shábáz Khán, Kásim Khán, Báz

Bahádur Khán, and an army of brave soldiers, were sent to capture Chámpánir. As it was reported at Baroda that the Mírzás had strengthened the fort of Súrat, and had joined their forces at Chámpánír, a large part of the imperial nobles and troops was necessarily sent there.

At this time, news arrived that Ibrahím Husain Mírzá was still in the fort of Bhroch, and was thinking of leaving it, with several others, to disturb the neighbouring country. The road by which he must pass was only eight koss distant from the imperial camp; and, though several of the great commanders, with their troops, had been already appointed to serve under Khání Azím Koká, and to drive out the Mírzás, leaving only a few select men with the Emperor, he himself resolved to go and punish Ibrahím Husain Mírzá with all possible despatch. Shábáz Khán Mír Bakhshí was therefore ordered to immediately proceed and order back the great commanders who had been previously sent to drive out the Mírzás, but who were now to join the Emperor. Mír Mohammed Khán, Khoájah Jahán, Shujár Khán, and Sádik Khán, were left behind in charge of the camp, whilst the imperial banners advanced against the Mírzá. It was also ordered that none from camp should follow in the rear of the party, lest the magnitude of its numbers might cause the enemy to resolve on flight; who, if they observed the smallness of the Emperor's party, would probably make a stand, and thus bring about their own punishment.

Two or three hours of the night had elapsed, when the Emperor, placing a firm reliance on God, mounted his horse, and, taking along with him, as a guide, Maliku-s-Shark Gujarátí, proceeded at a brisk pace. He continued to push on till the evening of the succeeding day had nearly closed, without seeing any thing of the enemy, when a Bráhman at length appearing, said that Ibrahím Husain Mírzá, having crossed the Mahindrí, by the ford of Bíakápúr, was encamped at the town of Sartál, with his troops, and was distant nearly four koss. The Emperor asked his followers, who were ready to die with him, what he might best do. Jalál Khán said, "that it would not be proper to attack the enemy in open day, before all the imperial troops had yet arrived; and, as their opponents were now on the alert, a night attack would be advisable." This advice was not approved of by the Emperor, who truly said, "that night murder formed no part of a good government, and that it would be better if he now attacked."

The town of Sartál, which is on a rising

ground, may be seen from a distance. When the troops came to the Mahindrí, they received orders to put on their quilted cotton jackets; and, at this time, Akbar had not more than forty persons with him. Immediately after that, however, intelligence of the remaining troops being close by was received; but, as the Emperor was annoyed at this delay, he angrily ordered that these men should not accompany him into battle. When he ascertained that the delay had arisen from having mistaken the road, however, he forgave them. After this junction, the party numbered about two hundred men, when the son of Mán Singh, with a few others, was sent in advance to cross the river.

Ibrahím Husain Mírzá, on perceiving the troops, knew that they were the Emperor's; and, resolving to stand a battle, took a position for his men on a rising ground, where he placed a gun. The imperial troops had received orders to cross the river at a place where there was much broken ground, called in the language of Gujarát Gotár; and, in their eagerness to advance, had taken different ways, so that the Emperor, with only a few associates, advanced to the gates of Sartál, which faced the river. The enemy, who possessed the place, endeavoured to drive them back; but Mukbil Khán

Kalmák and others, making a push at them, killed several. The Emperor, followed by those who accompanied him, entered the streets of the town, which were filled with quadrupeds and beasts of burden ; and, after squeezing through these with much difficulty, met the enemy and engaged them.

At this time, Bábá Khán Kákshál and several others were carried off by the enemy ; but the rest, defending themselves with the most obstinate bravery, slew many of their opponents. Several of those who had been kept back by the broken ground now arrived, when a smart action took place. The Emperor, on advancing to drive off his opponents, came to a bound hedge of euphorbium, where three of the enemy met him. One of these impelled his spear against Rájá Bhagwándás ; but the Rájá, having turned it aside, killed him. The two others made a push at the Emperor, but luckily did not reach him ; as Khán Álam, Sháh Kúlí Khán, and others, were at hand to give their assistance. Akbar, after causing the bay horse on which he rode to leap the euphorbium hedge, ordered a charge to be made against the two horsemen ; who, seeing that they could not resist, took to flight. Ibrahím Husain Mírzá, observing the success of the imperial party, also took to flight ;

and the remainder of his scattered followers retired, when the imperial party, pursuing, cut them down like grass. In this manner was the Emperor left victorious.

The troops encamped for the night at Sartál; whence Sháh Rúkh Bádakhshí was sent forward to announce the victory. The imperial troops returned to camp the following day, when Sháh Kúlí Khán and Sádik Khán were appointed to command an army, in advance against the fort of Súrat. After the troops had arrived in the neighbourhood of the place, Gúl Rúkh Begum, daughter of Mírzá Kámrán, and wife of Ibrahím Husain Mírzá, fled to the Dekhan; taking with her her son, Muzaffir Husain Mírzá. Though several of the nobles endeavoured to overtake her, none succeeded in the attempt.

At this time, some one represented to the Emperor that the Mírzás had strengthened the fort of Súrat, and had given it in charge to Hamzabán, who had been the imperial armour-bearer, and had joined the rebels. Akbar therefore determined to make the greatest possible exertions for its capture: and ordered Rája Todar Mall to arrange the disposition of the intrenched lines. Sháhm Khán Jalláir, who was made governor of Chámpánír, being allowed to depart for that place, was ordered to send from there the admiral, Kásim Khán, to join the Emperor; as the latter was very experienced in sapping[e] and mining. An order was also sent to Khán Azíz Koká, that he must exert himself in protecting Ahmadábád and other cities; and must punish the Mírzás, should they take flight in that direction. Shír Beg was also appointed to collect the revenue of Málwa, in order that Kutbu-d-dín, with the Zamíndárs of that quarter, might come to assist Khán Azíz Koká.

THE CAPTURE OF SÚRAT.

The Emperor's army encamped before Súrat
19th January, A.D. 1573. on Monday, the 17th of Ramazán, in the above year; and the besieged, vainly trusting to the abundance of their provisions, exerted themselves in defence of the place. Among the events which happened at this time, we may mention the capture of the Mírzá's elephants and baggage; which was effected in the following manner. These unhappy men, during the period of confusion, when they had separated, sent several elephants with their effects to Ráná Rám Deo, the Zamíndár of that part of the country, in order that he might take care of

(e) The practice of *sabat*, here translated sapping, is the construction of protected zig-zags of approach. An account may be found in Briggs's Ferishta, vol. ii. p. 230.

them; when the whole consequently fell into the hands of some camp followers, who had gone out on a plundering expedition. These men, who brought the whole to the Emperor, were all rewarded.

The other event which happened at this time was that of the nobles being sent to Agra; and of which the circumstances are these. Ibrahím Husain Mírzá, after his late defeat, joined Mohammed Husain Mírzá and Sháh Mírzá at Patan; but, as a dispute among the brothers happened there, at which Ibrahím Husain Mírzá was annoyed, he formed the resolution of undertaking an expedition against Agra. The Emperor, on learning his intentions, appointed Sayyid Mohammed Khán Barhá, Sháh Kúlí Khán Muharram, and Rájá Bhagwándas, to pursue and seize him; but the Mírzá soon after met his end in the vicinity of Multán.

The other two Mírzás now strengthened their connexion with the Faoládís, and went to Patan, where Sayyid Ahmad Khán exerted himself to maintain the imperial interest. Khán Azíz Koká, on learning this state of affairs, began to collect an army; when, by great good luck, Kutbu-d-dín Mohammed Khán, Súbahdár of Málwa, with the Zamíndárs from that quarter, joined Khán Azíz Koká, as did also Shaikh Mohammed Bokhárí, who was on his way from Dholka to join the Emperor.

Khán Azíz Koká now marched to Patan, where a battle took place between the two sides; in which the enemy's right, by advancing sharply against the imperial left, drove back several of Kutbu-d-dín Mohammed Khán's men. The Khán, with a select few, after most brave exertions and a severe contest, repulsed this attack of the Mírzás; who betook themselves to flight, and went towards the Dekhan, whilst Shír Khán Faoládí fled to Júnagarh. Khán Azíz Koká and the others resolved to pursue them; but, when the Emperor received the glad tidings of this fresh victory, he issued an order that Khán Azíz Koká should repair to court, while Kutbu-d-dín Mohammed Khán, Sháh Búdagh Khán, Murad Khán, and others, followed the Mírzás. Wherefore, Khán Azíz Koká obeyed the order; and, meeting the Emperor on the
21st February, A.D. 1573. 20th of Shawál, received many marks of the imperial favour.

At this time, the besieged, in the fort of Súrat, wishing to save themselves, were endeavouring to effect a union with the Portuguese at Goa, and had written to say that, if they came quickly to their assistance, they would give them up the fort. The Portuguese, under the pretence of an embassy, sent agents to Súrat, with rarities and valuables of their own country; who were instructed to get possession of the fort if possible, without disclosing their intentions; but, in the event of not obtaining their object, they were to pretend having come on a friendly embassy to the Emperor. They accordingly came; and, after observing the great train and power accompanying the Emperor, gave up all thoughts of the fort; but, assuming the name of ambassadors, paid their respects to Akbar, and presented a peshkah. They received in return many marks of favour, and were allowed to depart.

One month and seventeen days had been spent in besieging Súrat: at which time the mines were advanced to the door of the place, and the mounds for carrying it had been all prepared. The besieged despaired of assistance from any quarter; when Hamzabán sent a message to the Emperor, through his father-in-law, Múlá Nizámu-d-dín Lárí, saying that if his life was spared he would surrender the fort. Kásim Ali Khán and Khoájah Daolat were therefore ordered to promise safety to Hamzabán and the others, and were directed to conduct them to the Emperor. All of them appeared before him on Thursday the 23d of Shawál, in the above year ; and, being much ashamed of their conduct, had their lives and property respected. But Hamzabán, who was a great talker, and a foolish prattling fellow, had used no measured language in regard to the Emperor, and was doomed to lose his tongue. The following day, the imperial troops, accompanied by Akbar, walked into the fort, where they found a large gun, called Suleimání[f], of which the model was so exquisitive, that an order was given to have it transported to the capital of Agra. This is the very gun which belonged to Salím (Selim), the Emperor of Constantinople, whose troops were sent with several large guns to take the ports on the shores of Hindústán from the Europeans : but returned without effecting anything, as the force was discomfited, and received no assistance from the rulers of Gujarát. The Emperor not finding means for transporting the gun from Súrat, it consequently remains there.

A strange event happened at this time, when the Emperor was wounded in the hand, of which the following is an account. One night he was

([f]) It was so called from Suleimán I. of Constantinople, who reigned from A.D. 1520 to 1566; and who sent an expedition here mentioned from the Persian Gulf A.D.1553. The account of it is written in the Mirátu-l-Mamálik (See *Bombay Transactions*, vol. ii.)

elevated with wine, in an assembly of his friends, when the conversation turned on the carelessness which the Rájpúts manifest in regard to life. Some one said, such was their disregard of it, that two of them, when engaged, would run their breasts against a double-headed spear, held by a third person, until the same had gone through them; and that, in this manner, they would continue fighting with one another. On this, Akbar, who was bold and daring, fixing a sharp sword in the wall by its handle, and having the point towards himself, said that no one could better follow the example of the Rájpúts than he, as would be seen by his running against the sword. Those present, though astonished at this conduct, were afraid to speak for fear of offending him, and remained silent, until Ráná Mán Singh, in the sincerity of friendship, running forward, struck the sword so forcibly from the Emperor's hand, that it wounded him betwixt the thumb and forefinger. The latter, who was much enraged, threw Mán Singh on the ground; when Sayyid Muzaffir Sultán, brother of Sayyid Abdúlah Khán, imprudently released Mán Singh from the Emperor's gripe. During this scuffle, the wound became much enlarged; but this being soon healed, the Emperor was again able to join society.

Akbar, after the capture of Súrat, gave Kalíj Khán charge of the place; and on Monday
6th March, A.D. 1573. the 4th of Zú-l-kadah, marched back towards Ahmadábád. On his arrival at Bhroch, the mother of Jangíz Khán came to implore assistance against Shujár Khán Habshí, who had put her son to death under the cloak of friendship. On its being fully ascertained that Shujár Khán had committed an unjust murder, he was trod to death by the foot of an elephant. The troops arrived at Ahmadábád on the 29th
31st March, A.D. 1573. of the above month, when the Emperor began to make a settlement of the country.

CHAPTER III.

THE RETURN OF THE IMPERIAL BANNERS TO THE CAPITAL OF AGRA, AND THE APPOINTMENT OF KHÁN AZÍZ KOKÁ TO THE GOVERNMENT OF GUJARÁT, WITH WAJÍHU-L-MULK GUJARÁTÍ AS HIS DÍWÁN.

As soon as the Emperor has effected a settlement of the conquered territory of Gujarát, he conferred the government on Khán Azíz Koká, who was raised to the rank of five thousand; and was the first Súbahdár in this part, under the authority of Taimúr's family. The town, suburbs, and parganah of Ahmadábád, with the parganah of Pitlád, and other districts, were assigned him as a jágír. Núrang-Khán obtained Baroda, and Mír Mohammed Kilán, the uncle of Khán Azíz Koká, received the sirkar of Patan. Bhroch and the country round about were given to Kutbu-d-dín Mohammed Khán; and Dholka and Dhandúkáh were bestowed on Hámid Khán Bokhárí. In this manner the whole of the country was divided among the great nobles.

10th April, A.D. 1573. On Monday the 10th of Zú-l-hijjah, the Emperor set out for the capital of Agra by way of Patan and Jalore. Khán Azíz Koká, and the great nobles who had been appointed to situations in Gujarát, after being honoured with marks of distinction, were allowed to return from the neighbourhood of Sidhpúr.

Khán Azíz Koká, on his way back, heard that Ikhtiyáru-l-Mulk, through the assistance of Rái Náráyan, Zamíndár of Ídur, was creating disturbances in that neighbourhood, and that the sons of Shír Khán Faoládí, who were with him, were similarly engaged. The Khán, instead of returning to Ahmadábád, resolved to go in that direction, and drive out the enemy. The latter had collected in such force that Mírzá Mokím, who had a jágír in these parts, was obliged to quit his post, and joined Khán Azíz Koká, at Ahmadnagar, ten koss distant from Ídur. Mohammed Husain Mírzá, then in the neighbourhood of Daolatábád, on being made acquainted with Akbar's marching back to Agra, took this opportunity of advancing to the neighbourhood of Súrat, where he besieged Kalíj Khán in the fort. The latter did all that was necessary for the safety of the place, and the Mírzá, seeing no prospect of its capture, desisted from investing it. From thence he went to Bhroch, and obtained possession of it, from the faithless followers of Kutbu-d-dín Mohammed Khán, who was then at Baroda. Afterwards, going to Khambáyat, he became possessed of it, through the folly of Husain Khán, who offered him no opposition.

Husain Khán, then commandant of Khambáyat, went to Ahmadábád; from whence Khán Azíz Koká sent along with him Sayyid Hámid Bokhárí, Sayyid Bahá-ud-dín, and Shaikh Mohammed Múngírí, to assist Kutbu-d-dín Mohammed Khán in expelling Mohammed Husain Mírzá, then at Khambáyat, with six hundred cavalry. The above mentioned joined Kutbu-d-dín Mohammed Khán at the station of Samlí, five koss distant from the town of Dholka. At this time, Ikhtiyáru-l-Mulk advanced with a force from the fortresses of the mountains, when Khán Azíz Koká took up a strong position, where the rebels could not assail him. The enemy, having no other choice left, resolved on going to Ahmadábád, with the expectation of either possessing themselves of that place, or of being able to draw the Khán from his position, and bring on a battle. They therefore marched with this intent; but Khán Azíz Koká, well aware of their plans, set out for Ahmadábád late in the day, when the enemy could not attack him; and, after marching all night, entered the city next morning. On that very night, Mohammed Husain Mírzá, having been defeated and driven from Khambáyat, passed near Khán Azíz Koká's troops; when some of his baggage fell into possession of the latter. The Mírzá himself, now quite ruined, kept at a greater distance, and went to join the sons of Shír Khán Faoládí.

The account of Mohammed Husain Mírzá's defeat is the following. When Kutbu-d-dín Mohammed Khán, with Sayyid Hámid Khán Bokhárí, reached Khambáyat, the Mírzá engaged the imperial party, with the few men he had, but was defeated and quite ruined. The victors, thinking that they had done enough in defeating him, made no subsequent effort in pursuit: for, had they done so, they must have taken him prisoner. The latter, at length, formed a junction with the other rebels, and made every effort to reach Ahmadábád; but, three days having been spent by the Gujarátís in debating what ought to be done, Khán Azíz Koká, by great exertions, had in that time strengthened the place. The Gujarát nobles, at length, arrived before it, when continual skirmishes followed betwixt the imperial troops and the enemy. No general engagement, however, took place, as Khán Azíz Koká had not confidence in his own followers, nor in those of Kutbu-d-dín Mohammed Khán. He was, moreover, dissuaded from engaging the enemy, as the Emperor had particularly cautioned him against risking a battle in the event of disturbances, and requested that he would send to him immediately.

CHAPTER IV.

THE ARRIVAL OF THE EMPEROR, IN NINE DAYS, FROM THE SEAT OF GOVERNMENT, THEN AT FAT'HPÚR.

The Emperor, on hearing of the disturbances in Gujarát, determined to proceed to that quarter, with all possible expedition: and, as the shortness of the time would not allow of much preparation for the journey, he opened the doors of the treasury, to distribute as presents large sums of money among his attendants. He also issued a mandate that the chiefs of Málwa should expeditiously enter Gujarát; after which he himself set out, for that quarter,

24th July, A.D. 1573. on Sunday the 24th[g] of Rabí-ul-awal, in the year of the Hijra 981, A.D. 1573, being accompanied by a few faithful and select attendants, who were mounted on swift camels, or fleet horses.

On Monday the 25th, he arrived at Húns; and, proceeding by Moizzábád, pitched his tents at Ajmír, on the following Tuesday, when he visited the tomb of Moayyanu-d-dín Chístí. On Wednesday he was at Mírthá; from whence he went forward the same night; and, after halting to rest a little at Sojat, arrived, the following morning, in the neighbourhood of Banháriah, which is a dependancy of Jalore. Early on the morning of Friday, he reached Jalore; and, having halted there to the middle of the following night, he proceeded on a fleet steed, till he displayed his banners at the town of Dísa, on the following Monday. Here Sháh Ali Lingá,

(g) The Maásiru-l-Omará, in the life of Mírzá Azíz Koká, says it was the 4th of this month.

who was in authority at Patan, on the part of Khán Kilán, paid his respects to the Emperor. His Highness, having resolved not to go to Patan, ordered Khoájah Ghiásu-d-dín to join him, with the troops from thence; and, after leaving this place, arrived at the town of Bálísánah about noon, where the troops encamped. Here Khán Kilán, Wazír Khán, and Sháh Fakhru-d-dín, with the troops previously sent to prevent disturbances, then openly manifested, came and paid their respects, they having halted at Patan, on account of the dangers on the road.

The troops were now furnished with every thing they required. The Emperor, accompanied by a guard of a hundred horsemen, left this place on the evening of the same day, after sending a messenger to Ahmadábád, in order to tell the besieged that, as he was near at hand, they might prepare for war, and join him on his arrival. He continued to proceed on horseback at a quick pace, and arrived, a little after daybreak of Tuesday, at the town of Chotánáh, which is a dependancy of Karri. A party of the enemy, stationed there under the command of Auliá Khán, a follower of Shír Khán Faoládí, thinking that the imperial troops were those of Khán Kilán from Patan, came out and prepared for battle; but the former, having been ordered out against them, killed many; though the remainder, who fled, took shelter in the fort. The army was anxious to take the place; but the Emperor, who came up at this time, told them that he had not exerted himself, and taken all this trouble, in order to capture so insignificant a fortification, since he had come to punish the rebels of Gujarát, and that, after such had been accomplished, this fort would be captured without any difficulty. The troops were therefore ordered to quit the place, and continue to advance.

On Wednesday, when he had come to within three koss of Ahmadábád, he sent forward Asif Khán, in order to tell Khán Azíz Koká the glad tidings of his approach, and that he should be prepared accordingly. As the army now approached the enemy, he put on his armour, and mounted a white charger; at which time Rájá Bhagwándás came up, and congratulated him on the conquest of Gujarát, saying that he had observed three signs of his being victorious—1st, that the Emperor should be mounted on horseback at such a time—2nd, that the wind should be blowing from the rear of the troops, and wafting their inclinations against the faces of the enemy—3rd, that crowds of crows and kites continued to follow him.

The Emperor was pleased at these remarks; and, having thus terminated his march, in the space of nine days, prepared for battle, on Wednesday, the 5th of Jumádá-s-sání. As he approached the enemy, and saw no appearance of the Gujarát troops under Khán Azíz Koká joining him, he ordered the war-drum to be beaten. The enemy, proud of their numbers, amounting to more than twenty thousand persons, had closely invested the place, and were looking for Shír Khán Faoládí joining them. They were now, however, distressed by the arrival of the imperial troops, who were, at this time, ordered to cross the river in the order of formation they were then in. When the nobles beheld the numbers of the Gujarát army, they hesitated to advance. At this time, six hundred of the enemy's horsemen, having retired from Sirkej, came into view of the imperial musketmen, such as Sálbáhan, Kaddam Kúli, and Ranjít, who were ordered by the Emperor to direct a fire against them. The enemy, not able to make a stand, hastened to take shelter behind their intrenchments.

The Gujarát troops, on first hearing the sound of the imperial trumpets and war-drums, thought that either Shír Khán Faoládí had arrived, or that the troops of Khán Kilán had come from Patan to assist Khán Azíz Koká. Mohammed

Husain Mírzá, distracted with the noise, advanced before the others, and demanded in a loud voice to know of Subhán Kúli Turk, then on the bank of the river, What troops were these? To this the Turk replied (on seeing that the enemy were panic-struck), "Behold this army is commanded by the Emperor in person, and why do you abide to ask the question?" To this the other answered, "What! do you wish to intimidate me, by telling me this is the Emperor? And if this be he, where are his elephants and large army? Besides, only fourteen days have elapsed since my spies came from the capital of Fat'h-púr, and left him there." The Turk then said, "The Emperor, with a devoted few, had made the journey in nine days;" and the other, convinced that he spoke the truth, hastened back to his own camp, that the line might be got under arms.

The Emperor, now aware that the enemy had remained in complete ignorance of his movements, ordered his troops to cross the river without delay. As he was anxiously looking for the junction of Khán Kilán's troops from Patan, some one said, "that as the Gujarát army was numerous, he had better remain on this side of the river till the troops from Ahmadábád came up." To this the Emperor replied, "The enemy being now aware of our condition, what time is there for delay, and what necessity is there for waiting longer in expectation? for, had we rested our hopes on external parade, what cause was there for all this haste in coming here?" As his soldiers were cautious, and looked to consequences, they still hesitated to pass the river, and put off the time by speaking and jesting with the Emperor. The latter, soon after, observing their spirit roused, plunged into the stream with a few select friends; and, at this very time, having taken off his helmet, gave it to Rájá Deva Chand, whom he ordered to accompany him. While they were riding along at a quick pace, the helmet by chance fell, and the Emperor remarked that this was a good omen of the road being open before him. To give weight to this prediction, some person brought the head of one of the enemy, on which the nobles overcame their scruples, and began to pass the river.

Succeeding this, Mohammed Husain Mírzá advanced to oppose their passage, and gave command of his right to Dúli Khán, who had the Abyssinians and Gujarátís; whilst he entrusted his left to Mohammed Khán Faoládí, who had a large body of Afghans. His centre was occupied by Sháh Mírzá, supported by the Abyssinians and people of Ma-wará-ul-Nahr.

The Emperor, after crossing the river, took his station on a rising ground, and was looking at the troops, when Asif Khán came to say that Mírzá Azíz Koká, though not aware of the imperial army being so close, was now ready to join them. These troops had not, however, yet come up, when part of the enemy's troops appeared from among the trees. On this occasion, as Mohammed Kúlí Khán Tírkhán, and several other bowmen had retired, after a slight skirmish, the Emperor, addressing Rájá Bhagwándás, observed, " that, though the army of the enemy might be numerous, God's favour was on his side; and that it behoved all who were with him to make a simultaneous and determined attack on the red ensigns of the former, without fearing the result, as he felt assured of Mohammed Husain Mírzá having adopted the red canopy to establish his claim to the throne.

Mohammed Husain Mírzá, advancing at a brisk pace, was at this time a considerable way before the rest of the troops. Sháh Kúlí Khán Muharram, and Husain Khán, saying it was the period for making a charge, the Emperor remarked that, as yet, the distance between them and the enemy was too great. He then gave orders that, after advancing in a firm and compact line till they met the latter, they should make a charge. The line, however, being broken in the advance, some of the troops on the right gave way on coming to close quarters, and just as the Emperor was about to charge. But Happá Chárun calling out the word, the charge and shout of "Allah Akbar!" became general. One of the enemy's own elephants, frightened by a rocket, happening at this time to rush into their own ranks, threw the whole into confusion, when the Emperor was left standing on the plain, with only Tárá Chand and Balawál Khán by his side.

Mohammed Husain Mírzá, with a considerable body of men, now made an attack on some of the imperial troops, when a trooper, riding up to the Emperor, struck his horse on the head with a sword, and made the animal rear. His Highness, however, holding on by his left hand, kept his seat, and speared his opponent. Another, also, threw a spear at him, but, missing his aim, immediately fled; and a third, who made an attack, was speared by a Gújar. The imperial main body now joined the Emperor, who placed himself in the centre, and ordered a general charge to be made. This was immediately obeyed, and Mohammed Husain Mírzá being taken, the victory was complete.

The troops subsequently marched to Ahmadábád; and Mohammed Husain Mírzá, when brought before the Emperor, was given over in charge to Rájá Mán Singh Darbárí. The Mírzá's foster-brother, Shaikh Maddú, having been also brought before Akbar, at this time, was speared by him on the spot, for having been concerned with the Mírzá in rebellion.

The day was far spent, when as yet Khán Azíz Koká had not come up; and another large body of the enemy came in sight. The greater part of the imperial troops, having dispersed in different directions, left the Emperor attended by only a hundred followers. The enemy, however, without making a stand, fled in the direction of Mahmúdábád; when it was ascertained that these were the followers of Ikhtiyáru-l-Mulk. As the small party of the imperial troops became alarmed on seeing this body, his Highness gave orders to sound the war-drums and trumpets, whilst he encouraged his men by placing himself in the centre. The person whose duty it was to beat the war-drum was so overcome with fear, that he neither heard the Emperor's orders nor sounded the drum, till roused by the point of a spear. During this confusion, Rái Singh, at the instigation of Rájá Bhagwándás, put Mohammed Husain Mírzá to death.

This body had been investing Ahmadábád, as would appear, and had kept Khán Azíz Koká, with Kutbu-d-dín, Mohammed Khán from joining the Emperor. During these contests, the imperial troops lost about a hundred men, and the enemy twelve hundred.

Khán Azíz Koká and his troops at length arrived, when the Emperor, much pleased, embraced the Khán at meeting. The Gujarát nobles subsequently came up to pay their respects; and Sohráb Túrk, having presented the head of Ikhtiyáru-l-Mulk, at this time, was praised for his conduct. Orders were now issued that the heads of the slain rebels should be built into a pyramid, in order that it might serve as an example of terror to the people and a lesson to the nobles.

The Emperor, after entering Ahmadábád, issued a proclamation announcing his success to all the neighbouring districts. After dismissing several persons presented to him at this time, he was informed that one of the Gujarát poets had found the date of his coming in the words *Kahri Gujarát ámadah*, "The scourge of Gujarát has come." The poet, on being sent for, was asked why he had been guilty of such disrespect, when the same denied having used these words, but that he had found the date in this sentence, *Sháhi Gujarát ámadáh*, "The Prince of Gujarát has come." He was accordingly dismissed with a present.

The imperial head-quarters were now fixed at Itimád Khán's former residence; where the mode of governing the country was agreed upon. Sháh Mírzá having fled to Bhroch, Kutbu-d-dín Mohammed Khán, Núrang Khán, and some others, were sent there; whilst Rájá Bhagwándás and Sháh Kúli Khán were sent with a large army to punish the Ráná of Ídur. The government of Patan was entrusted to Khán Kilán; while Dholka and Dhandúkah were given in jágír to Wazír Khán. It was also ordered that the country of Sorath, then in possession of Amín Khán Ghorí, should be allowed to remain with him. But, after the imperial troops marched, Wazír Khán hastened into Sorath, and endeavoured to wrest the country from the latter. He fought several battles, but, not being successful in the attempt, returned to Court.

CHAPTER V.

THE RETURN OF THE EMPEROR TO HIS CAPITAL, AFTER CONFERRING THE GOVERNMENT OF GUJÁRAT ON KHÁN AZÍZ KOKÁ A SECOND TIME.

Akbar, after having settled in eleven days the whole affairs of Gujarát, set out for his capital

14th August. on Saturday the 12th of Jumádá-ul-awal, and carried along with him Sayyid Hámid, his family and domestics. The first day's march was to Mahmúdábád, the next to Dholka; where, having halted a day, he gave Khán Azíz Koká leave to return. After conferring on Khoájah Ghiásu-d-dín the title of Asif Khán, he promoted him to the important situation of paymaster in Gujarát; in which office he was to be guided by the provincial governor's advice. Here all the important affairs of the province were finally arranged; and the Emperor marched from thence to Karkí. From this he went to Sidhpúr, in two marches; and halted till the capture of Barnagar, and the seizure of Auliá Khán, by the troops sent under Rájá Bhagwándás, were reported to him. He then continued his journey; and sent Rájá Todar Mall to investigate and purify the revenue settlement of Gujarát. It was expected that the Rájá, from his great experience, would fix the assessment at what was just; and that, when the same had been arranged, without observing a selfish or avaricious policy, he would submit it to the Emperor, for the future guidance of the revenue accountants in all that concerned the military or the cultivators. He accordingly amended the revenue settlement of the country in a very short time, and, returning to the imperial presence, delivered his account of it into the register office.

The Emperor, interested in the welfare of the Gujarát nobles who had served him, conferred the rank of one thousand horse on Itimád Khán,
A. Hij. 983. A. D. 1575. in the year of the Hijra 983, A.D. 1575. As the same was celebrated for prudence and outward parade, he was also entrusted to arrange and decorate the imperial *darbár* ; having the traffic in jewels and ornaments connected therewith particularly confided to him. His son, Shír Khán, also received the rank of four hundred ; Alagh Khán Habshí had similar rank, and a jágír conferred on him : and Malíku-s-Shark was honoured with a command at the city of Thánesar.

Some districts of Gujarát had been already set aside, as assignments to the nobles serving in the province ; but several places were this year appropriated to the government exchequer, and Wajíhu-l-Mulk Gujarátí was sent as Díwán of the province. He was, therefore, the first collector-general appointed from Dehlí. Some of the Emperor's ladies, in this same year, went to Mekka, having come through Gujarát ; and Khán Azíz Koká returned by order to Court.

A regulation had been passed, previously to

the Khán's return, that the different troops of cavalry, in the service of government, should be specially marked. Khán Azíz Koká was, therefore, the first who was to carry into effect this order, on his arrival at Court: since he, being the greatest of the nobles, might, by commencing this practice, leave no room for others to cavil. Presuming on his intimacy, however, he did not comply with the order; and, retiring to a solitary place, in a garden near Agra, commenced a hermit's life. The Emperor, in deference to the feelings of the Khán's mother, and out of regard to his own services, wished to send him back to Gujarát, if he would repent of his ungracious conduct; but the same showed his independence by telling the Emperor that, having now renounced a soldier's life, he must be numbered among his well-wishers.

It being absolutely necessary that Akbar should now otherwise provide for the government of Gujarát, he conferred this office on Mírzá Khán, the son of Beirám Khán, who had then the rank of four thousand horse, and afterwards obtained the exalted title of Khán Khánán, or chief of the nobles. Wazír Khán, Mír Alá-uddín Kazwíní, Sayyid Muzaffir, and Prágdás, were sent to accompany and assist him; but, being yet in the flower of his youth, and this the first service he had ever performed, he was ordered to follow the advice of the former in all things. At the same time, Mír Alá-ud-dín was made Amín of the province.

Prágdás, who was one of the experienced government writers, was next appointed Díwán, in place of Wajíhu-l-Mulk. In the month of Rabí-us-sání of the same year, the imperial standards arrived at Ajmír, when Wazír Khán left Gujarát to meet the Emperor, and was made deputy governor of the province. Sayyid Háshim and Rái Singh were ordered, on this occasion, to remain at the town of Nadote, and to keep in subjection the refractory of that quarter. A suitable army was also sent to subdue Ídur; and Tarsú Khán, who was at this time commandant of Patan, captured the fort of Sirohí.

In the year of the Hijra 984, A.D. 1576, Kalíj Khán, government clerk of Súrat, received permission to accompany the caravan, going on a pilgrimage to the Hijáz. The Rájá of Ídur, being overwhelmed by the multitude of the imperial army, took refuge in the mountains; but at length, advancing to give the latter battle, sustained a defeat. Ídur was at the same time taken.

Akbar, hearing that the country did not prosper under the thoughtless administration of

Wazír Khán, despatched Mutamadu-d-Daolah Rájá Todar Mall into Gujarát, for the purpose of bringing the province into order. On the latter arriving in the neighbourhood of Jalore, the Zamíndár of Sirohí was induced to pay him a visit, having been instigated thereto by Pahár Khán Jalorí; and as the Sirohí Zamíndár presented a tribute of five hundred rupees, with one hundred gold mohurs, Rájá Todar Mall gave him in return an honorary dress, a jewelled head ornament, and an elephant, after making an agreement with him, on the part of the Dehlí government, that he was to serve the governor of Gujarát with two thousand cavalry. Rájá Todar Mall went from thence to Súrat; and, on the way thither, having had a meeting at Bhroch with the Zamíndár of Rámnagar, who presented a tribute of twelve thousand rupees and four horses, he made him suitable presents in return. The Zamíndár was at this time permitted to assume the rank of fifteen hundred horse, and agreed to serve the governor of Gujarát with one thousand cavalry.

Gul Rúkh Begum, daughter of Kámrán Mírzá, and who, as before mentioned, had fled into the Dekhan, now returned; and, accompanied by her son, Muzaffir Husain Mírzá, with a crowd of other rebels, raised disturbances in the country. Wazír Khán, having many seditious persons among his followers, was obliged to act with great caution; and, having shut himself up at Ahmadábád, sent a messenger to Rájá Todar Mall, at Patan, acquainting him that he had done so. While the enemy's troops were at Sultánpúr, in Khándesh, several of the government servants proving faithless, joined them. From thence they advanced on Baroda, when the imperial Faojdár fled without making any effort to oppose them. Wazír Khán now sent Báz Bahádur and the Díwán Prágdás, with troops, to drive back the enemy; but, having been met by the latter, in the parganah of Sirtal, they experienced a defeat. These contentions increased the audacity of the rebels; and, though Rájá Todar Mall had completed the revenue settlement of the country, and was about to leave Patan for the capital, he immediately returned to Ahmadábád, on receiving Wazír Khán's letter. After his arrival there, he induced Wazír Khán to leave the fort and prepare for war. The imperial troops were only four koss from Baroda, when the enemy fled to Khambáyat; where they were opposed by the force under Sayyid Háshim, chief of the government exchequer. The latter, having been severely wounded on this occasion, shut himself up in the citadel, and was besieged by the rebels; who were closely followed in their flight to Khambáyat. When the imperial troops arrived there, the enemy abandoned the siege and retired on Júnagarh; but the former, continuing the pursuit, overtook the rebels near Dholka; where an engagement was fought, in which several women, dressed in men's clothes, acted the part of bowmen, and shot their arrows. The engagement was fiercely contested by both sides; but the rebels, who at length gave way, took to flight. On this occasion many of the latter were either killed or taken prisoners, among whom were several women who had been employed as archers.

Rájá Todar Mall, after collecting the prisoners and plunder, sent the whole to the Emperor, in charge of his son Sidhárí, and left Gujarát for the capital. On the road thither, he received a visit from Ráná Sáhsmall, Zamíndár of Dúngarpúr, when this chief was presented with an honorary dress, and the rank of two thousand five hundred cavalry. He was also permitted to take leave at Mírtha, after having agreed to serve in the province of Gujarát.

Subsequently to Todar Mall's departure for the capital, a set of robbers, who had assembled about Muzaffir Husain Mírzá, plundered the city of Khambáyat; and, as many opulent merchants dwelt there, they thus obtained possession of much wealth and valuables. Wazír Khán now left Ahmadábád to pursue them; but, learning on the way that the enemy were in great force, and suspecting the fidelity of his own troops, he returned to Ahmadábád, and there shut himself up in the citadel. Many of his followers deserted him on the march, and joined the enemy; who, at length, appearing with all the parade they could exhibit, invested Ahmadábád.

Wazír Khán, at this time, suspecting several of his followers, put them in chains; and, by encouraging his old and trustworthy servants, made every necessary effort to defend the place. The men in the citadel, being much frightened, were relieved every day from the batteries, whilst the Khán, taking on himself the task of going the rounds, remained on the alert. The enemy, who had some accomplices among the besieged, had at one time applied the scaling ladders, and were about to make an assault on all quarters, when Mihr Ali, their commander, and leader of the rebellion, was luckily shot dead. The whole now took to flight, though some had even ascended the wall; and the besieged, though wavering, did not prove untrue. Wazír Khán, and those who had been ransomed, returned thanks for their unexpected success. Muzaffir Husain Mírzá, having subsequently fled to Khándesh, was seized by Ali Khán Farúkí, and sent to the Emperor Akbar, with which ended the rebellion of the Mírzás[h].

CHAPTER VI.

THE GOVERNMENT OF SHAHÁBU-D-DÍN AHMAD KHÁN, AND THE DÍWÁNSHIP OF PRÁGDÁS, WITH THE FLIGHT AND RETURN OF MUZAFFIR SULTÁN TO GUJARÁT.

As Wazír Khán had not successfully accomplished the settlement of Gujarát, Shahábu-d-dín Ahmad Khán, governor of Málwa, who had the rank of five thousand cavalry, was ordered to assume the former government in the end of the
A. Hij. 985, A.D. 1577. year of the Hijra, 985, AD. 1577. The following noblemen, who had permission to accompany him thither, were also to assist in the administration of the province, namely, Kásim Khán Saifu-l-Mulk, Mír Ghiásu-d-dín, Ali Nakíb, Kamar Khán, Ghází Khán, nephew of Na-

(h) It would appear, from Ferishta's history, that the Mírzá was not delivered up before A.Hij. 986, A.D. 1578.

kíb Khán, Fíroz Khán Kábúlí, Shaikh Mozim, and Shaikh Jadíd. Wazír Khán was, at this time, ordered to subdue the country about Ídur.

A. Hij. 986, A.D. 1578. In the year of the Hijra 986, A.D. 1578, the ladies of the Emperor's family, who had gone on a pilgrimage to Mekka, returned in safety; and Shahábu-d-dín Ahmad Khán was ordered to assist them on their journey to the capital.

As the Emperor was wholly given in these days to beneficent acts, he yearly appointed one of the nobles as chief of the caravan going to Mekka; and supplied him with money and valuables, to be given away among the attendants and visiters at that holy place. Mír Abú Túráb, who, at this time, obtained permission to make a pilgrimage to the Hijáz, was therefore made chief of the caravan; and Itimád Khán Gujarátí was also permitted to accompany it.

Mír Abú Túráb, on returning from this pilgrimage, brought with him an impression of the Prophet Mohammed's foot, which belonged to the temple of Mekka; and, after landing this relic at the port of Súrat, prepared to send it to Akbar, then at Fat'hpúr. He accordingly appointed seven or eight hundred people of Hijáz to accompany it; and, after wrapping it in a portion of the veil which had covered the temple of Mekka, set forward with it in a covered litter. Letters were also sent to acquaint the Emperor of having obtained this precious prize; when an order was issued, complimenting the chief of the pilgrims. Instructions were also sent that due notice of its arrival within one stage of the royal residence should be given, in order that the Emperor, to show the relic due respect, might advance and welcome its arrival.

Due notice was accordingly given; when the ladies of the Emperor's family, with all the nobles, went out to meet it, and were blessed by having thus made the pilgrimage. All ranks flocked to kiss this model of the Prophet's foot; and the Emperor, after wrapping it in a splendid covering, carried it the distance of a hundred feet, in the direction of the city. It was subsequently entrusted to the particular charge of Mír Abú Túráb, chief of the pilgrims; when all the ministers, judges, and principal nobles, relieved each other in conveying it to the foot of the throne. This impression of the foot was kept for one year contiguous to the palace, and here the people made pilgrimages. But Mír Abú Túráb, having been allowed to go into Gu-
A. Hij. 988. A.D. 1580. jarát, about the year of the Hijra 988, A D. 1580, requested to carry the foot along

with him, that he might build a temple for it in this country, which is, as it were, the gate of the holy Mekka. He moreover petitioned that, after preparing a place for its reception, he might be appointed superintendent of the same. His wishes were after some time complied with; and Mír Abú Túráb conveyed this impression of the Prophet's foot to Asawal, near Ahmadábád, where, in the course of six years, he built a mosque for it. As must be generally known, the same became a place where great numbers were wont to walk round in religious veneration: and the practice was continued for many years. But, when disorder and anarchy in Gujarát had rendered Asawal and other places desolate, the heirs of Mír Abú Túráb brought the sacred foot into the city, where it yet remains in their possession.

Subsequently, Sháh Fakhru-d-dín was ordered to go from Ujain to the government of Patan, and to send Tarsú Khán to court. Hájí Ibrahím Sirhindí was promoted to the chief-justiceship of Gujarát; and Asif Khán, on receiving the appointment of Bakhshí, was ordered first to put the imperial mark on the cavalry of Málwa, according to regulation; and then to do the same to those of Gujarát, on arriving there, provided the concurrence of Shahábu-d-dín Ahmad Khán and Kalíj Khán was obtained.

A short time after these events, Sultán Muzaffir, who had been kept in close attendance on the Emperor, fled to Gujarát, and remained for some time at Tarwárí, with the Zamíndár of Rájpípalah, without the circumstance being known by Kutbu-d-dín Mohammed Khán, then at Bhroch. After leaving this place, he took up his residence among the Kattís of Karrein, in the parganah of Sordhar, one of the dependancies of Sorath; where he remained so completely concealed, that it was the only period during the government of Shahábu-d-dín Ahmad Khán when the seditious were at rest, and the people in quiet.

Fat'h Khán Shírwání, who commanded the troops of Amín Khán Ghorí, being annoyed at his master, made a proposition to Shahábu-d-dín Ahmad Khán to wrest Júnagarh and the country of Sorath from the latter, and to render it subject to the Emperor, provided he was supplied with troops. Shahábu-d-dín Ahmad Khán accordingly appointed his own brother, Mírzá Khán, with four thousand horse, to accompany Fat'h Khán on this expedition. When the troops arrived in the neighbourhood of Sorath, Amín Khán Ghorí sent a messenger to say that he would pay tribute, and mark his cavalry, according to imperial regulation, provided a sufficient jágír was assigned him for this purpose. He also stipulated that they would permit him to retain Júnagarh for the sake of his dignity, whilst the rest of the country should remain with them. To this Mírzá Khán answered that such could not be conceded, without taking Júnagarh; and, having afterwards advanced, captured the city of Júnagarh, named Mustafábád, through the efforts of Fat'h Khán. Amín Khán Ghorí now strengthened the upper fort, and took refuge there. Fat'h Khán, at whose instigation this expedition had been undertaken, fell sick at this time and died; when Mírzá Khán, abandoning the siege, marched to Manglúr, distant twenty koss, where he took up a position, having this town between him and the enemy. Amín Khán Ghorí, now assisted by the Jám with four thousand cavalry, left his stronghold, and hastened to Manglúr; and, on his approach, Mírzá Khán, retreating to the mountain of Dínar, risked a battle there and met with a defeat. The whole of his baggage fell into the hands of the enemy, and he himself, after having been severely wounded, came to Ahmadábád.

Shahábu-d-dín Ahmad Khán now built fortifications at Morásah and other towns, where the people were disaffected; and, having there stationed parties of cavalry, thus completely settled the country. On a complaint from the cultivators of Ahmadábád and several other parganahs, he made a second admeasurement of all arable dry lands, and brought them into cultivation.

CHAPTER VII.

THE GOVERNMENT OF ITIMÁD KHÁN GUJARÁTÍ, WITH THE DÍWÁNSHIP OF ABÚ-L-KÁSIM, AND THE CAPTURE OF AHMADÁBÁD BY SULTÁN MUZAFFIR.

As already related in these pages, Itimád Khán obtained permission to proceed to Mekka on a pilgrimage; and, returning from thence, joined the Emperor. Having had expectations held out to him that he would obtain the government of Gujarát when the latter conquered the country, Itimád Khán made several representations on this subject, at the time when Shahábu-d-dín Ahmad Khán was raised to the dignity of governor. Among other things, he represented that he was a well-wisher to the Emperor, and promised both an increase of revenue and prosperity in the province. His Highness consequently caused him to be raised to the distinguished post of governing Gujarát,

about the end of the year of the Hijra 991, A.D.
A.Hij. 991, A.D. 1583. 1583; although many of the imperial advisers said that he had not the capacity to settle the country. But, a promise having been passed, and the business settled, the Emperor would not listen to them, and accordingly gave Itimád Khán permission to go to his government. On this occasion, Mír Abú Túráb was raised to the dignity of Amín, and Khoájah Nizámu-d-dín Ahmad to that of Bakhshí [i]. The Emperor also appointed Khoájah Abú-l-Kásim to be collector-general, and sent along with him, as assistants, Mohammed Husain, Shaikh Mír, Muzaffir Beg, Mohammed Beg, Mír Mohábullah, Mír Sharfu-d-dín, Mír Saláh, Sháh Beg, Mír Háshim, Mír Másúm Bhakrí [k], Zainu-d-dín Kamboh, Sayyid Jalál Bhakrí, Sayyid Abú Is'hák, Faiz-ullah Beg, and Pehlwán Alí Sístání.

The son of Mehtar Ramazán, superintendent of the perfume department, who was named Karm Alí, was appointed to conduct Shahábu-d-dín Ahmad Khán to Court, after Itimád Khán's arrival in Ahmadábád. At this time,

(i) This is the distinguished author of the history called the Tabakát Akbarí.

(k) Mír Másúm is the author of a history of Sind, and assisted, it is said, Nizámu-d-dín Ahmad in compiling the Tabakát Akbarí.

crowds of people complained against Hájí Ibrahím Sirhindí, chief judge of the province, on which the Emperor removed him from office and recalled him to Court. Clear proofs of his crime having been established, he was imprisoned in the fort of Rentumbhore.

When Itimád Khán was about to join his government, there were several rebellious wretches in Ahmadábád, who had been once retainers of the Mírzás, but, after their overthrow, had continued in the service of whatever person held the government of the province. These people watched every fit opportunity for rebellion, and, during the government of Wazír Khán, had actively excited an insurrection, which Shahábu-d-dín Ahmad Khán opportunely put down, whilst he entertained several of them in his service. Akbar, on then hearing the state of the matter, ordered that they should be dismissed from service, and expelled that country, and that others more trustworthy should be taken to replace them. He, in the mean time, marched for Kábúl; and Shahábu-d-dín Ahmad Khán, not thinking it advisable to expel them, increased their munsubs and jágírs ; and, by various other means, endeavoured to make them contented. Orders were again issued for expelling them, when Itimád Khán went to Gujarát; and these seditious men, hearing of these, were thinking what they should do. Mír Ábid, chief of these vagabonds, in consultation with Mohammed Yúsaf Balkhí and Khalíl Beg Bádakhshí, agreed that they ought to put Ahmad Khán to death, before Itimád Khán had arrived in Gujarát, and that, after electing Muzaffir for their leader, they should take possession of Ahmadábád. One of the mutineers, named Jahángír, informed Ahmad Khán of this iniquitous plot; but he, being about to leave the government, made no inquiry into the matter, and merely sent a message to Khalíl Beg and Mohammed Yúsaf, that they must quit the city. They perceived that by doing so they would strengthen their cause, and went accordingly to their jágír at Matur, where they began to make preparations. They at the same time wrote to Sultán Muzaffir, intimating their submission to him, and requesting that he would join them. Mír Ábid outwardly professed that he was ready to accompany Shahábu-d-dín Ahmad Khán; but, by secretly plotting evil, induced Moghul Beg Wafádár and Taimúr Husain, chief men about Shahábu-d-dín Ahmad Khán, to unite with him in the insurrection.

At this time, Itimád Khán, Khoájah Abú-l-Kásim Díwán, and Khoájah Nizámu-d-din Ahmad

Bakhshí, arrived at Patan; while Karm Alí, who had been sent on deputation to Shahábu-d-dín Ahmad Khán, reached Ahmadábád, along with Itimád Khán's agent. Shahábu-d-dín Ahmad Khán, who came forth to meet the horse and honorary dress, which accompanied the imperial commands, conducted Karm Alí to the city, and, on being made acquainted with the Emperor's instructions, delivered over the keys of the town to Itimád Khán's agent. He also caused the parties of cavalry to be withdrawn from the different posts, which were nearly eighty in number; but, as soon as the troops left, the Kúlis and Grássiahs destroyed several fortifications, and excited disturbances. In the mean time, Shahábu-d-dín Ahmad Khán, leaving Ahmadábád, encamped at Osmánpúr, on the Sabarmatí river, while Itimád Khán, with the others, entered the city. Mír Ábid and the rebels, in number about five hundred persons, took up a position near the reservoir of Batwáh. The latter sent Itimád Khán a message, that, being in distress, he could not accompany Shahábu-d-dín Ahmad Khán to Court, but was willing to perform whatever service might be required of him, provided he was put in possession of the jágír formerly belonging to him, and that, if the last was not conceded, he would be under the necessity of following a vagabond life. Itimád Khán replied, that, though he could not, contrary to the Emperor's orders, assign them a jágír, he would do as much as he had personally power to do. These unfortunates now became altogether desperate; and, going to Khalíl Beg and Mohammed Yúsaf, at Mátar, joined them in insurrection.

The force destined to assist Itimád Khán had not yet arrived from the capital; and this officer, therefore, deemed it advisable to detain Shahábu-d-dín Ahmad Khán for some days, that, by his assistance, he might act with vigour against the disobedient. Wherefore, when Sháh Abú Túráb, and Khoájah Nizámu-d-dín Ahmad Bakhshí, went to consult Shahábu-d-dín Ahmad Khán in this matter, he advised that the rebels should have their jágírs on former conditions, in order that the peace of the country might be preserved. But, if this could not be done, he recommended the imperial commanders to sow dissension among the mutineers, by going against them with a force, before the former had been joined by any men of note, or were agreed among themselves what to do. To this Itimád Khán replied, that if Shahábu-d-dín Ahmad Khán returned to the city, he would do whatever might appear most advisable. Shahábu-d-dín Ahmad Khán excused himself from remaining, as he had already expended considerable sums of money on account of the journey, and as his people, having left the city with their families, were distressed and disgusted. Itimád Khán, therefore, agreed to assist him with money from the government exchequer; but, as there was no ready money in the treasury, several days were spent in correspondence regarding the means of raising the sum wanted.

Itimád Khán, by discussing this matter, only wished to gain time, and detain the other till the troops from the capital had arrived; after which he would abandon him. He therefore marched from Ahmadábád, and went to Karkí: when a crowd of vagabonds, who had collected in the parganah of Matur, thinking this a fit time for plundering, went into Kahtiwar and joined Sũltán Muzaffir. On joining the latter, they represented to him the richness of the country; and he, through avarice and desire of plunder, taking the Karkí chiefs along with him, turned towards Ahmadábád. The rebels, having assembled nearly fifteen hundred Karkí cavalry, made all possible expedition till they arrived at the town of Dholka, where, having encamped, they proposed for the general safety to make a night attack on the camp of Shahábu-d-dín Ahmad Khán. Sultán Muzaffir, however, wished to go to Khambáyat, and plunder that populous town. But, when Itimád Khán heard that the enemy had arrived at Dholka, he lost all self-possession, and, not knowing what to do, followed Shahábu-d-dín Ahmad Khán to Karkí, with a view of inducing him to return to Ahmadábád. The former, after much wavering and hesitation, thus committed one grand mistake, namely, in leaving the enemy within ten koss of the gates, and actually going eighteen to seek assistance. This was unwise, as he had no confidential person to whom he could well entrust the charge of the city; while the more judicious and candid endeavoured to dissuade him from such a resolution. He would not listen to their advice, however; and, after giving his son, Shír Khán, charge of the city, left Ahmadábád for Karkí, accompanied by Nizámu-d-dín Ahmad Bakhshí. On this occasion he gave the city gates in charge to Mír Másúm Bhakrí, Faiz-ullah Beg Aka, and Zainu-d-din Kamboh, while Mujáhid Khán Gujarátí was stationed at the Rámkhir gate.

Several of the discontented people of Gujarát, who were in league with the rebels, sent messengers to represent his departure in the manner of a flight; and such happy intelligence arrived at the very time when the rebels were about to retire, not knowing what to do. They now, however, made all possible haste to Ahmadábád; whilst their numbers continued to increase every minute. On arriving there, they made an assault on the Rámkhir gate, and, after the interchange of a few blows, entered the city. The confusion consequently increased; and while Shír Khán, Mír Másúm, and others, withdrew from their dangerous situation, the rebels plundered everywhere. Sultán Muzaffir, who had prayed for the present crisis, entered the dwellings of the Gujarát kings, and obtained his desire of sitting on their throne. Thus, in an instant, this populous city, filled with gold, jewels, and fine clothes, was left a prey to plunderers.

Itimád Khán induced Shahábu-d-dín Ahmad Khán to return after some preliminary agreement, but, mistrusting the fidelity of some of his followers, made them swear on the Koran to be faithful. The chief of these ungrateful men was the first to join the enemy.

When the imperial confederates came within eight koss of Ahmadábád, they were met by Shír Khán, Mír Másúm Bhakrí, and others; who separately made known the frightful intelligence of the city being taken. Shahábu-d-dín

Ahmad Khán, on hearing this, was much puzzled how to act, and consulted the others in this matter. Each having given counsel to the best of his ability, it was finally agreed on, that, after advancing to Ahmadábád, they ought to give the enemy battle, if the latter would meet them; or, if not, that after surrounding the place, they must besiege it, until such time as the troops from the capital arrived. In effecting this plan, they committed an error by carrying along with them the men's wives and children, instead of leaving them in a place of security.

The imperial party arrived at Osmánpúr, within sight of Ahmadábád, by morning, and had just fixed on the ground for encamping, when the enemy, aware of their arrival, came out, mounted and prepared for battle. Some of Shahábu-d-dín Ahmad Khán's men were at this time engaged in pitching the tents; and others were taking care of their families and baggage. But, though the main body which came up with him were on the alert, nearly two thousand of the enemy's cavalry left the city, and drew up on the river bank. Sultán Muzaffir, having there taken up his position in the centre, placed the Kahtí chiefs around him, and detached Mohammed Yúsaf Bádakhshí, and Khalíl Beg, as his advanced guard. Shahábu-d-dín Ahmad Khán, observing this, quietly mounted his horse, and put his troops in order of battle; while Itimád Khán, under a pretence of retaining possession of the ford at Osmánpúr, and of thus preventing the enemy passing the river, kept aloof with Mír Abú Túráb and the Gujarát troops, and was only looking for an opportunity to fly.

Shahábu-d-dín Ahmad Khán, who had taken possession of a rising ground with seven or eight hundred cavalry, determined to make a stand against the rebels. He therefore detached from his centre two hundred horsemen to cross the river and make an attack. Though the commanders were in league with their opponents, those under their command twice drove back the latter. One of the commanders, named Shaibak, restrained his men from fighting, and, by constantly sending messages to the enemy, continued inviting them to advance. Badr Beg Turkmán, who had gallantly exerted himself for the Imperialists, was at this time killed; when Shaibak and others, to the amount of five hundred, went over and joined the enemy, who now crossed the river.

Shahábu-d-dín Ahmad Khán, who had not more than two hundred horsemen left, endeavoured to retain his position, and animated his companions to repel the enemy's attack; his horse had, however, received an arrow wound, while several of his relations and brothers had fallen around him, and, being attacked by great numbers, he was thus reduced to extremities. Some of his friends at this time seized the reins of his horse, and forced him from the field of battle; when one of the deserters, coming behind, made a blow at him with a sword, from which he escaped unhurt.

The Kahtís and people of the city, who had come for plunder, now committed depredations on the property of the imperial party, and made their wives and daughters prisoners. Money and other valuables, with horses and elephants, were carried away in the confusion. Sultán Muzaffir, thus loaded with plunder, afterwards went to Ahmadábád; and took up his abode in the citadel; where, with the confidence of a great man, he commenced to administer the government of Gujarát; and, having promoted Shaibak, who had deserted to him from the service of Shahábu-d-dín Ahmad Khán, assigned him a jágír. On the succeeding day, accompanied by several of the rebel chiefs, he went to the principal mosque: and, after causing the oration to be read in his own name, sent for Shír Khán Faoládí from Júnagarh, where he was living in disgrace and indigence. This chief joined Sultán Muzaffir soon after with two hundred ill-mounted horsemen. But, as the latter was not quite at ease regarding Kutbu-d-dín Mohammed Khán, then in the neighbourhood of Sultánpúr and Nadarbár, he left Mír Ábid in charge of Ahmadábád, and then marched to that neighbourhood. He at the same time sent Shír Khán Faoládí to keep in check Shahábu-d-dín Ahmad Khán at Patan; and the former, having enlisted all the imperial soldiery in this part of the country, collected fourteen or fifteen thousand men in the course of a fortnight.

Soon after this, the force sent to assist Itimád Khán, amounting to two thousand men, joined Shahábu-d-dín Ahmad Khán at Patan, and the Imperialists, after strengthening the garrison there, represented the state of affairs to Court. Kutbu-d-dín Mohammed Khán, hearing of these events, marched by successive stages to Baroda. During this confusion, as Sayyidu-d-Daolat, the servant of Kalian Ráo, of Khambáyat, had collected troops and seized on this place, he thus obtained a considerable sum of money; and, after increasing his force to four thousand men, acquainted Sultán Muzaffir of what he had done. Sultán Muzaffir gave him the title of Rustam Khán; and, presenting him with an honorary dress, wrote him in reply to remain where he was, until sent for. Moreover, Auliá Khán, a servant of Shír Khán Faoládí, excited an insurrection at the town of Chotánáh; and, as Mohammed Beg, then in his neighbourhood, had defeated him, Shír Khán Faoládí sent his son-in-law, Husain Khán, to assist him. The Imperialists, under Mohammed Husain, and Khoájah Nizámu-d-dín Ahmad Bakhshí, had by this time joined Mohammed Beg, who now came up with the enemy and defeated them. Shír Khán Faoládí, hearing of this event, advanced in turn, when Itimád Khán, and Shahábu-d-dín Ahmad Khán, resolving to remain at Patan, sent the son of the former, with others of the imperial troops, to oppose him. The contending parties met within eighteen miles of Patan, where the rebels were defeated, and the son-in-law of Shír Khán Faoládí killed.

Sultán Muzaffir, as already mentioned, had marched against Kutbu-d-dín Mohammed Khán from Ahmadábád. Sayyidu-d-Daolat, on this occasion, joined him in the neighbourhood of Nariád, with four thousand men from Khambáyat; while Kutbu-d-dín Mohammed Khán, detaching Mohammed Afzal and Mohammed Mírak to guard the ferries of Khánpúr and Vankánír, ordered them to prevent the enemy from crossing the Tapti. These commanders, who were secretly in league with rebels, fled after a little skirmishing, when Sultán Muzaffir came to the ford at Khánpúr.

Kutbu-d-dín Mohammed Khán now shut himself up in the walled town of Baroda, with some trusty followers; while the enemy, advancing, besieged the place. Though twenty thousand horse and foot of Rájpúts or Kúlis had collected around Muzaffir, Kutbu-d-dín Mohammed Khán, nevertheless, held out the fort against them for twenty-two days; and exerted himself to the utmost, as he could not trust his own men. At this time, Mohammed Mírak and Chirkash Khán Rúmí sent, from the trenches, to tell Muzaffir that, as they were there watched by the imperial spies, he must, under pretence of concluding a peace, send for them, along with Zainu-d-dín Kamboh, Sayyid Jalál Bhakrí, and Khoájah Yahyá, the agent of Naorang Khán; and that, if after imprisoning them and Khoájah Yahyá, he would put the other two to death, he might attack the fort on the succeeding day, without meeting with any opposition from the troops of Kutbu-d-dín Mohammed Khán. Sultán Muzaffir followed the advice of these dissemblers; and, as Kutbu-d-din Mohammed Khán sent him a deputation of the five persons mentioned, he instantly imprisoned them, and caused Zainu-d-dín Kamboh to be put to death the same day, by ordering that he should be trodden under the feet of an elephant. Sayyid Ahmad Bokhárí, however, having interceded for Sayyid Jalál Khán, obtained his release, and carried him to his own house.

Succeeding this, Sultán Muzaffir, mounting his horse, gave orders to surround the fort, when the besiegers, having closely invested the town with the guns brought from Ahmadábád, Kutbu-d-dín Mohammed Khán thought his followers had quite deserted him, and shut himself up in the citadel. The next day, Sultán Muzaffir took an oath that he would not injure Kutbu-d-dín Mohammed Khán's person; and, after making a compact to this effect, sent for him. Kutbu-d-dín Mohammed Khán, thus reduced to extremities, visited Sultán Muzaffir, who instantly imprisoned him, and soon after put him to death, along with his sister's son, Jalálu-d-dín.

Sultán Muzaffir, after remaining at Baroda for two days, marched to the neighbourhood of Bhroch; where the mother of Kutbu-d-dín Mohammed Khán and several slaves were residing. On the third day after Muzaffir had encamped before Bhroch, the slaves, proving traitorous, left the fort, and, having gone to visit the Sultán, delivered to him the keys of the place. By this means the whole treasure and effects of Kutbu-d-dín Mohammed Khán fell into his hands. Sultán Muzaffir remained at Bhroch fifteen days; but, during that time, having heard that Mírzá Khán, son of Beirám Khán, was marching on Ahmadábád, he suddenly decamped, and moved to that quarter.

CHAPTER VIII.

THE GOVERNMENT OF MÍRZÁ KHÁN, WITH THE DEFEAT OF MUZAFFIR, AND CAPTURE OF AHMADÁBÁD. THE EXALTATION OF MÍRZÁ KHÁN TO THE RANK OF FIVE THOUSAND, AND THE TITLE OF KHÁN KHÁNÁN, WITH THE FOUNDATION OF THE FAT'H BÁGH, AT THE TOWN WHERE THE BATTLE WAS FOUGHT. THE DÍWÁNSHIP OF KHOÁJAH ABÚ-L-KÁSIM, AND THE ORDER FOR ADOPTING THE ILÁHÍ ERA IN THE COUNTRY OF HINDÚSTÁN.

The news of the Gujarát insurrection having
A. Hij. 991, A.D. 1583. reached the Emperor, in the end of A. Hij. 991, A.D. 1583, at a time when the imperial standards turned eastward, the government of the province was conferred on Mírzá Khán, son of Beirám Khán, who, then only a youth, had been brought up through the favour and kindness of Akbar. Several brave and enterprizing leaders, such as Rái Durga, Mediní

Rái, Shaikh Kabír, entitled Shujáat Khán, and Nasíb Khán, who were sent to assist Mírzá Khán, were ordered to take the direct road to Gujarát. Kalíj Khán and Naorang Khán were, moreover, ordered to proceed by the way of Málwa ; and, entering Gujarát by that route, to take along with them all who were commanding in these parts. Sultán Muzaffir, hearing of Mírzá Khán's intended march, returned to Ahmadábád.

Shahábu-d-dín Ahmad Khán, and the imperial nobles then at Patan, on learning that Mírzá Khán was approaching, sent forward a messenger to him, and soon after joined him at Mírthá. Mírzá Khán, judging wisely, did not generally make known the unfortunate fate of Kutbu-d-dín Mohammed Khán; but, having called the different leaders, asked their advice, when every one gave it to the best of his ability. It was at length settled that they, trusting to the good fortune which had ever accompanied the imperial cause, must expeditiously bring on a battle ; and, having made the necessary dispositions, they exerted themselves to do so.

Muharram, A. Hij. 992, January 22, A.D. 1584. Sultán Muzaffir, on the 9th of Muharram, A. Hij. 992, A.D. 1584, advancing with a large force and many guns, took up a position at Mohammednagar, contiguous to Osmánpúr, on the bank of the Sabarmatí river, where he waited their attack. Mírzá Khán accordingly proclaimed publicly that they must immediately engage the enemy; but, expecting that the army from Málwa would soon join him, he delayed the attack for some days, and marched, on the 11th of the same month, to the town of Sirkej. Here he encamped on the banks of the Sabarmatí, having the town on one flank and a grove of trees on the other.

At first, a party of the enemy came and made a night attack, but returned without accomplishing their wishes. The expected arrival of the Málwa troops was currently rumoured abroad; and Sultán Muzaffir, thinking the present a fit opportunity for marching from Mohammednagar, crossed the river, and began skirmishing. The imperial army now necessarily made its dispositions, and hastened to oppose the enemy; but, as its front rank and right flank were passing a small stream, whose banks were covered with brushwood, they fell into confusion. Notwithstanding this, having soon after engaged their opponents, they behaved gallantly. Mírzá Khán, who, with five hundred horsemen and one hundred elephants, had taken up a position, and was watching the recent manifestations of the imperial good fortune, beheld Sultán Muzaffir, with five or six thousand cavalry, confidently occupying the plain, and saw that there were evident signs of the enemy proving victorious.

Several of Mírzá Khán's friends wished him at this time to leave the scene of action; but he, deeming such conduct pusillanimous, determined to maintain his ground, and urged his men forward. On this the elephants threw the enemy's army into disorder; and Sultán Muzaffir, giving all up as lost, took to flight. Several of his associates fled along with him to Mahmúdábád, on the banks of the Mahindrí river; and, though his whole army was dispersed, and many had been killed by the sword, the Imperialists could not follow him, as the day was now far spent. These events happened on the
Jan. 26, A.D. 1584. 13th of Muharram in the above year.

On the day of Sultán Muzaffir's defeat, Kalíj Khán, Sharíf Khán, and Naorang Khán, from Málwa, arrived at Baroda, and, having there received intelligence of the victory, halted. Naorang Khán detached Mírzá Záhid to obtain possession of Bhroch; but Hájí Beg Chirkash and Nasír Khán, who had charge of the treasure in the place, closed the gates and attacked the Imperialists.

Sultán Muzaffir, after his flight, went to Khambáyat, where, having raised a money contribution from the merchants and inhabitants, he collected ten or twelve thousand vagabonds, by distributing his gold to all discontented and seditious characters. The cultivators, also, thinking he was the lawfully-born prince, exhibited proofs of their fidelity, and were joining him from all quarters. Mírzá Khán, receiving intelligence of these things, left Ahmadábád in charge of Sayyid Kásim, who had been wounded, and, with the intention of dispersing the rebels, marched, on the 2d of
Feb. 4, A.D. 1584. Safar, against Sultán Muzaffir, having at the same time ordered the troops of Málwa, then besieging Bhroch, to join him.

The enemy detached Sayyidu-d-Daolat, with a force, to Dholka, and the sons of Ikhtiyáru-l-Mulk, with Mustafá Khán Shírwání, to Mahmúdábád. The Málwa commanders, with their troops, joined Mírzá Khán at the town of Barayáh; and Sultán Muzaffir, hearing of this, left Khambáyat, and marched to Baroda. Mírzá Khán pursued him to the latter place, whence he despatched Naorang Khán against Sayyidu-d-Daolat, whilst he himself continued the pursuit of Sultán Muzaffir. The enemy at length resolved to risk a battle, when victory declared for the Imperialists, after some sharp work on both sides. Naorang Khán, having also proved victorious, joined the main body; and Sultán Muzaffir, crossing the Nerbuddah, took refuge among the mountains of Ihániyah. The imperial commanders, at the town of Nadote (Nandode), now put their troops in motion, with the intention of extirpating the vagabonds, several of whom, after having separated, came and visited Mírzá Khán, and others went into the Dekhan. Nearly two thousand persons were slain during the campaign, and five hundred, having been made prisoners, were put to death.

When the glad tidings were communicated to the Emperor, he gave Mírzá Khán the title of Khán Khánán, with the rank of five thousand cavalry, and exalted others according to their merits, giving to each suitable assignments for the support of their ranks.

The Khán Khánán, now leaving Nadote, came to Ahmadábád, where he laboured for the prosperity of the country and the relief of the oppressed. He also established a garden near the town of Keshápúr Sirkej, on the spot where he had defeated Sultán Muzaffir, giving it the name of Fat'h Bágh. Several of the buildings and remains of the summer-house belonging to this garden are yet there, and the collection from the ground still cultivated is counted distinct from that of the above-named town.

In fine, Sultán Muzaffir, whose cause was now totally ruined, left the defiles of the Rájpípalah mountains, and marched to Patan. And, as Abid Mírak, Yúsaf, Abdullah, and others of the enemy, had at this time excited an insurrection in his favour near the town of Múndah, an army, under Shadmán Beg, was sent against them. Sultán Muzaffir, not being able to make a stand here, fled towards Ídur, and from thence to Kathiyáwár and the town of Kharrí, among the Lonah Kathís. Mírzá Khán Khánán, having accordingly equipped another force, sent it under the command of Khoájah Nizámu-d-dín Ahmad Bakhshí, and Mír Abú-l-Muzaffir, to drive out the rebels; but, by the time the troops reached Dholka, the insurrection had altogether ceased, and many of the enemy were wandering about in a distressed condition. On this account, Shír Khán Faoládí took refuge with the Zamíndár of Baglánah.

While Kalíj Khán and Naorang Khán, with the army of Málwa, sent against Bhroch, were unsuccessfully besieging it, Nasír Khán, who was in the fort, thinking he should recommend himself to the imperial troops, treacherously put to death Hájí Beg. The Khán Khánán consequently sent Shahábu-d-dín Ahmad Khán with troops to that quarter, and gave him Bhroch in jágír. One of the gunners from the fort came to tell Shahábu-d-dín Ahmad Khán that the men within were quite harassed by the siege, and that he and his associates would open the doors, provided the imperial troops directed their efforts there. As the man appeared to speak truth, a party was instantly detached to the gates, and easily got possession of the place. Nasír Khán and Charkish Khán escaped, with much difficulty; and the latter, falling into the hands of the Imperialists as a prisoner, was put to death.

When Sultán Muzaffir, now much distressed, went at the end of this year to Júnagarh, the Imperialists returned to Ahmadábád, while several of the commanders of the subsidized troops of Gujarát returned to their jágírs. But, as the collection from the jágírs, on account of the disturbances in the country, was at this time less than usual, the troops were much distressed for want of pay.

The rebels, who only waited for a fit opportunity, again collected; and the Khán Khánán, leaving Ahmadábád in charge of Kalíj Khán, marched against the enemy, with troops under

Naorang Khán and Khoájah Nizámu-d-dín Ahmad Bakhshí; after previously detaching Sayyid Kásim Báráh to Patan, and stationing detachments wherever they were required. Sultán Muzaffir, having come to Múrbí, plundered Rádhanpúr, and continued forcibly to seize whatever he could find. While he was looking for assistance from the Zamíndárs of this quarter, the imperial troops arrived; when he, having fled before them, was pursued by Khán Khánán, as far as the mountainous country of Barnagar. The Zamíndárs of this part, wishing to be received into imperial favour, sent forward their agents, and, though they had previously accompanied Sultán Muzaffir, they yet perceived that being thus received would be the means of saving themselves. They, therefore, came in submissively, and made their complaints. Amín Khán Ghorí, the commandant of Júnagarh, agreed to send his son to attend the Khán Khánán: and the Jám Rájá, to show how well disposed he was to the imperial government, sent to say that Sultán Muzaffir was in a certain place, and that he might possibly be taken prisoner, if a party of the light troops were quickly sent to do so. The Khán Khánán went in person; and, as he found no traces of Sultán Muzaffir on entering the mountainous country, divided his troops into four portions. After retaining the command of one of these for himself, he appointed Naorang Khán, Khoájah Nizámud-dín Ahmad Bakhshí, and Daolat Khán Lódí, to the other three, with orders to enter the cultivated country and plunder it.

It was at this time rumoured abroad that Sultán Muzaffir, leaving his son in charge of the Jám, had gone to Ahmadábád. This disappointment did not dismay the Khán Khánán, who determined to punish the Jám; and, on this occasion, many of the Rájpúts were slain, and much plunder obtained by the imperial troops. When the latter came within four koss of Nawanagar, the Jám sent in his submission; and, after having obtained the intercession of Rái Durga and Kalián Rái, sent his son to present the Khán Khánán with an elephant and other valuables. The Khán Khánán, being victorious, respected the offer made him, and returned.

Sultán Muzaffir, who, with great boldness and presumption, had gone towards Ahmadábád, having arrived at the post of Puránti, the troops there, with those of Nahrwálah, happening to be together, made an effort to expel him. These, having come to action with his followers, slew many of them. When the glad tidings of this victory reached the Khán Khánán on the road, he returned thanks for this great mark of kindness shown by Providence.

Shahábu-d-dín Ahmad Khán, who from the Zillah of Bhroch had been promoted to the government of Málwa, went there in the year
A. Hij. 993, A.D. 1585. of the Hijra 993, A.D. 1585. In this year, the Khán Khánán, having completed the arrangement of the country of Gujarát, went to the imperial presence, where he was honoured in various ways; and, a short time after, having obtained permission to leave Dehlí, returned to Gujarát.

A. Hij. 994, A.D. 1586. In A. Hij. 994, A.D. 1586, Khán Azíz Koká, who held the government of the Dekhan, being at enmity with the commanders of the subsidized troops, there under his orders, quitted them; and, coming alone to Ahmadábád, requested the assistance of the Khán Khánán against those who were hostile to him. The Khán Khánán, who much respected him, and went to give him an honorary meeting, was about to comply with his request; but, after hearing the representations of those opposed to him, abandoned this intention. Wherefore, Khán Azíz Koká, without obtaining his wishes, went into Málwa.

A. Hij. 995, A.D. 1586-7. In A. Hij. 995, A.D. 1586-7, the

Khán Khánán went to Court, agreeably to order, as the celebration of the marriage festival of Sultán Morad then took place; and, having left Kalíj Khán as his deputy, the same continued to perform the duties of his office at Ahmadábád.

The Khán Khánán, whose original name was Abdu-r-Rahím, was brought from Gujarát to Court, at the death of his father, Beirám Khán, and was then only four years of age, as has been already mentioned in this work. After receiving instruction, under the immediate care and kindness of the Emperor, he was first dignified with the title of Mírzá Khán; and was
A. Hij. 983, A.D. 1575. promoted, in A. Hij. 983, A.D. 1575, to the government of Gujarát. Being soon after recalled to Court, Wazír Khán was appointed his deputy, and continued to perform the office of the Nizámat. Mírzá Khán, on obtaining the government of Gujarát a second time, received his father's title of Khán Khánán, after his victory over Sultán Muzaffir. He was an excellent man, who constantly kept company with the good; and most distinguished men were continually entertained in his service. He was so well acquainted with military matters, and the mode of defeating his enemies, that no words could here explain his character. He

was even more graceful and liberal than Hátim Tái; and if all his rare qualities, which are generally known, were to be detailed, such would require a distinct volume.

In this same year, an order for the establishment and adoption of the Iláhí Era[l], and code of regulations in all the countries of Hindústán, was issued, and all government servants were to observe the same. Wherefore a copy of these two orders is inserted in the present work.

COPY OF THE IMPERIAL FIRMÁN FOR THE ESTABLISHMENT OF THE ILÁHÍ ERA.

After a cycle[m] of the Emperor's reign had elapsed, an order to this effect was issued. Be it known to governors of provinces, and government writers, in their several ranks and departments, that, as the Emperor's endeavour has ever been to make both great and small happy and prosperous, all such should esteem these precious times, and employ themselves in works

(l) The Iláhí Era was established A. Hij. 992, according to Gladwin's translation of the Ayín Akbarí, and not in 995, as before inserted. Mr. Gladwin has, however, made an error of one year, as the order was issued in A. Hij. 993.

(m) A *karn*, or cycle, is a period of time usually counted by the Mohammedans, from ten to eighty years. As Akbar commenced reigning in A. Hij. 963, it is here meant for thirty years.

agreeable to God. And let them, at the same time, beware of adopting this opinion, that the founders of religion and of systems, being perfect men, and secluded from the world, have completely explained the perfections and imperfections of faiths[n]; but let them, on the contrary, follow the example of philosophers, and never wholly trust their pretensions, without some one as their guide; nor undertake any thing, either great or small, without due consideration; so that. conscious of rectitude, and a desire to attain perfection, they may attend to the truths of theology, and the subtilties of science, till, by the favour and guidance of God, they obtain and are entrusted with the grace of his revelations and designs; and be especially informed of past and future things.

At this time, his Highness, while studying the almanacks of the Hindús, called by them *Patra*, observed that, according to the *Kál-Patra*, the commencement of the lunar month is reckoned from the conjunction, or the time when the darkness is increasing, called in Hindí *Kishn-Pach (Krishna Paksha.)* But, as these

(n) I have made the translation of this passage as explained by the very learned Mír Khairát Ali Munshí, commonly called Mushták; but the original Persian would imply a more severe censure of the difference of religions, and indirectly intimates that Akbar had some designs of founding a new system.

people ignorantly, and from custom, make the month commence with the darkness, and as such practice is not sanctioned by authority, it becomes necessary to demonstrate this to them. Wherefore, the Emperor was informed by the chiefs of their religion that such is their practice; and, their old and celebrated works being produced, it was discovered that the commencement of the lunar month was once reckoned from the time of the new moon's appearance, a period called by the Hindús *Shukal-Pach (Sukla Paksha)* ; though, from the days of Vikramajit (Vikramáditya,) this enlightened practice has, through various causes of confusion, fallen into disuse. But, still more wonderful, though these people acknowledge that the month commences with the appearance of the light, they do not practically follow this opinion. Wherefore, it is ordered that all astrologers, and keepers of the calendar, with all other accountants under the government, shall regulate their almanacks on the practice of reckoning from the *Shukal-Pach*. Moreover, having prepared a calendar with much care and attention, to facilitate the use of this method, and having stamped it with the royal seal, the Emperor has distributed the same that all men may follow it.

The grandees, on this occasion, said—Doubtless, the Emperor's intention, in establishing this Era, must be to facilitate a knowledge of important events and commercial transactions ; so that no one may have the power of wrangling in any matter : for, in the instance of a person agreeing to a contract, a lease, or the payment of a debt, within four years and four months, the period cannot be accurately ascertained, if the commencement of it be not fixed.

The establishment of new eras, moreover, has ever been with a view of facilitating a knowledge of certain events, happening after a considerable period had elapsed from the original commencement of some other era. Historians must also be aware, that such has been the practice of former great kings; and that, through their care in fixing new eras, men of business have been relieved from doubt and difficulty. And now, said they, a thousand years of the Hijra having nearly elapsed, while the eras of Sikandar and Yezdijerd, though used in calendars, are not accurately known, the people of Hindústán, therefore, use a variety of eras, such as that in Bengal, dated from the reign of Lakhsman Singh, now in its 465th [o] year ; in the country of Gujarát the era of Sál-

([o]) In two copies of the Akbar Námah which I have consulted, this is the number of the year corresponding to that of the Hijra ; but

báhan (Sáliváhana), now dating in its 1506th year, A.D. 1584; in the country of Málwa and Dehlí, the era of Vikramajit (Vikramáditya), now in its 1640th year, A.D. 1584; whilst the people of Nágrakót date from the government of every individual who rules over that fortress.

As the learned are also of opinion, added they, that the eras of Hindústán do not commence from any great event, and have no true foundation, if the Emperor, through his universal clemency and paternal care, would establish a new era to remove such discrepancies, he will be rewarded and blessed both now and hereafter. It is, moreover, ordered in astronomical books, such as the Ílkhání and Gúrkání tables, that the eras should be made to commence from some great transaction, either the establishment of a religion or a dynasty: and, though many great and glorious occurrences of the present reign are each suited to this purpose, let the Emperor fix the same from the period he came to the sovereignty, (now in its thirtieth lunar year, and the greatest manifestation of God's favour and grace,) and he will be certainly repaid with thanks for this good work, as having complied with the wishes of the

but in a third I find that the 1165th year is called the corresponding one. The former is, however, the true date.

learned. By having done so, the era of the Hijra, established at the flight of the best of men from the honoured Mekka to the sacred Medina, will lose nothing of its dignity: for, though this, in the time of Malik Sháh, had not reached its present lengthened period of duration, and business had not then become so difficult, the Jalalí era was nevertheless established, in order that, in all affairs of difficulty, mankind might be relieved from perplexity. The same is now used in the calendars of all Mohammedan countries, as those of Arabia, Constantinople, Má-wará-ul-Nahr, Khorásán, and Irák; and all the written obligations of the faithful are drawn up from these almanacks.

In consequence of the repeated requests of these people, and to quiet their importunities, the Emperor, giving his consent, has issued this order: "Let the gates of felicity and rejoicing be opened, by dating the Iláhí Era from the day of the year corresponding with the first of the king's reign." A command to this effect is also sent to the learned; "Let all compilers of almanacks used in the country of Islám, in which are inserted the Arabí, Rúmí, Farsí, and Jalálí eras, open the door of facility, by therein using the new era; and, in the almanacks of the Hindús, let the same be written, that their various eras may fall into disuse, particularly that of Vikramajit, which had its foundation in falsehood." As the years in the common calendars are solar, and the months lunar, we hereby command that the months of the new era shall be also solar.

The learned of all religions and systems, having set aside certain days of the year, which are agreeable to heaven and favourable to spirituality, have specially appropriated them for the delight of all men: and named them the days of festival, in order that such may give rise to charity and beneficence. Having moreover pointed out the efficacy of prayer, at such joyful seasons, when men are to observe the customary homage and veneration for the great God, they have thus spread the table of beneficence, and opened the gates of gladness, for both rich and poor. Wherefore, agreeably to this order, several festivals, formerly known in this country, which, though long neglected, had been observed for the last thousand years, will be thus fixed: and let all men use their utmost endeavour to observe such; and not disregard the same as here detailed: viz. the nineteenth of the month of Farwardín of the Iláhí Era; the third of Ardíbehisht; the sixth of Khurdád; the thirteenth of Sir; the seventh of Mirdád;

the fourth of Sharíwar; the sixteenth of Mehr; the tenth of Abán; the ninth of Azar; the fifteenth and twenty-third of Dai; the second of Bahman; and the ninth of Isfendiár. Written by order of the Emperor.

COPY OF THE ORDER REGARDING VENERATION FOR GOD AND ATTENTION TO THE GOVERNMENT REGULATIONS.

All government servants, nobles, and other persons, are to observe the following commands, in administering the affairs of cities, villages, towns, and other places.

1st. It is essential that all such endeavour to please God in whatever they undertake; and, as suppliants at his shrine, that they act impartially to themselves and others.

2d. They must not seclude themselves from society, as such is the practice of dervishes; nor must they keep company with the commonalty, and be constantly engaged in worldly matters, as such is the way of the market people; but, in following a middle course, let them choose moderation, and be neither too much in society nor too much in solitude.

3d. Let them honour the incomparable God, by watching night and day; and let them more particularly observe his worship at morning, noon, evening, and midnight.

4th. When not conducting the affairs of mankind, let them study the writings of the good, and books of morality, which are as spiritual medicine, and the essential part of science. Among these, let them use the Akhláki Násirí[p], or Morals of Násir; the Munajiát; the Máhulákát; the Ahiyá[q]; the Kímiá[r]; and Masnaví of Múlá Rúmí[s]; till, having become acquainted with the various systems of faith, they cannot, by the illusion of impostors, be shaken in their belief that the worship of God is best in this world, and the great object with his creatures[t].

(p) The Akhláki Násiri is a system of ethics and politics, translated from its original Arabic by Násiru-d-din of Tús, who lived in the middle of the thirteenth century of our Era. Some extracts from it have been translated into English and published in the Transactions of the Bombay Literary Society, vol. 1., and in the Transactions of the Royal Asiatic Society, vol. 1, p. 514, &c.

(q) The Ahiyá, an esteemed work on Theology, written in Arabic, was composed by Imán Abú Hámid Mohammed-ul-Ghazálí of Tús, now Meshid, about the beginning of the twelfth century.

(r) The Kímiá-i-Saádat, a General System of Ethics, by the author of the Ahiyá.

(s) This poetical work treats of religion, morality, and politics: the author was Jalálu-d-dín Rúmí, who lived in the city of Koniyáh, or Iconium, in Asiatic Turkey.

(t) It is well known that the infidelity of the celebrated Akbar, in regard to the Mohammedan creed, led him to investigate the doctrines of other religions. Christian Monks, the Dastúrs of the Fire-worshippers, the Bráhmans of the Hindús, were each assembled, and called on to explain the principles of their belief to Akbar. As the Emperor lent a willing ear to the expounders of all faiths, they were each alternately convinced he had become a follower

Wherefore, by making no distinction between friend or enemy, a relation or a stranger, let them act with fearless independence.

5th. Let them be charitable, according to their means, to all religious mendicants, and to all poor, indigent, and naked persons, who will not open their mouths to ask for the means of subsistence, and have secluded themselves from the world.

6th. Bring back the discontented to their duty, by alternative severity and kindness, according to their various ranks; and, when the matter admits not of admonition, let them be fettered, beaten, or put to death in various ways. With regard to the latter punishment, reflect well, and be not too ready to use it: for, according to the verse, "one cannot restore the head of him who is slain." Moreover, wherever it is possible, send all such as are worthy of death to court, forwarding along with them an account of their case; and subsequently they will comply with the Emperor's orders. But if, by retaining or sending to court such rebellious characters, there be a chance of sedition, let them be put to death; in doing so, however, abstain from mangling them in any way.

lower of their creed. His true belief, however, appears to have been a system of Theism, similar to that of the Súfí philosophers.

7th. Let them release whosoever is venerated for wisdom or religious opinions; and, if they perceive any thing improper in his conduct, let them warn him of it in secret. As the advisers, however, may be sometimes in error, let them not reproach such a person in anger; since, by doing so, they prevent him offering a reply. Let all those who, by the grace of God, speak the truth, be held in particular veneration, as men who do so are very rare: and many are the evil-disposed who have no mind to speak truth, but have hearts unfortunately inclined to the contrary. Men of good intentions are very cautious in what they say, lest he who hears them should be annoyed, and they themselves fall into misfortune. Consider all men, therefore, who are ready to give up their own interests for the sake of others to be precious as the philosophers' stone.

8th. They must not befriend flatterers; since, by the advice of such, business is improperly performed. They must not, however, be suddenly displeased with those who speak in a flattering manner, as it is proper for servants to discourse politely.

9th. Regarding those who petition for justice, let their cause be inquired into by yourself in person, and in the order in which their names have been filed; so that those coming first may not have the trouble of waiting in expectation. In this matter let not the inferior agents of business invert the natural order of precedence; but, according to this verse, let them represent the complaint to the master, as from him perhaps the complainant will obtain redress.

10th. Be not hasty in punishing those who speak ill of their neighbours, yet investigate the matter; as there are many who find fault with other people, and those who speak good of them are very rare. In this case do not, through passion, forget what is reasonable, but do what is necessary in a deliberate manner and with patience. In the time of sorrow or anger, let such acquaintances, or servants, as are distinguished for their wisdom and friendship, have authority over you; and wise men, on such occasions, will confine themselves to repeating the confession of faith.

11th. Become not habituated to taking oaths, as men who do so expose themselves to the suspicion of telling lies, if at any time they take an oath; and thus obtain a name for bad faith.

12th. Become not addicted to the custom of giving abuse, as such is the practice of mean men.

13th. Let them use their endeavours to increase the cultivation, to conciliate the cultivator, and give him advances in money ; so that villages, towns, and cities, may yearly increase; and let them collect the rent from the subjects in an easy manner, in order that all lands may be cultivated and blessed with population. After such, moreover, let them strive to increase the production of useful articles, being strictly guided in their conduct by the regulations which have been separately detailed. In collecting rent from the cultivators, do so piecemeal, and deviate in no degree from the agreement which has been made.

14th. Have a care that soldiers or others take not up their abode in any one's house without his permission.

15th. Be not entirely guided by self-opinion in any matter ; and let them consult those wiser than themselves. Though no one wiser may be found, let them still seek for counsel ; as the ignorant may discover truth, according to the saying, "it happens that the old and wise man does not always think aright, while the ignorant child sometimes hits the mark by mistake." Let them not, however, consult every one, as the wisdom fit for business, being the gift of God, cannot be obtained by reading or by length of life. As the ignorant may advise, through enmity, it is necessary to be suspicious in this matter, and to retain good men of business, who are rarely to be found.

16th. Let them not permit any thing to be done by their children, when it may be accomplished by their servants: and let them not become accountable for any thing done by the former; since it is difficult to alter it should it miscarry.

17th. Let them readily hear men's excuses, and wink at their faults: as man, who cannot be without faults, sometimes becomes more hardened by punishment, or takes to flight through fear of it. In short, there may be one man who must be punished for one fault, and another who must be forgiven for a thousand: knowing then that punishment is the most important business of a government, let them execute it with mildness and discernment.

18th. Let them entrust the care of the high roads to such as fear God; and, holding these responsible for the good or evil there committed, let them be well informed regarding such matters: for as government, or command, is but another word for keeping watch, such cannot be accomplished without good information.

19th. Punish each man according to his tribe; and, though it may be necessary to kill the proud, a blow to a man of meaner disposition benefits him nothing.

20th. Let them not afflict men on account of their faith, their sect, or their religion ; for a wise man does not, in this transitory world, wish for his own destruction ; and in the matter of religion, will follow such as he knows or hears of. The truth may be with him or them, perhaps ; act not towards him, therefore, with enmity or oppressure : and, if the truth be with them, though he pursues an opposite course, it is fit to pity, and assist such an unfortunate, instead of oppressing and detesting him. In this matter, be friendly to all who are distinguished for virtuous actions or benevolent opinions.

21st. Indulge not beyond measure, or what is necessary, in sleeping or in eating; so that men may be distinguished from the brutes ; and let them watch at night when they can, but not delay till that season the performance of what should be done by day.

22d. In weighing the faults or sins of others, let them do so by the standard of their own ; after which, let them decree their punishment. In this matter, however, let them nicely determine what faults it is necessary to forgive, and what it is necessary to punish ; for many slight faults require great punishments, and many great faults must be overlooked, and a light punishment awarded.

23d. It is not proper to entertain an inveterate enmity to any one, or to make the breast the prison of revenge. When much annoyed, therefore, with any individual, let such be discharged: as the foundation of action is the inscrutable God, and to him should be left the investigation of all that relates to quarrels.

24th. Let them be on their guard with respect to spies, and not implicitly trust any individual; as such are very rarely faithful and without avarice. Wherefore, let them have several spies in every business, and station them in such a manner that they may have no communication with each other. By thus comparing their different accounts, form an opinion of what should be done, and remove from office such spies in the city as are well known.

25th. Let them hold no intercourse with evil disposed persons; and, though the business of great men, in regard to other evil doers, cannot be at all times carried on without them, let them not implicitly rely on them in such matter, but, on the contrary, hold them in suspicion, lest, in the garb of friendship, they have designs against the lives of good men, while their employers have no leisure to discover their intentions.

26th. Let them be on their guard against smooth-tongued deceivers, who meditate enmity under the cloak of friendship, lest sedition be accidentally produced by confiding in such men, who have much leisure, while their employers, through multiplicity of business, have none.

27th. Let them occasionally ask for grace, in the company of the solitary, who seek God.

28th. Let them collect information regarding every part of their neighbourhood; and, without being too communicative, let them represent things worthy of being known to the imperial court.

29th. Let them labour in diffusing science, and acquiring knowledge, so that men of genius, in whatever tribe, may not be neglected.

30th. Let them look carefully after every soldier's accoutrements and arms, so that he may spend less than his income; while the equipment of every person is a contract; for, according to the saying, he is a fool who spends more than his income, whilst he who adapts his expences to his pay, if not a wise man, is still no fool.

31st. Let them have no fixed place of residence, but remain in constant expectation of being recalled to court.

32d. Let them not delay in fulfilling whatever they have promised; and let them speak uprightly, more particularly revenue writers, wherever they have held forth expectations.

33d. Let them be continually employed in the practice of archery and ball firing, so that they may teach the soldiers a habit in such things.

34th. Let them not be too much addicted to the pleasures of the chase, and only engage in them so far as they are necessary for the military profession and for relaxation in this world.

35th. Let them labour in instructing their old domestics, and abstain from frequently laughing or jesting with them.

36th. Let them beat the nukaráh, or great drum, at sunrise and midnight; as from that time day may be said to commence.

37th. During the course of the sun through the signs of the zodiac, let them salute him by firing muskets and great guns, so that all men may give thanks for the favour he confers.

38th. Let them look after their intimates and servants, lest, presuming on their intimacy, such may commit oppression.

39th. Let them retain one person specially in their service to present petitions.

40th. Let them be attentive to the regulations of the *Kutwál*, or police magistrate; and, if in any of the cities there be no such person, let them strive in giving effect to the sections of the regulations hereafter detailed, and endeavour to execute this office to the best of their ability. As one person, however, cannot execute every thing relating to this office, let them use their utmost efforts to entrust the different departments to good men. In this matter, let them assign each his portion of business, of which the different departments will be here detailed. Let them, therefore, entrust this office to a well-informed person, and let them not ignorantly suppose that it is not fit to be attended to; but, knowing, on the contrary, that it is one of great responsibility, let them labour in this department according to the following detail:

1st. The *Kutwál,* in all cities, towns, and villages, must, in connexion with the government writers, keep a list of the houses and buildings, and must enter in a book the inhabitants of each quarter, mentioning the individual houses, the men who inhabit them, the number of cultivators, the tradesmen, the soldiers, and others. By also taking bail from every house, he must thus unite the community, and, apportioning the place into divisions, must station a superintendent of every quarter, to be answerable for the good or evil deeds there committed.

He must also station a spy in each quarter to give a daily account of every transaction that takes place, and to make arrangements for all the neighbours assisting, whenever a theft, a fire, or other such event, happens. In such matters, let all persons in the neighbourhood assist the superintendent of a division and the government police; and, should they not do so on all necessary occasions, they will be to blame, and must be set down as having acted improperly. When any person quits his house, let him give it in charge to a neighbour, or the government policeman appointed to that quarter; and, whenever a guest is in any one's house, whether friend or stranger, let the master of the same acquaint the superintendent of the division of such a one's arrival, whose name will be written in a register. In short, let one or more guards be stationed in every quarter to write down the arrivals and departures, with other transactions in the place; and, when any one comes alone to the division, let them demand bail of him, and not permit him to live there, unless he can give such. Let them send all such as cannot find bail to live in a separate quarter; where a superintendent and a police must be stationed, in order secretly to discover the income and expences of each individual.

Any person whose income is less than his expences must be certainly in fault, and let them inquire into such accordingly; but, in this matter, by not forgetting what is proper and virtuous, let them know that such an investigation is necessary for good regulation, and not for the purpose of seizing on men's property.

2d. The *Kutwál* must appoint one or more brokers, to transact the various kinds of commercial business; and, after taking security from them, must station such in the market-places, that they may afford information regarding such things as are bought or sold. He must also make it a rule that every person buying or selling, without the advice of the above-mentioned brokers, will be deemed in fault; and that both the name of the buyer and seller must be written in the register of daily transactions. Every thing, therefore, must be bought or sold in connexion with the superintendent of that particular division and the government policemen.

3d. Let him station a nightly guard, for the protection of the division in the by-paths and neighbourhood of the city.

4th. Let him take care that there be no strange persons in the division, by-streets, or market-places.

5th. Let him search after and find out thieves, through the aid of pickpockets, shoplifters, and other such persons; and, whenever any thing in the neighbourhood may be lost or plundered, such persons must either produce the thief or forfeit the benefit of their contract with government in this matter.

6th. Let him look after the effects of deceased persons, and give them up to the relations, or heirs of such; but, if there be none to claim the property, let him place it in security, sending, at the same time, an account of such to Court, so that when the true heir appears he may obtain the same. In fine, let him act conscientiously and virtuously in this matter, lest it should be the same here as in the kingdom of Constantinople.

7th. Let him be very careful that there should be no wine within his limits; and let the judge punish the drinker, the seller, and the maker of such, in such a manner as to be an example to other men.

8th. Let him endeavour to keep down the market prices, and not permit that the wealthy, while possessing large heaps of things for sale, should sell them in small portions.

9th. Let him do every thing that is proper to be done at the festival of the Nao-Roz, a feast of great consequence, which commences at the time when the sun enters Aries, and is the beginning of the month of Farwardín. The other festivals are, one on the 19th of the above month, which is a day to be particularly honoured; one, on the 3rd of the month of Ardíbehisht; one, on the 6th of the month of Khurdád; one, on the 10th of the month of Abán; and one, on the 9th of the month of Azar. In the month of Dai, there are three festivals to be respectively observed, on the 8th, 15th, and 23rd days of the month. On the 2nd of the month of Bahman there is one festival. On the 9th of the month of Isfendiár there is another, besides which, let people observe all the other usual festivals.

10th. Let the night of the Nao-Roz be held in similar honour as that of Burat. Wherefore, let the lamps be lighted, and let the *nukaráh* be beaten during the part of the night, which is the commencement of the festival. During the day of the Nao-Roz, the great drums must be beaten at the top of every mountain.

11th. Women must not ride on horseback, without an absolute necessity for doing so.

12th. Let the stations on the river, where people go to bathe, be appointed separately from those where they draw water; and distinct ones must be set aside for the women.

CHAPTER IX.

THE GOVERMENT OF MÍRZÁ AZÍZ KOKÁ, FOR A SECOND TIME IN GUJARÁT, AND COPY OF THE ORDER WHICH WAS ISSUED ABOLISHING THE TRANSIT DUTY ON ARTICLES OF COMMERCE.

A. Hij. 997, A.D. 1588-9. Mírzá Azíz Koká, who, in A. Hij. 997, A.D. 1588-9, had been promoted from the government of Málwa to that of Gujarát, arrived the following year, and carried on the important concerns of the country.

While Khán Khánán was at this period leaving the neighbourhood of Jalore, Ghazní Khán Jalorí, who had come with an intention of joining Sultán Muzaffir's insurrection, not being able to effect a junction with the latter, committed many acts of folly. The Khán Khánán, on the 9th of Muharram, A. Hij. 998, A.D. 1589-90, sent a force against him; but the latter, on learning this, and perceiving that he was not in a fit condition to offer opposition, went submissively to Court. The Emperor, at this time, taking compassion on him, confirmed to him his hereditary patrimony of Jalore, as a subsistence.

A.D. 1590-1. In A. Hij. 999, A.D. 1590-1, an imperial order was issued abolishing transit duties in all the countries of Hindústán; and the following is an exact copy of the same.

COPY OF AN ORDER ISSUED FOR ABOLISHING TRANSIT DUTY.

Be it known to all government writers, both now and hereafter, and to all executive officers, in every part of Hindústán, that, in this auspicious period, being the seventh year of the second cycle from the commencement of the imperial reign, an order has been issued to this effect. "As the divine government of the glorious and blessed God has, in conformity with its greatness and purity, and with a knowledge exalted as eternity, deemed it necessary that the dominion of countries, and the government of cities, (which must provide for friend and stranger, and must arrange the affairs of the merchant and trader,) should be accomplished by means of just kings, a tax was therefore established on all articles brought into the market; that from this source of revenue, troops might be kept up, and proper guardians appointed to protect the property of the State and of individuals. But, as such tax, when not justly collected, must be a source of confusion, and detrimental to business, (though, praised be God! since the Emperor's just reign commenced, the attention and consideration of his heart have ever been exerted for the necessary comfort of the common people, and the encouragement of his subjects,) an order is hereby issued exempting from taxation and registry the following articles: all kinds of grain, or seeds; herbs, whether edible or medicinal; oils, sugar, essences; cotton and woollen cloths; things made of leather; copper articles; madder, wood, reeds, and grass; with such like things and effects as are in common use among the people: excepting, however, horses, elephants, camels, sheep, goats, military arms, and silken stuffs, the taxes on which, besides one per cent., are claimed, as vested rights, toll, or for benevolent purposes[u]. The government writers, and other executive officers, are hereby commanded to give effect to this order, so that the powerful may not oppress the weak, nor the tyrannical commit aggressions on those who are at their mercy; and, now that respect for the imperial greatness and magnificence exists in every breast, and that the light of justice and clemency has appeared; let us give thanks for all these presents to Him who is the beneficent author of truth.

"It is therefore necessary that all executive officers and commanders, all provincial writers and governors of cities, with all Jágírdárs, admi-

([u]) These three sources of taxation are respectedly called by the Mohammedans, Tumghá, تمغا Báj, باج and Zakát, زكات.

nistrators of government lands, custom-house officers, keepers of the highways or passes, landholders, and all other government authorities, should attend to this order, and use their utmost efforts to obey it; without attempting in any way to evade the same.

"Finally, during the government of Mírzá Azíz Koká, the Desáyas, Mukaddams[x], and inhabitants of several parganahs, made a complaint at court that the agents of the Názims and Jágírdárs were possessing themselves of all revenue dues; and that the Rájpúts, Kúlis, and Mohammedans of these villages, which they had been in possession of, previously to the country becoming tributary to Dehlí, were in rebellion, and squandered the land revenues, so as to occasion the ruin of the subjects and a deficiency of the government collections. Wherefore, it was ordered that the Díwán of the province, with the approbation of the Desáyas, Mukaddams, and Amíls, should set aside two and a half per cent. from the collections of the Khalsah, or government lands, and those of Jágírdárs, as a perquisite for the Mukaddams of villages; and on

(x) A Desáya is the chief of a district, who inherits lands and money perquisites; but on which the government intendant of revenue had a claim of from two to ten per cent. The Mukaddam is chief of a village.

this account, nothing more than the above was to be demanded. It was further ordered, that the Kúlis should be permitted to retain one fourth of the land, with its revenue, on producing good security for their conduct, and that all landholders of villages should put the government mark on their cavalry contingents, in order that they might attend the provincial governor on all necessary occasions. One half of the usual collection was also to be taken from the purchaser of all saleable lands, and, while the province was managed agreeably to the above regulations, it continued to increase in prosperity.

"The Rájpúts and Kúlis before mentioned originally possessed the country. But, when the Sultáns of Gujarát had completely subdued the same, they continued to punish these people, and forcibly to exact the tribute from them; till, at length, the original possessors consented to perform service and to pay a quit rent [y], for retaining one fourth of their villages and hereditary estates, which portion is called Banta; whilst the other three-fourths were given up as the government share, and named Talpat lands. An agreement was also made with the greater landholders, who possessed several parganahs,

(y) The term in the original is Málguzárí مالگذاري.

that they were to serve the State in war time with infantry and çavalry, according to the size of their jágírs, and extent of their means ; till at length the Kúlis and Rájpúts, who possessed the Banta of different villages, in consideration for the military services they performed, made themselves masters of this share, and presented in the harvest time a free gift to the Jágírdárs.

" In the course of time, the Rájpúts and Kúlis, who had become powerful, excited disturbances, carried away the cattle from towns, and murdered the inhabitants, during the harvest season. The people, having no means of redress, purchased exemption from these evils, by giving the authors of them a yearly payment in money, or by yielding up possession of one or more fields fit for cultivation ; and such claim for exemption is called Grás, or Dol. This custom, gradually established, has been so matured through the weakness of the provincial governors, that there are very few places in the parganahs where some of the Rájpút, Kúli, or Mohammedan inhabitants do not possess the right to Grás.

As these people are naturally disobedient, addicted to theft, highway robbery, and sedition, they therefore excited insurrections, whenever the government of the provincial rulers indicated the least weakness. On this account, several of the governors, both in past and present times, after strengthening the fortifications of the province, stationed a sufficient party of soldiers therein: and these posts are named Tahnahs. The payment of each Tahnah has been fixed by government, and certain lands are set aside for this purpose, in order that the party of men may never leave the post, lest disturbances might be set on foot. Now that the unsettled state of the province goes on increasing, the seditious tribes already mentioned have levelled the small forts, where there were formerly Tahnahs, and, by establishing themselves in others, have obtained possession, in many towns, of the Talpat government share instead of Grás.

"Many of the great landholders, who were Jágírdárs, performed the usual services until the time of Aurangzíb; but, at present, the provincial governor raises a force, and collects a tribute from the Bantútárs, in possession of the Talpat, in proportion to the capability of each place; while he takes security from his own Ámildárs. But, when the great landholders refuse to pay the tribute, what power has the provincial governor to enforce it? and so faithless have they become, that he cannot pass the city gate without an escort from them."

In fine, Mírzá Azíz Koká, in A. Hij. 999, A.D.
A.Hij. 999. A.D. 1590. 1590, gave the Emperor an introductory present of elephants and fine things.

CHAPTER X.

SULTÁN MUZAFFIR, SURNAMED NATHÚ, EXCITES THE JÁM, OR LANDHOLDER OF NAWANAGAR, TO RAISE A TUMULT; THE LATTER IS DEFEATED, AND JÚNAGARH TAKEN.

Among the events which happened in this year, we may mention the disturbances excited by Sultán Muzaffir, of which the account is briefly this. When Mírzá Azíz Koká arrived in Gujarát, the Jám, who is the great landholder in the district of Sorath, was bent on rebellion and war, and only waited for a suitable opportunity. About this time, Sultán Muzaffir, who quitted his place of concealment, made exertions to collect together a crowd of discontented vagabonds; and was joined by Daolat Khán, son of Amín Khán Ghorí, and by Khangar, Zamíndár of Kach. Mírzá Azíz Koká, after making the necessary preparations, marched to quell the disturbance; though the brothers of Kalíj Khán (who were the children of Ismael Kalíj Khán, and had a jágír at Sorath,) would not accompany him. After his arrival at Víramgám, he had a meeting with Fat'h Khán, son of Amín Khán Ghorí, Chandar Sen, Zamíndár of Halwád, and Káran Parmál, Zamíndár of Morbí; while Sayyid Kásim and Khoájah Suleimán Bakhshí, were sent with a force in advance. The troops came to Morbí, distant twenty-five koss from the enemy, where they halted: and, at this time, some proposals for peace passed between the imperial commanders and the latter. This endeavour to treat made them more arrogant; and, having resolved on war, they advanced to battle. Mírzá Azíz Koká, who was much enraged at their conduct, prepared to receive them; not pausing to consider that the enemy's strength was thirty thousand, whilst his own was only ten thousand cavalry. Muzaffir, who advanced, was accompanied by a great crowd of Gujarátís and Rájpúts.

At this time it rained heavily, and continued to do so without intermission for two days and nights. The enemy encamped on an elevated plain, while the imperial troops were on a low spot of ground; and, as the severity of the rain prevented large quantities of grain being brought into the camp of the latter, the men were straitened for provisions. Khán Azíz Koká, not thinking it advisable to offer battle, marched towards Nawanagar, in order that his soldiers might more easily be supplied with provisions and grain, and that dissensions among the enemy might spring up in the mean time. The Imperialists took up their position within four koss of a flourishing town, where the troops obtained much grain and other things by plunder; many of the enemy, in the mean time, went to their homes and families.

Muzaffir had encamped at the edge of a river which divided the two armies; and one day, soon after, an engagement having taken place between them, each bravely contended for victory. The Rájpúts, dismounting from their horses, formed a compact line, and advanced with their knives and daggers; but the right of the Imperialists having driven back the enemy's left, threw them into confusion; and Khán Azíz Koká, who, with a reserve of chosen men, was watching an opportunity, having made a rapid advance at this time, broke their line. The brother and two sons of Jásá Bábá, with five hundred Rájpúts, were killed on this occasion. Muzaffir and the Jám, not knowing what to do, took to flight; and Daolat Khán, who was wounded, went to Júnagarh. The enemy had two thousand killed and wounded, and the Imperialists only seven hundred.

Subsequently to this victory, Mírzá Azíz Koká marched to Nawanagar, where he obtained large booty; and, as Muzaffir and the Jám had taken refuge in the defiles of the mountains, he lingered for some time in that neighbourhood. Naorang Khán and Sayyid Kásim were sent from thence with a force to take Júnagarh. As Daolat Khán, who had been wounded in the late engagement, died at this time, the people in the fortress asked for quarter, and agreed to come out; but, when Muzaffir soon after joined them, they changed their intentions. On this account, Mírzá Azíz Koká went in person to capture the place; and Muzaffir, thinking it unsafe to remain there, abandoned it, and spread a report that he had gone to Ahmadábád. Mírzá Azíz Koká sent his son with a force to follow him; while he himself invested Júnagarh. Intelligence was at this time brought to the former that the Jám was passing in the neighbourhood of the imperial troops to his hereditary estate; and, though every possible expedition was made in pursuit of him, the latter fled like a wild beast before his pursuers.

In consequence of the length of the march and the privations experienced by the troops, Mírzá Azíz Koká did not take Júnagarh in that year, but returned to Ahmadábád, when the nobles were for once permitted to remain quiet on their own estates.

CAPTURE OF JÚNAGARH.

In the year of the Hijra 1000, A.D. 1591, A.Hij. 1000. A.D. 1591. Mírzá Azíz Koká, after having equipped another force, marched with the determination of capturing Júnagarh and punishing the enemy; at which time, the son of the Jám, Jalál Khán, Ghazí Khán, and Malik Husain, came and met him. The ports of Gogar, Manglúr, and Somnáth, with sixteen others, were taken possession of without a blow; and from thence Mírzá Azíz Koká marched against Júnagarh, then in possession of the sons of Amín Khán Ghorí. After having established his entrenchments for capturing the place, he sent Naorang Khán to take up a position on the high road, from which provisions and supplies were brought into the fortress. At this time, a fire broke out in the latter, by which a great part of the provisions and implements of the besieged were consumed. During this conflagration, the enemy kept up a sharp fire on the besiegers, who, after taking possession of a small hill in the vicinity of the fort, threw up a breastwork and brought up a gun. From this position, the latter ascertained the exact range of their shot, and occasioned great annoyance to the besieged; who, when at length straitened, asked permission to treat, and delivered up the keys of the place. The sons of Amín Khán and Daolat Khán, with five other persons of consequence, came out and waited on Mírzá Azíz Koká, who conferred on each, according to their rank, a horse, honorary dress, office, or jágír.

As this fortress, in the district of Sorath, came into the power of the imperial government, the author will here insert what is necessary to be known regarding this country, and the appellation of Júnagarh. This territory is bounded on the south and west by the sea; on the east by the Zillah of Jhalawár; and on the north by the boundaries of the provinces of Thattah, where the black soil of the hills and stony grounds become so swampy after a little rain that one can with difficulty walk over it. It is generally destitute of wood, though the mango, khirny, tamarind, and mimosa trees are to be found in the hilly parts. The inhabitants are a mixed race of Kúlis and Rájpúts, who, being for the most part armed horsemen, wear a quilted cotton jacket as armour, and carry a spear. They are addicted to robbery, and will not pay the revenue without the presence of troops to enforce it. This country is divided into five Zillahs, which are named Hallar, Kathiyáwar, Golwár, Babrewar, and Jaitwar; comprehending several ports, rivers, fortifications, and places of Hindú worship, such as Dwarka, Somnáth, and Shatrinjáh[z]. A greater produce is obtained from the spring than the autumnal crop; and such is the natural strength of the soil, that it requires no manure previously to being sown. After the rainy season, the wheat and nukhod[a] are sown, and do not require to be irrigated, but are brought forward by the natural moisture of the soil and the assistance of the dews, which are heavy in this quarter. The species of wheat called kath, which is very fine, is a product of this country. In the collected revenue of Sorath, that of Islámnagar is included.

Sultán Ahmad, who founded Ahmadábád, made two separate attempts to gain possession of this country, but without success. At length, Mahmúd Bígarrah having taken the Rájá Ráo Mandalik, as before detailed, built a fortified city, and named it Mustafábád.

In regard to the appellation of Júnagarh, the

(z) This is said to be the same place as that otherwise named Hinglaj; which is sometimes, however, included in the Súbah of Thattah.

(a) *Cicer Arietinum.*

people of Sorath generally relate that the Rájá of the country, who was named Mandalik, and was contemporary with Mahmúd Bígarrah, was the last of a race that had possessed dominion there for nineteen hundred years. His ancestors had succeeded each other in the Ráj during that time, and had their seat of government at the town of Bhantullí, distant from Júnagarh five koss. Formerly an impenetrable forest existed in this neighbourhood, and had not been explored. One day, however, a woodcutter penetrated so far as to discover the fortress, and, returning, informed the Rájá of what he had seen. The latter, after having caused the trees to be cut down, went in person to view the place, and beheld a wonderful fortification, constructed on the western side of Mount Girnar, whose walls had been scarped from the surrounding rock, above which a kind of battlement had been erected. It was entered by three doors, one of which is on the east, the other on the west; but within the latter there was a third door, towards the north, which cannot be passed without first entering the outer one. The water of the fortress was supplied by two deep wells and two smaller ones. During this visit, the Rájá Mandalik, having asked his followers regarding the name of this place, and the time of its construction, received for answer they did not know. He therefore called it Júnagarh, or the ancient fortress; the first part of the appellation signifying old, and the last a fort, according to the language of the country. The place has ever since retained this name.

CHAPTER XI.

THE SEIZURE AND SUICIDE OF SULTÁN MUZAFFIR, THE PILGRIMAGE OF MÍRZÁ AZÍZ KOKÁ TO MEKKA; THE GOVERNMENT OF THE PRINCE SULTÁN MORÁD, WITH SÚRJ SINGH AS HIS DEPUTY, SUCCEEDED BY THAT OF MÍRZÁ AZÍZ KOKÁ, ON HIS RETURN FROM THE PILGRIMAGE, AND THE DEATH OF AKBAR.

As Mírzá Azíz Koká, after capturing Júnagarh, made every possible endeavour to discover the retreat of Muzaffir, intelligence was at length received that this unfortunate had taken refuge with the landholder of Haraw [b], in the territory of Dwarka. He therefore sent a suitable force in search of the fugitive, and gave command of the same to Naorang Khán, who was accompanied by Gujar Khán, Nizámu-d-dín Ahmad Bakhshí, and Mohammed Anwar, the son of Mírzá Azíz Koká. These commanders, after

(b) I cannot find this place in the map, but it is probably the same as Aramraw, opposite the Bate Pagoda.

arriving at Dwarka, took the place, and established a mosque; and, having there left a party of troops, marched in pursuit of Muzaffir. But, as the landholder of that part had heard of the expedition, he conveyed Muzaffir by sea to a fortified island, and went along with him. The Imperialists followed the enemy, who now made a stand on ground where cavalry could not act; but the troops of the former dismounted and engaged their opponents. Many of the latter were slain; and, as the landholder had been at this time killed by an arrow, Muzaffir, much distressed and perplexed, took refuge with the Bharah Zamíndár of Kach.

When intelligence of these events was brought to Mírzá Azíz Koká, then at Júnagarh, he sent another force to that quarter, and gave command of it to his son, Abdullah. The Jám, in token of submission and good wishes, met the latter on the way, and, having indicated a wish to be received with favour by the imperial government, concluded a treaty. The Zamíndár of Kach also sent his agents, who agreed to send the son of their master to the imperial camp; but, as Mírza Azíz Koká, who would not favourably receive this proposition, told them that if they had any real intention of serving the imperial government, or wish to be received into favour, they must deliver up Muzaffir to the servants of the latter. An attempt was made to procrastinate and deceive; but, as Mírzá Azíz Koká had yielded up some territory to the Jám, a force was in the mean time sent to assist him in this matter; and he, being afraid of the consequences, sent to say that he would deliver up Muzaffir, provided the parganah of Murbí, which had been formerly part of his territory, was given to him as a reward for his services. Mírzá Azíz Koká gladly accepted his proposal; and a party, detached for the purpose of seizing Muzaffir, was guided to the spot by the Jám, who sent on a messenger to say that the Bharah Zamíndár was about to pay him a visit; when the latter, coming out to meet him, having been surrounded by the men of the detachment, was made a prisoner.

The party, after thus accomplishing the object for which it had been sent, hastened to return, and marched all night with their prisoners; who, when morning dawned, having alighted for a little, retired behind a tree under some pretext, and cut his throat with a razor, which had been kept concealed in his pocket. He thus liberated himself from the contentions of this world; and, such was the celerity with which the act was accomplished, that, in the time it could have been known he was dead, Mírzá Azíz Koká sent his head to Court along with Nizámu-d-dín Bakhshí. These events happened at Dharrol, fifteen koss from Murbí.

When the news of Muzaffir's death, and the capture of Júnagarh, reached the ear of Akbar, an affectionate order, recalling Mírzá Azíz Koká, was issued. Notwithstanding the latter had done such service, he could not, for various reasons and suspicions, make up his mind to go to Court; and excused himself, by saying that he intended to take Diú from the Portuguese. Having first permitted Naorang Khán, Gujar Khán, and Khoájah Ashraf, with others of the nobles, to return to their jágírs, he at the same time wrote to the commanders at the different sea-ports, that they must prevent the merchants from trading to the harbour of Diú; in order that, by thus reducing the Portuguese to extremity, they might procure for him a licence to go to sea. He at the same time sent to the Bharah Zamíndár and the Jám, saying that he intended to return to Court by way of Sind. After his arrival at Somnáth, he confined Mír Abdu-r-Rizzák Bakhshí and Sayyid Báyázíd Díwán, but on what account the author is not aware; and at this time a letter of licence to go to sea was received from the Portuguese. In A. Hij. 1001, A.D. 1592. the year of the Hijra 1001, A.D. 1592, having embarked with his family, and about one hundred followers, he sailed from Bilâwal Patan, in a vessel called the Ilahí, with the intention of making the pilgrimage to Mekka. On the day he went on shipboard, the whole of the troops had been drawn out in line; and the great drums were sounding, when Mírzá Azíz Koká bade his companions farewell with tears in his eyes. He at the same time released the persons he had confined, and asked them for forgiveness. Akbar, on hearing of these things, was greatly vexed; but, after conferring the rank of one thousand horse on the Mírzá's eldest son, then at Court, and giving to another that of five hundred, he entrusted the government of Gujarát to the Prince Sultán Morád Bakht.

As the prince had been appointed to the government of the Dekhan, previous to these events, and had delayed taking charge of it, in endeavouring to assemble troops in Málwa, Gujarát was now granted him in place of the other. He at the same time received instructions to leave Málwa and go to Ahmadábád, whence he was to lead the troops of both provinces into the Dekhan, and endeavour to mend the state of affairs in that quarter.

A. Hij. 1002, A.D. 1593-4. In A. Hij. 1002, A.D. 1593-4, Mírzá Azíz Koká returned from the pilgrimage, and went to Court by way of Gujarát, and, as the Prince Morád Bakht, in the following year, went into the Dekhan, Súrj Singh came to Ahmadábád as his deputy.

Bahádur, the son of the late Sultán Muzaffir,
A. Hij. 1003, A.D. 1594-5. in A. Hij. 1003, A.D. 1594-5, excited an insurrection in the province, and met with defeat. At the death of Muzaffir, two sons and two daughters had been left behind, who took refuge with the Parwar Zamíndár of Loárí. The Jágírdárs of Gujarát had been sent to assist in the conquest of the Dekhan; and, as a favourable opportunity for exciting an insurrection in the former province now appeared, Muzaffir's eldest son raised the standard of insurrection, and plundered the towns and villages. Rájá Súrj Singh went against him with a force; and the enemy, being overtaken, made a demonstration as if they resolved to fight, but fled at the first onset. Subsequently to this, Bahádur withdrew into retirement.

A. Hij. 1007, A. D. 1598. In A. Hij. 1007, A.D. 1598, the fortress of Asír, which, from the time of Sultán Bahádur Gujarátí, had been possessed by Ikhtiyár Khán, Alagh Khán, and Murján, sons of Yákút Sultán, was incorporated with the provinces of the Dehlí empire[c].

A. Hij. 1009, A.D. 1600. The death of Prince Sultán Morád having taken place in the Dekhan A. Hij. 1009[d], A.D. 1600, Mírzá Azíz Koká was for a third time made governor of Gujarát. In this same year, Shamsu-d-dín Husain was sent as deputy governor to Ahmadábád, and one of his sons was appointed Faojdár of Sorath.

The revenue of the province had been assigned over to Mírzá Azíz Koká and his family, in A. Hij. 1011, A.D. 1602; when, at his request, the Emperor conferred on his son Shádmán the deputyship of the province, and made his other son, Abdullah, governor of Júnagarh. In this same year, the sum of one lak of rupees, from the revenue of the port of Khambáyat, was assigned as an annual gift to the Prince Salím[e].

(c) There is an inscription on the minaret of the great mosque at Burhánpúr, written by Mír Másúm of Bhákar, which records the capture of Asír in the 44th year of the Iláhí Era. As Akbar commenced to reign in A. Hij. 963, the 44th year of that Era would therefore correspond to the Hijra year 1007; but, if the inscription has been correctly copied, this year of the reign is there called 1009. The last is an error; and Ferishta, in converting the years into each other, appears to have committed a similar one.

(d) This appears to be wrong; it had happened two years before.

(e) The same who succeeded Akbar on the throne.

On Wednesday the 12th of Jumádá-s-sání, in
12th of October, A.D. 1605.
A. Hij. 1014, A.D. 1605, Akbar, by the will of God, left this transitory world for the mansions of eternity.

THE END.